The Paradox of Aging in
Place in Assisted Living

The Paradox of Aging in Place in Assisted Living

Jacquelyn Beth Frank

BERGIN & GARVEY
Westport, Connecticut • London

Library of Congress Cataloging-in-Publication Data

Frank, Jacquelyn Beth.
    The paradox of aging in place in assisted living / Jacquelyn Beth Frank.
      p. cm.
    Includes bibliographical references (p.   ) and index.
    ISBN 0–89789–678–5 (alk. paper)
    1. Congregate housing—Illinois—Chicago—Sociological aspects.
    2. Aged—Housing—Illinois—Chicago.   I. Title.
    HD7287.92.U5F7   2002
    362.6′1—dc21   2001052791

British Library Cataloguing in Publication Data is available.

Library of Congress Catalog Card Number: 2001052791
ISBN: 0–89789–678–5

First published in 2002

Bergin & Garvey, 88 Post Road West, Westport, CT 06881
An imprint of Greenwood Publishing Group, Inc.
www.greenwood.com

Printed in the United States of America

The paper used in this book complies with the
Permanent Paper Standard issued by the National
Information Standards Organization (Z39.48–1984).

10 9 8 7 6 5 4 3 2 1

Copyright Acknowledgment

The author and publisher gratefully acknowledge permission for use of the following material:

Excerpts from Schwarz, Benyamin, and Ruth Brent, eds. *Aging, Autonomy, and Architecture: Advances in Assisted Living*, pp. 166–182. © 1999 The Johns Hopkins University Press. Reprinted with permission of The Johns Hopkins University Press.

TO MY PARENTS

Contents

Preface

My interest in assisted living grew out of my ongoing fascination with the concept of home: its meaning and importance in people's lives. Throughout graduate school I had been curious about the perceptual differences between architects and users in regard to residential environments. Starting as an undergraduate, my anthropological training taught me to look at the issue of housing from a holistic perspective and to consider the viewpoints of everyone involved, not simply those who possessed the power, control, or education. I credit Dr. Philippe Bourgois as the person responsible for sparking my initial interest in urban anthropology and housing issues.

My early examination of public housing environments and housing environments for the elderly led me to a shocking conclusion: no one was asking the residents about *their* needs or perceptions of their environment. Many designers, policymakers, and planners were simply acting on the residents' behalf, and creating residential environments that *they* believed would be functional for residents.

I began my research on assisted living in 1991. When I told local providers that I planned to interview residents about their experiences, and spend protracted amounts of time conducting participant-observation fieldwork, I was confronted with looks of amazement. Providers would respond to my stated plan with the phrase, "what a great idea," as if I had just discovered fire. I was astonished that spending time with residents seemed to be such a novel idea because, as an anthropologist, it seemed like an obvious idea. After all, if assisted living operators wanted to improve the residential environment, then they must understand the perspective of those who *live* there. This book has thus grown from a continuing concern that residents' experiences in different environments were being unintentionally overlooked by those designing, planning, regulating, and administering the settings.

Over the extended period of time it has taken me to assemble this body of work, a number of people have been critical to my learning process, both academic and personal. First, I would like to thank Dr. Karen Tranberg Hansen, my thesis advisor. She was there when it all began and helped to guide me through graduate school, to advise me during the research process, and to make me appreciate the value of interdisciplinary research. I would also like to acknowledge my mentor in the field of gerontology, Dr. Madelyn Iris. Dr. Iris and the Buehler Center on Aging introduced me to the field of aging and helped me to realize the unique contribution that social scientists can make to aging research.

I would like to thank the providers at all of the assisted living sites I visited, especially those at Kramer and Wood Glen. The staff and administrators were always very open, honest, and eager to assist me with my research. I must express even greater gratitude toward the residents of Kramer and Wood Glen. Although it was initially difficult for the residents to trust me and to understand my role as a researcher, they were willing to emotionally express their thoughts and feelings about life in assisted living. Their contribution to this book is immeasurable.

In the process of writing this book, technical assistance was graciously provided by many people. Thanks to JoAnne Geigner for her skillful work on the figures and tables. I consider myself lucky to have two wonderful graduate assistants who have helped me with some of the less desirable aspects of the research process. Specifically, I thank Keri Katko for her tireless library research and assistance with the compiling of my bibliography. Angelia Bowman has also been a wonderful graduate assistant, researcher, and proofreader. She has provided me with insightful feedback during the writing process.

Thanks to Dr. Sue Sprecher for her friendship and latenight e-mails. Thanks to my department chair, Dr. Nick Maroules, for his caring nature and for showing wonderful support for his junior faculty. I am extremely grateful to Dr. Barbara Heyl for her willingness to be a mentor and a sounding board during my entire writing process. Her enthusiastic attitude helped to keep me going during times of frustration. Barbara unselfishly volunteered to read multiple drafts of my book and spent a significant amount of time meeting with me, providing crucial feedback and suggestions. I am also indebted to Barbara's late mother, Augusta Sherman. Through the course of her death, Mrs. Sherman helped to shed new light on the importance of aging in place in our last years.

With great fondness I would like to recognize the contributions of my friends. A special thanks to my friend Lisa Hinchliffe for commiserating with me during our mutual book-writing experiences and for her expert assistance during the research process. Thank you to Ingrid Sato for listening to me for over a decade! Thanks to Darryl Chew, Leigh Woodard, Marion Willetts, and Steve Yovits, for reminding me to take time out and enjoy life. To my longtime friends Karen Kandl, Laura Raymond, Mary Knappenberger, Becky Sattin, and Michele Siegel—my friendships with you have spanned between thirteen and twenty-eight years in length—it has been wonderful to share the process of growing up with all of you. In the coming years I look forward to sharing the process of growing old with all of you in my life. To my family—Jeff, Abby, Evan, the Friedberg family, Mary Dow, the Rubinwitch family, and the Frank family—thank you for listening to me and bearing with my stress. Thank you for all of your support and encouragement, past and present. An extra special thanks to my four-legged family members Betty and Awesome, who gave me unconditional love and support every step of the way (and they never criticized my work!).

Finally, and most important, I would like to thank my parents, Bruce and Linda Frank. Your caring, love, and support mean more to me than I can ever express. I am so glad to have you both accompanying me on the journey of life. Thank you for encouraging me to follow my own path. I love you both very much.

The Paradox of Aging in Place in Assisted Living

Introduction

In the past several years, the idea of aging in place has been embraced by older adults and by those advocating on their behalf. However, aging in place, or "remaining in the same residence where one has spent his or her earlier years" (Harris 1988:18), is not always possible because the older person's longtime home may not adequately support his or her evolving needs. This reality has produced a reinterpretation of aging in place by the long-term care and senior housing industries. The ultimate result of this reinterpretation is the emergence of senior residential options that offer services and assistance to older adults so that they may live in a more supportive environment that meets their changing needs (Bernard 2001). At the forefront of this wave of options is assisted living. What makes assisted living unique is its "supportive services, personalized assistance and health care, designed to respond to the individual needs of those who require help with activities of daily living and instrumental activities of daily living" (ALFA 1999:6).

The past fifteen years have witnessed an explosion in the senior housing industry in the number of assisted living communities constructed. By the end of 2000, an estimated 32,900 assisted living sites were present in the United States.[1] The growth of this housing/health care option created new residential opportunities for semi-independent and frail elderly. No longer does disability or advanced age translate into life in a nursing home. Instead, a frail older adult can move to a homelike environment designed to meet his or her needs. This creative new option appears to offer the perfect setting in which to age in place. Indeed, the assisted living industry has touted aging in place as one of the primary benefits of assisted living. Aging in place, however, may not be a reality for assisted living residents, because in order for aging in place to occur, many considerations come into play involving the licensure, regulation, marketing, and design of this housing option. Considerations in these various domains raise critical questions about the ability of assisted living to offer older adults a real opportunity to age in place.

The following chapters seek to systematically address a number of critical research questions that provide the framework for this book: (1) What exactly *does* aging in place mean in a setting such as assisted living? (2) How do the plethora of assisted living definitions and licensure categories affect aging in place? (3) What role does the continuum of care play for aging in place in assisted living? (4) Why are many residents unable to feel "at home" in assisted living and how is this reality linked to aging in place?

I will address these strategic research questions through the lens of anthropology. Anthropologists' holistic approach focuses on the interdependence of different parts of an issue in order to comprehend the larger picture. In the case of assisted living, the anthropological perspective can reveal the challenges facing assisted living residents and providers across the United States. It is critical to listen to the voices of those who encounter the consequences of policies and regulations on a daily basis so that we may better understand how the ideals and realities of assisted living translate on an individual level.

PROVIDERS AND RESIDENTS: DIFFERENT PERSPECTIVES ON ASSISTED LIVING

Assisted living is growing at a rapid rate across the country. Developers see the potential benefits that such a housing/health care alternative may offer frail adults. Accompanying the option of assisted living are a number of guiding ideals (known as the philosophy of assisted living). Providers adhering to the philosophy of assisted living hope that residents will maintain their independence and feel at home in assisted living and, ideally, that residents will not move on to another level of care but rather that they will die while residing in this more homelike setting. It is hoped that assisted living can serve as a viable alternative for older adults who do not yet require twenty-four-hour nursing care, thereby sparing them the institutional design and atmosphere of a nursing home environment. Finally, by permitting residents to assume the type of risks they would face in their own home (e.g., cooking, making repairs, smoking) assisted living promoters are optimistic that residents will learn to treat assisted living as their own home.

Few studies have investigated the individual's experience in assisted living compared with the industry's promises and the operator's procedures. This gap is crucial to bridge because the people who have the most to gain or lose in assisted living are the elderly residents themselves. It is they who will be living and possibly dying in assisted living environments; therefore, their stories must be known.

Equally as important, though not as overlooked, is the perspective of assisted living providers. The perceptions of residents, staff, and administrators at the local level should be brought into focus in order to approach the wider policy issues arising in the field of elderly housing and health care. The daily workings of assisted living must be understood from the perspectives of both residents and providers. How do administrators approach their residents? What is their philosophy? How do they perceive that assisted living fits into the established continuum of elderly care? Do administrators' perceptions differ from those of their staff? For residents, there is an equally compelling set of questions. How much independence, control, and autonomy do residents believe they have? How do they feel about other residents? What are their day-to-day experiences? Is assisted living home for them?

THE RESEARCH

Currently, qualitative and ethnographic research on assisted living is almost nonexistent. Although scholars have surveyed providers and evaluated resident characteristics, there are few studies in which the residents' perspective is represented. Notable exceptions include Barry (1999), Oh (1998), Knoerl (1993), Frank (1994), and Lucas (1999); however, all of these studies are unpublished dissertations and theses. The lack of a body of substantive research that focuses on the views of residents makes it almost impossible to test the ideals of assisted living against the residents' reality. This text focuses much attention on residents in order to capture the differences between the ideals and the realities of assisted living.

Qualitative research is especially timely because of the ongoing confusion that stems from the vast differences in assisted living from state to state. Assisted living advocates must understand the fact that, ideally, these various definitions of assisted living offer great flexibility for this housing option; at the same time, however, these differences often confuse residents and providers who have to interpret these definitions. Assisted living is still in its adolescence. Proponents and residents may still play an active role in shaping both the future of this option and its potential as "home" for the elderly, as long as their voices are heard. The anthropological approach certainly helps to shine new light on the assisted living industry by acknowledging the experiences of everyone involved with it.

Throughout the following chapters, the elderly women and men of two assisted living communities will offer their insights on issues such as design, quality of life, and aging in place. The qualitative data presented in this book are the result of eighteen months of research in the Chicago, Illinois, metropolitan area. Ethnographic fieldwork was conducted at two primary assisted living sites. The first site, Kramer, is a freestanding building housing twenty-nine residents in suburban Chicago. The second fieldwork site, Wood Glen, is actually a nursing home containing one floor devoted to assisted living.[2] Wood Glen is located in the city of Chicago and its assisted living floor houses up to seventeen residents.

A major part of the methodology for this research was participant-observation fieldwork conducted at both Kramer and Wood Glen. Not only is this particular research method absent from almost all of the studies cited above, but, at press time, there were no published studies on assisted living utilizing ongoing participant-observation fieldwork. Accordingly, in these studies researchers were removed from the opportunity to understand day-to-day life and happenings in assisted living.

My fieldwork at Wood Glen and Kramer included multiple tape-recorded interviews with residents and providers, informal interviews and discussions with both groups, participation in resident activities, and the administration of anonymous surveys.[3] During the year and a half spent at these two sites my daily interactions and in-depth interviews reveal that providers and especially residents are concerned with the issue of aging in place in assisted living and what it means for their future. Eight additional assisted living sites in the Chicago area were also visited and interviews were conducted with administrators at each setting. This was necessary so that data could be gathered from a diverse group of providers rather than just those at the two primary research sites.

OBJECTIVES

While addressing the research questions above, this book aims to accomplish three primary objectives:

1. to present residents' ideals and realities of life in assisted living,
2. to illustrate the differences between residents' ideals and realities and those of assisted living providers, and to convey what can be learned from these differences,
3. to utilize the ethnographic data gathered from residents and providers to direct the attention of scholars and the assisted living industry toward making assisted living a place residents can truly call home.

Through the unique details that residents and providers offer, assisted living proponents can direct their energy toward the impact that assisted living policies and regulations have on the different stakeholders involved in this housing/health care option. Should we maintain the current place of assisted living in the continuum of care, or should we adopt a controversial alternative that allows older adults to remain in one residential setting until they die? This question is undoubtedly the most pressing policy issue facing assisted living scholars in the United States today. Because this policy issue is so critical, the three objectives for this book will be pursued in tandem with my four research questions, all of which focus on aging in place. After all, it is the issue of aging in place that raises questions of regulation for policymakers, of interpretation for providers, and of daily life for residents. It is also the issue of aging in place that will determine the future of assisted living.

OVERVIEW OF CHAPTERS

Interwoven throughout the book are the voices of assisted living residents and providers. Although each chapter examines broad issues swirling around assisted living, providers' and residents' narratives serve to ground the topics in the reality of everyday experiences in assisted living.

Chapter 1 creates a foundation for the rest of the text by addressing the role of anthropology in studies of the elderly in residential environments. The chapter outlines the methods I used in my research and the role that "the elderly mystique" (Rosenfelt 1965) plays in our society. In conclusion, I discuss the critical role that ethnographic research can have in setting the stage for policymaking for assisted living.

Chapter 2 begins with the meaning of home for the residents of Kramer and Wood Glen. Residents express their thoughts and personal definitions of home. Analysis of tape-recorded interviews reveals how notions of identity, autonomy, and privacy are encompassed in what is known as a *sense of home*. Next, I turn to the importance of assisted living's physical design and the role its homelike atmosphere plays in the uniqueness of this housing option. Ultimately, residents offer explanations as to why they do not consider Kramer or Wood Glen their home. The reasons are complex and help set the stage for chapter 3.

In chapter 3 I speak to the nature of assisted living: its origin, history, and variations. From here I describe the philosophy of assisted living and the need to consider it when addressing resident satisfaction. Also highlighted in this chapter are various interpretations of what it means to age in place in senior housing. I close this chapter by presenting demographic data on the population currently residing in assisted living and how the population has evolved along with this residential option.

Chapter 4 narrows the focus to an examination of assisted living providers' experiences in the state of Illinois. Administrators from Kramer, Wood Glen, and other sites in Illinois present their perspectives on various aspects of assisted living, including admission and discharge criteria; the definition of assisted living; increasing frailty of residents; and the true benefits of assisted living for their residents. Nurses, activity directors, physicians, and assisted living directors from Illinois all speak to these issues, based on their experiences with residents, policies, and licensure. These providers have varying views on assisted living, all of which reflect the diversity of this residential option.

From the providers' view, I move on to an in-depth exploration in chapter 5 of the residents' reality. Kramer and Wood Glen residents speak about where they used to live and the circumstances surrounding their move to assisted living. Residents discuss their adjustment to assisted living, their feelings about their fellow residents, and their struggle to find purposeful tasks to accomplish. Residents also elaborate on friendships, social life, and the uncertainty of their lives at Kramer and Wood Glen.

Chapter 6 widens the focus back to the national level. Data from national studies on assisted living are presented in the context of several issues currently being debated in the assisted living industry. I discuss regulatory confusion across states and the obstacles it can present for assisted living providers and residents. First, marketing materials are carefully analyzed in relation to the philosophy of assisted living. Next, resident contracts are examined in order to highlight contradictions between the notion of aging in place and operator's policies. Resident rights are then probed on both the national and local levels. Wood Glen and Kramer are spotlighted here to convey the difference in perspectives regarding policies and resident freedoms. It appears staff and residents hold very different ideas about the flexibility of this residential option. Finally, this chapter closes by returning to the issue of aging in place: its interpretation by providers across the country and its impact on licensure, regulations, and a sense of home.

The final chapter of the book attempts to weave the various themes from chapters 1 through 6 together in order to address the research questions presented in the Introduction. The chapter begins by examining the close connection between the meaning of home and the philosophy of assisted living. Next, I explore the issue of autonomy for elders in long-term care settings. As part of this discussion I analyze the different types of autonomy and how seniors exercise their autonomy(ies) in different living environments. After this discussion, I re-examine assisted living as both part of and independent from the continuum of care. I examine this issue through the eyes of residents in order to highlight their conflicted feelings about what it means to age in place. The residents' perspective will then serve as a backdrop for a discussion of aging in place and dying in place in assisted living environments. Finally, I conclude by revisiting the phenomena of prolonged residence. I stress the urgent need for the assisted living industry to remedy the problem of prolonged residence if the industry wishes to make assisted living a place that elders can truly call "home."

NOTES

1. This number is according to Mollica (2000). It should be pointed out, however, that it is difficult to obtain a precise number of assisted living communities due to differences in terminology and state licensure. In addition, new assisted living communities are opening each month, making it difficult to pinpoint an exact number.

2. All names of persons and places are pseudonyms.

3. The survey administered to residents is the Sheltered Care Environment Scale (SCES) and was developed by Moos and Lemke (1996, 1984, 1988). The SCES is part of a larger tool developed by Moos and Lemke called the Multiphasic Environment Assessment Procedure (MEAP). For a full discussion of the MEAP and its use in my study, see Appendix I.

CHAPTER 1

Home, Housing for the Elderly, and Anthropology: A Conceptual Framework

People develop relationships with their physical dwellings that lead them to view their houses as homes. Occupants can see a house on one level as merely a structure and also experience the deeper level of house as home. Universally, homes function for people in so many important ways, both physical and psychological, that they become symbols that involve all aspects of our lives. Specifically, anthropological scholars such as Werner (1987), Dovey (1985), Rapoport (1976), and Duncan (1985) claim that our dwellings symbolize order, identity, social roles, and values.

THE CULTURAL SIGNIFICANCE OF HOME

The importance of home is evidenced in cultures around the world. Groups from Africa, Asia, the United States, and Europe all illustrate the use of housing as an expression of culture. Anthropological literature from the past century highlights the strong cultural link people have with their homes.

An examination of Navajo house structures, known as hogans, illustrates how important nature is to the Navajo way of life with the sun itself represented in the circular shape of the dwelling's floor. For the Navajo, the sun symbolizes power, protection, and life, and this is reflected in the function of the hogan, which "offers protection from evil" (Art 1979:2). The four directions and the four seasons are also illustrated through the hogan. "East is the direction of the home of the sun, and is associated with spring and birth. Hence the doorway into the hogan faces east, as a place to begin 'entrance' into the life cycle" (Frank 1989:2). The total structure of the hogan also symbolizes nature.

The domelike roof and the dirt floor represent the sky and the earth. Every time they enter the hogan, Navajos are reminded of their cosmology: what they consider important to the cyclical and eternal order of their lives.

Homes can also serve as a symbol of identity. Our homes allow us to show others how we wish them to perceive us. This identity is not only reflexive but can lead people to actually personify their homes. The Batammaliba of Togo and Benin vividly describe their homes as human. "In a variety of ways, the Batammaliba suggest that their houses are human, that they represent men and women. The fabric of this house complements that of the human body; the earthen core is its flesh . . . the water used in moistening the earth is its blood, the numerous pebbles are its bones, and the smooth plaster surface is its skin" (Blier 1987:119).

Within any given society houses also symbolize social rules and cultural values: Social rules describe what behaviors are appropriate and expected in settings at particular times, thereby giving meaning to the settings, people, and their behaviors. In all societies, social norms and roles dictate how homes should be used, the time and places for entering, entertaining, sleeping, and eating as well as a myriad of other behaviors and symbolic practices. Social norms and roles are also reflected in the very designs and configurations of residences, the types and locations of furniture and objects, and the like. (Werner, Altman, and Oxley 1985:3–4)

Once again the reciprocal relationships between people and their homes is clear. Our social structures and cultural values produce the physical form and arrangement of our homes; and the homes themselves serve as a symbolic reminder of those values our society holds dear.

Homes can symbolize social structure through either their physical design and use or by cultural rituals. For example, in the Trobriand Islands, hereditary chiefs have absolute rights over the rest of their village. This is reflected in the positioning and size of their homes. "The political power of the chiefs was symbolized by their [homes'] location in the center [of the village] and the possession of elaborately decorated yam storage houses" (Duncan 1985:141).

Duncan (1985) shows in Sri Lanka, how the location, decoration, and use of homes reflect the caste system. First, the castes live in different areas of the village and build their houses from different materials. And, although castes may interact in the public realm, the private or home realm is "not for mixing." On those rare occasions when lower caste people must visit the houses of higher caste persons, the inequality of the social structure manifests itself through the behavior in the homes. Usually, lower caste persons may not even enter the house. They must sit on the porch outside of the dwelling. For Sri Lankans, "the home is the place of ritual honor, of the etiquette and hierarchy that constitutes the heart of a caste system whose guiding principle is, of course, inequality. It is here in the home where caste identity is strongest" (Duncan 1985:144).

This discussion of the symbolic properties of homes is significant for a number of reasons. There can be no doubt that homes, in the capacities of order, identity, and social rules, certainly fulfill many psychological functions. It is also quite evident that social and cultural qualities of homes are developed through the interaction of residents with the physical environment that surrounds them. The question is, how does understanding social qualities of dwellings relate to elderly housing problems and the present state of assisted living?

HOUSING FOR THE ELDERLY: YOU CAN'T GO HOME AGAIN

Housing and health care settings for the elderly have been historically designed with little or no acknowledgment of the residents' cultural needs and sense of home. For fulfillment of these needs there must be certain features present in the built environment that will encourage residents' sense of order, identity, and social structure. Characteristics such as carpeting (rather than linoleum floors), private bathrooms, the ability to bring one's own furniture and personal items, and access to cooking facilities can all help to make an environment feel more like home. If these features are absent, the environment may be rendered a social failure for the occupants. Residents of housing developments for the elderly tend to suffer much frustration and anger because of their lack of choice regarding their health status, their move, and their new living arrangement. If residents had the chance to contribute to the design process they would probably choose structural features that are culturally and socially relevant to their own lives, whereas architects might not. Sometimes this problem is also evident in the marketing of housing for the elderly. Frequently advertisers and developers market the residence toward the older person's adult children, thereby choosing styles and furnishings that are not necessarily pleasing or helpful to the older person but are to their family members. This issue will be discussed in greater detail in chapter 6.

Choice is also an important element regarding behavior in the environment. The amount of choice that the environment offers can greatly affect the inhabitants in that setting. "Freedom of choice is a critical aspect of man's behavior in relation to his physical environment. Whatever the primary purpose that brings the individual to a given physical setting, the setting must not only have the capacity to satisfy the primary need and other relevant subsidiary needs, but it must also allow for goal satisfactions that are only remotely related to the major purpose" (Proshansky, Ittleson, and Rivlin 1970:175). Housing environments for the elderly are often regarded as socially constraining by the residents for a number of reasons. Meals are scheduled at designated times, the thermostat is set at a particular temperature, and residents do not have choices regarding who they live with. How can social and cultural goals be attained in an environment that is potentially "disabling" to its inhabitants?

There can be major repercussions for residents if their housing is not socially or emotionally enabling. One major problem is the negative self-identity assumed by many residents. If our environments reflect ourselves, and if residents are unable to achieve social satisfaction within the environment, then they will begin to relate negatively to the environment. In addition, residents living in senior housing, especially more medicalized environments, may believe their identity is stigmatized. Although the following statement by Rapoport (1981) refers to public housing, it poignantly applies to housing for the elderly: "Identity, particularly seen from the outside, can be either positive or negative, so that identity communicated to outsiders can become so negative as to constitute a *stigma*. Public housing projects are known for taking on such characteristics; their residents are given a negative identity and are stereotyped, leading to a process of stigmatization" (Rapoport 1981:12). This stigma is certainly assigned to residents of housing for the elderly. Outsiders believe that everyone inside is sick, helpless, and dying. It seems likely that this stigma and sense of frustration are due to a combination of social and architectural factors because the creation of a sense of home itself results from more than architectural design or physical experience. It arises from the *relationship* between people and their environment. When conditions in seniors' housing inhibit them from creating any sort of positive relationship with the environment, the living conditions can actually take on qualities of a total institution (Goffman 1961).

Our relationships with our homes, as well as the wider meaning of home in our culture, are important concepts to bear in mind while examining assisted living. Developers and designers of assisted living are specifically hoping to get past the stigma of housing for the elderly. Although in many ways this goal has been achieved, it has fallen short when it comes to aging in place. This point will become clearer through a discussion of the history of anthropological approaches to studying the aged.

ANTHROPOLOGICAL APPROACHES TO AGING

Anthropology has made important contributions to gerontology and the study of aging. Anthropologists first became involved with aging in the mid-1940s. Until that time it has been said, "anthropology had a long history of being interested in age, but not in aging or the aged" (Fry 1980:1). In 1945 Leo Simmons wrote the first cross-cultural book on aging, titled *The Role of the Aged in Primitive Society*. For twenty years after this seminal work was printed, however, little additional work in the field was published. The few writings that did address the elderly in the 1950s and early 1960s were "based on observations incidental to research focused on some other central problem" (Clark 1973:79). The observations on aging were "buried in ethnographic accounts, and were almost never singled out for special presentation in journal articles" (Clark 1973:79).

In the late 1960s anthropological interest in the aged began to grow. In 1967 Margaret Clark and Barbara Anderson published *Culture and Aging*, ushering in a new wave of aging studies. In addition, in 1977 the Association for Anthropology and Gerontology (AAGE) was formed.

By the early 1970s cultural anthropologists began to concentrate more on aging as a specific subject for research. By 1973 six "principal concepts of aging" emerged (Clark 1973). The concepts included: (1) aging as dying; (2) aging as decrement and disengagement; (3) aging as disease; (4) aging as dependency and regression; (5) aging as minority group status; and (6) aging as development. Interestingly, almost all of these principal concepts focused on the negative aspects of aging and shed a decidedly depressing light on the process of growing older. As the 1970s ended, different topics began to emerge as the central point of anthropological scholarship of the aged. Community formation, cultural adaptation to aging, and the status of the elderly began to be examined in more detail.

As aging research advanced, three themes came to distinguish the anthropological approach: (1) an emic perspective; (2) a documentation of diversity; and (3) a holistic view of aging. The emic, or insider, perspective is important for aging research because it helps anthropologists refute stereotypes typically associated with aged people. Anthropologists sought to understand the elderly by eliciting the feelings and experiences of older adults in various cultures in order to understand the older adults' reality, not interpretations of their reality by others.

Anthropology also contributed to aging studies by documenting the great diversity of older people between societies. The roles, situations, and attitudes of the aged were shown to be complex and very different across cultures. The most important contribution of ethnography in relation to this theme was that we began to see "the diversity among old people, seen by outsiders to be the same" (Keith 1981:287).

Finally, anthropology made a critical contribution to gerontological studies by highlighting the "holistic view of cultural context as it affects the old" (Keith 1981:286). Anthropologists revealed the importance of understanding the contexts that produce certain attitudes and behavior toward the aged rather than judging them by our own biased standards. They also pointed out the need to understand how the notion of aging fits into a society's culture as a whole. What is the role of elders in a society? What responsibilities and powers do older adults carry? What are the interconnections between generations within individual societies?

Since these early contributions to gerontological studies, anthropology's involvement in aging studies has become much more complex as anthropologists have expanded their research to include studies on culture, person, and age; community studies on aging; and medical/health analysis of older people. Anthropology and aging research continues to grow and develop, branching out into a number of different areas including medical anthropology, community studies, disease specific studies, and studies of age-segregated communities. Since assisted living represents a type of age-segregated community, it will be useful to understand the history of anthropological research in this arena.

As research progressed, age-segregated community studies began to be divided into two types: those communities that are institutions or nursing homes and those that are not. Age-segregated, noninstitutional community studies often center on retirement communities (Jacobs 1974) or public housing for the elderly (Smithers 1985). Anthropologists frequently examine the nature of community formation and adjustment by residents. Janice Smithers, for example, in her 1985 ethnography titled *Determined Survivors: Community Life among the Urban Elderly,* was very interested in how the poor elderly residents of a housing project in Los Angeles (called St. Regis) managed to "stay at home" so long. She learned that residents looked out for one another and created a system of reciprocity whereby they exchanged goods and services with each other as needed. This system allowed St. Regis residents to age in place longer, with many residents actually dying there (an achievement the residents hoped for). Thus, Smithers found that there was actual community formation among these poor frail elderly and that their secret for survival was being able to rely on each other. As she puts it, "being aided by similar others is minimally threatening to self-esteem" (Smithers 1985:181). The importance of reciprocity will be developed further in this book as the assisted living residents speak about friendships and social interactions in their living environments.

Many researchers studying age-segregated communities have focused on nursing homes. Scholars such as Gubrium (1975), Kidder (1993), Kayser-Jones (1981), and Savishinsky (1991) have all examined the institution of the nursing home. Unlike the studies of retirement communities and public housing, this research tends to focus on medical issues, socialization, and staff-resident relationships. Part of the reason for anthropologists' interest in nursing homes is that the majority of nursing home residents do not place themselves there. Rather, a concerned family member or physician places the older adult in the nursing home for "his or her own good."

Uneasy Endings: Daily Life in an American Nursing Home (1988) by Renee Rose Shield examined the lives and relationships between seniors in a New England nursing home. The Franklin nursing home houses 250 primarily Jewish residents. Shield spent fourteen months between 1981 and 1983 conducting fieldwork at the nursing home and interviewing a number of residents and staff. I have chosen to highlight Shield's ethnography because her findings and experiences were very similar to my own. She found that there was no basic community formation among the residents of the Franklin nursing home. Instead, the residents at Franklin were isolated and "only superficially involved with each other" (Shield 1990:332). Through issues such as dependency, control, reciprocity, liminality, and quality of life, Shield examined the relationships of residents to staff and of residents to each other in order to understand why community formation does not occur. *Uneasy Endings* focuses on the anthropological topic of rites of passage and how moving into a nursing home is an unfinished rite of passage. "When the residents leave behind independent life in the community, dependency is dramatized. Unlike other rites of passage and unlike degradation ceremonies, however, there is no explicit next stage for which admission to the nursing home prepares the entrant" (Shield 1988:126). Shield presents a hypothesis for the lack of community formation by discussing reciprocity and control and how they relate to incomplete rites of passage. Shield's hypothesis will be explored in greater detail in later chapters. Specifically, I will examine the concepts of liminality and the incomplete rite of passage in relation to residents at Wood Glen and Kramer. In order to fully understand how and why liminality occurs for many older adults living in institutional environments, it is important to examine anthropological rites of passage in depth.

RITES OF PASSAGE, LIMINALITY, AND ASSISTED LIVING

Entering assisted living means giving up one's home and, often, the outside world. The process of leaving one's dwelling is referred to as "breaking up the home" (Shield 1988, 1990), a time during which the elderly person must decide what items to take along and what items to dispose. "Breaking up a home means losing ties with many people, objects, and places. Most recall the loss of loved ones—a spouse, children, a friend—with whom they once made a home. Their histories store memories of birthdays, weddings, and other times when someone now gone was somehow linked to them. . . . Breaking ties with objects blurs a set of sentiments as does breaking ties with people" (Gubrium as quoted in Shield 1988:132). The loss of one's home encompasses every other loss an elderly person experiences. Perhaps that is why remaining in their own homes is so important to older adults.

The transition to assisted living can also be quite difficult for older adults. The activities, meal choices, and services that providers offer do not mirror the freedom and independence residents experienced in their own homes. Residents at both Kramer and Wood Glen share this opinion. Eighty-nine-year-old Kramer resident Katie Jacobs, who has been in group living for more than ten years, claims, "I've been in these places [group living] long enough to know that no place is better than your own home." One reason residents do not think of assisted living as home is because home is a place where they have complete control. Residents at Kramer and Wood Glen claim they do not have a sense of control over their lives. Instead they feel a sense of loss.

What happens after these elderly people move into assisted living and try to settle in? Many residents of Kramer and Wood Glen never complete the transition from their homes to their assisted living community. They reside in a limbo of sorts. An explanation of how and why this occurs can be found in the anthropological literature on rites of passage.

In cultures throughout the world, rites of passage mark the transition from one stage of life to another. According to Van Gennup (1960), rites of passage have three components: *separation* from the old status, *transition* (or liminality) between old and new roles, and *reincorporation* into the new life role. During rites of passage, initiates must learn about the new position they are about to acquire. Rituals that take place during such rites help to make the transition less stressful for the initiates. The liminal, or transition, phase is considered the most precarious of the three stages because the person has no defined role. Turner (1977) further developed the idea of liminality, applying it to any situation in which people are defined as belonging to neither one category nor another. Turner also stresses the idea of *communitas,* or the bonding that initiates usually experience when they undergo a rite of passage together.

In Shield's *Uneasy Endings* (1988), she applied these concepts to residents in one particular nursing home. She argues that elderly residents experience an incomplete rite of passage when they enter a nursing home because they have no new role to assume in the nursing home. According to her, residents experience no *communitas*; they do not bond with others when they move into the nursing home, and they do not assume new roles once they settle in. My research at Kramer and Wood Glen reveals that much of the same process occurs in assisted living. Residents claim they feel lost and useless, not knowing what they should be *doing* while they live in assisted living.

This limbo has been discussed by other anthropologists who study the elderly. For example, anthropologist Haim Hazan addressed liminality and the concept of time among Jewish seniors in a London senior center in his book, *The Limbo People* (1980). In another example, Carobeth Laird (1979) wrote a personal account of her own life in a nursing home. Due to failing health, this anthropologist entered a nursing home at the age of seventy-nine. Her book, *Limbo: Memoir of Life in a Nursing Home by a Survivor,* chronicles her experiences in an Arizona nursing home. Finally, Joel Savishinsky (1991) examined the realities of living and working in a nursing home in his book, *The Ends of Time: Life and Work in a Nursing Home.* Savishinsky looked at how residents deal with losses and build relationships with staff and volunteers at Elmwood Grove nursing home in upstate New York.

Residents in assisted living environments experience this same limbo, caused from an incomplete rite of passage (Frank 1994, 1999). Further, residents in assisted living endure a heightened sense of liminality because they do not know how long they can stay in assisted living. The site may operate according to one of the varying definitions of assisted living, based on the laws in that state, creating a strong sense of uncertainty among residents. Liminality creates prolonged residence for older adults in assisted living. Prolonged residence does not allow residents to feel "at home" in their residential environment because their separation from their old status and roles will continue for an unspecified period of time, possibly months or years. The point is that because residents cannot fully age in place (meaning remain where they are until they die) they remain in a suspended state and are very uneasy with this situation. Hence, it is critical to understand that prolonged residence is not *fully* aging in place. And while assisted living may be preferable to living in a more restrictive environment, the uncertainty of their length of residence does not help residents psychologically or socially, as will be explained in detail in subsequent chapters.

FIELDWORK CHALLENGES AND EPISTEMOLOGICAL WINDOWS

Several challenges arose during my fieldwork and research at Kramer and Wood Glen that opened rich epistemological windows. An epistemological window is defined as "any situation during the ethnographic process that potentially enhances the discovery of new insights into the cultural knowledge of the people under study" (Werner 1987:57). Simply put, epistemological windows are new opportunities for learning and they are critical for any qualitative research.

The first challenge I faced was the lack of a universally accepted definition of assisted living. Because no standard definition exists, I have compiled over twenty definitions during my research. Many of these definitions overlap but they are different enough to be considered separate definitions. The ramifications of this lack of a uniform definition will be discussed in greater detail in chapters 3 and 6.

I experienced several hurdles involving the residents of Kramer and Wood Glen. First, it was difficult to remove myself from the role in which residents had initially placed me. For many residents, my role was somewhat unclear. Although I constantly reminded tenants why I was spending time at their assisted living communities, they were still somewhat confused. Some residents clearly believed that by complaining to me about the food, the activities, or the other residents, I would somehow be able to change things; after all, they were *sure* I was a social worker. On the other hand, several residents expressed the opposite opinion. They told me that they would not discuss their dislikes with me because, as they said, "what are you going to be able to do about it? Nothing. So, why discuss it?" Still, other residents gave me the impression they believed they would "get into trouble" if they said anything negative to me about Kramer or Wood Glen. Even though I assured residents that anything they said to me would be held in the strictest of confidence, they were still reluctant to voice negative feelings about many issues. Possible reasons for their reluctance will be analyzed in chapters 5 and 6.

The second hurdle and epistemological window involving residents resulted from my attempts to interview residents at Wood Glen and Kramer. I planned to conduct an extensive series of interviews with many residents at both locations. These plans were quickly altered once the fieldwork began. The reality of my situation turned out to be that getting tape-recorded interviews with residents was, to quote one Kramer administrator, "like pulling teeth." Although residents were very willing to sit and chat with me on subjects ranging from politics to the aging process, when it came to formal, tape-recorded interviews, I always encountered the same barrier. A pattern of reasons and excuses began to surface, such as "oh honey, I don't have anything interesting to tell you, my life wasn't that exciting," or "I've participated in surveys and interviews before and I don't want to do it again," or the very popular "I don't have anything to say, what could you possibly learn from me?" Almost every single resident I spoke with, both those I ended up interviewing on tape and those I did not, began our interaction with one of the above statements. After hearing these phrases several times, I began to respond by suggesting that they have plenty to offer because every person has a unique perspective on life in assisted living and everyone's life experiences are different. My comments were usually met with "oh, but my life was boring, what do you want to know from me?" or "honey, you're young, what do you want to waste your time talking to old people for?—You must have a lot of patience."

In a 1988 study of an East Coast nursing home, Renee Rose Shield encountered similar problems when trying to interview elderly residents at the Franklin Home. Shield referred to residents' methods to close a conversation as "enders."

As though they expected to be considered rambling and boring, several residents pepper their speech with "enders" such as "and that's all dear," or "what can I say?" These linguistic enders allow the resident to take the initiative to stop the conversation, sparing the speaker embarrassment if his audience is impatient. If I allowed the pause ensuing after an ender to persist and did not follow up the resident's invitation to end the conversation, he often continued to talk—until the next ender, which he inserted a minute or so later. This mechanism protects the speaker from seeming [to be] unaware that the talk is repetitive or overly long. This talk-stop behavior is adaptive because residents are critical of each other and are often quick to note repetitiveness or other similar traits. But these self-monitoring devices muffle free-flowing talk and create a laborious self-consciousness. (Shield 1988:167)

I experienced much the same scenario with residents from Wood Glen and Kramer. I would be led out of the conversation if the resident thought that he or she was rambling. It was as though residents were testing my interest level, making sure it was safe to really speak in an in-depth manner about their lives.

The process of getting interviews was initially very discouraging. The interesting part of the whole process is that once I did succeed in convincing residents to sit down for interviews, almost all of the residents told me afterward how much they enjoyed talking with me. Before the interview, many residents told me, "My life is basically over, so why would anyone want to hear the reminiscing of an old lady?" They did not react this way after the interview. I believe that this process created an important epistemological window. Residents seemed to enjoy the special individualized attention that I gave them. They needed to be persuaded that I was genuinely interested in listening to what they had to say. Insights regarding why residents were hesitant to speak with me and used many "enders" in our early conversations can be found from an examination of "the elderly mystique."

The Elderly Mystique: An Epistemological Window on My Fieldwork

In 1965, researcher Rosalie Rosenfelt, inspired by Betty Friedan's 1963 book, *The Feminine Mystique*, introduced a term called "the elderly mystique." According to Rosenfelt, the term "refers to a core of ideas and attitudes, explicit or not, held by an in-group with respect to a particular concept—in the present instance, old age" (1965:27). Rosenfelt asserts that the elderly mystique arose during and after World War II and has continued to evolve ever since. According to her 1965 article, there are several facets associated with the elderly mystique. First, there is the assumption that society regards older people as declining in their health and vitality. Society assumes that older persons lose their mental faculties, leaving "adventure and creativity for the young and courageous" (p. 39). Second, the elderly mystique maintains that society perceives older people as "behind the times," rigid, and incapable of working any longer. These qualities eventually lead to isolation and loneliness for the elderly individual. Family ties may be lost as the older person assumes his or her grown children need to focus on their own nuclear families. "Nothing is to be expected from the children, they have their own lives to lead" (p. 39).

The central point of the elderly mystique is that many older people themselves embrace the ageist notions outlined here. "The participant in the elderly mystique knows society finds it hard to accept, let alone forgive, his existence" (p. 40). Interestingly, Rosenfelt links her elderly mystique with Goffman's idea of stigma. Rosenfelt says that older people are strongly stigmatized due to their age and assumed frailty. She says this stigmatization results in the formation of a subculture among older adults whereby they cling together and find some solace in their shared state of rejection. Other older adults may instead attempt to fight the elderly mystique (and aging) by "acting young" or choosing not to retire, thereby thwarting their stigmatized role as "elderly."

Later scholars such as Cohen (1988, 1990) expanded on the elderly mystique, saying that as times have changed, so too has this mystique. No longer aimed at *all* older adults, the elderly mystique is now reserved for application to frail and disabled elders. And, Cohen (1988) argues, much of this frail and disabled population lives in settings such as nursing homes and long-term care facilities. I maintain that assisted living shelters as much of this same frail and disabled population as nursing homes and long-term care facilities. Implications of this assertion will be revealed as the book progresses.

In 1965 Rosenfelt outlined some serious consequences for those who embrace the elderly mystique. These consequences lead me to reflect on many of my experiences with residents at Kramer and Wood Glen.

What are the consequences of belief in the elderly mystique? As with the feminine mystique, *acceptance of so limited and limiting a view ends by not only blinding its holders to the full range of possibilities available to them but also by so deforming them in conformity with its warped image that they become as restricted as the mystique would have them.* A vicious circle is then set in motion. There is no hope in old age, and those who grow older are quite hopeless. That, in essence, is the elderly mystique. Clearly, the world pays dearly for this myopic view of what are sardonically called "The Golden Years." (Rosenfelt 1965:41)

As I will argue in more detail later, I believe many of the residents of Wood Glen and Kramer subscribe to the elderly mystique. They negate themselves, view themselves as less than "full persons," and restrict their own autonomy and self-expression because they hold to the stigma of the elderly mystique. Their statements and apprehensions noted above about participating in my research illustrate this point. Many residents use "enders" or self-deprecating language that is certainly connected to the elderly mystique. They focus on their decrements and tell me they feel useless to society. As I will also discuss later, it appears that many providers in the assisted living industry also adhere to the elderly mystique when creating and administering their policies and procedures.

A review of anthropological studies on aging presages the discussion for this book on assisted living housing for the elderly. Since assisted living is a combination of a housing environment and a health care environment, it has been useful to see how anthropological studies of institutional as well as noninstitutional environments for the elderly set a foundation for a study of assisted living. Likewise useful to explore are the notions of home and the relationships between individuals and their homes. This book now turns to a detailed explanation of the special relationship that many older adults have with their homes. This relationship shapes their lives in assisted living and their perspectives on aging in place.

CHAPTER 2

Home Is Where the Heart Is

House n.
  (1) a building for human beings to live in, something regarded as a house; a place that provides shelter, living space et cetera.
  (2) any place where something is thought of living, resting, etc.

Home n.
  (1) a dwelling place; the place in which one resides; the seat of domestic life and interests.
  (2) the abiding place of one's affections; a place where one likes to be; restful or congenial place; as home is where the heart is.
  (3) a place or institution provided for the needy and the homeless, as a home for orphans or veterans.
  (4) the grave or death.

Homelike adj.
  (1) having qualities usually associated with home; comfortable, familiar, friendly, cozy, etc.
        Webster's New Twentieth Century Unabridged Dictionary 1977: 869

"A home is the idea of who you are."
                    Mr. Anderson, homeless man (Brown 1993:18)

Few words in the English language embody as much emotional symbolism as home. The word "home" carries meanings of shelter, security, and protection. At the same time, home is also an intensely personal idea. Experiences conveyed in the notion of home span one's entire lifetime. During childhood we become familiar with the idea of home as the place where we not only live but also find comfort and security. As we grow older the concept of home stays with us; yet, its meaning expands to encompass more intangible qualities: cultural norms, social values, and personal memories. Ultimately, home seems to be a word whose meaning is enhanced with the passing of time: the older we become the more enriched and fulfilling our notions of home become. By the time we reach our elderly years, our sense of home is more than place: it has been integrated into our personal identities.

Although the meaning of home can be separated from a physical place, home is still considered to be "where the heart is." This may be especially true for elderly people who no longer live in their own dwellings and often associate home with somewhere they used to live rather than with their current residence. Older adults living in life care facilities do not automatically feel "at home" in their new living arrangement. This problem can lead to feelings of despair, depression, and health problems, both physical and psychological.

Home is also a word that conveys multiple meanings to people. Americans use the word almost daily yet rarely stop and think about what it really means to be "going home" or to be "at home." Yet, at the same time we all understand the phrase "there's no place like home." Why is the notion of home so complex and why is it so important when examining life in assisted living?

ASSISTED LIVING: A HOMELIKE ENVIRONMENT

Assisted living is currently considered to be a promising residential alternative for those older adults whose needs exceed their ability to live independently yet do not require twenty-four-hour skilled nursing care. The primary purpose of assisted living is to help residents with activities of daily living, otherwise known as ADLs. This housing option developed in reaction to a strictly medical model of care that often placed elderly persons in a much more constraining and institutionalized care setting like a nursing home or hospital.

The elderly person entering a nursing home environment often faces the feeling of instant institutionalization. A revealing definition of "home" cited at the beginning of this chapter defines home as a place or institution for the needy or homeless. Certainly our idea of nursing "homes" fits into this depressing definition. Elderly people see nursing homes as a place they go to die not to live; yet, the usual idea of home we tend to carry with us invokes life, contentment, and happiness.

Assisted living pioneers believe that a more homelike environment needed to be introduced into housing for the elderly. As a philosophy of care that emphasizes restorative health, control, choice, privacy, independence, and dignity for residents, advocates believe that assisted living accomplishes this goal (Regnier 1991; Kane et al. 1990). In fact "homelike" even appears in several major definitions of assisted living. Victor Regnier, architect and well-known leader in the design and research of assisted living, defines assisted living as "a model of residential long term care where professionally managed and administered services are provided in an effort to keep residents physically and psychologically independent in a residential homelike environment" (Regnier 1992:4). Another popular definition of assisted living is as follows: "Assisted living emphasizes 'home-like' living units, privacy, resident choice, independence, shared risk, and the shared responsibility in which residents actively participate in the accomplishment of regular tasks and activities" (Mollica et al. 1992:1).

In order to fully comprehend the homelike aspects of assisted living, it will be useful to examine the word "homelike." It is defined as "having qualities usually associated with home; comfortable, familiar, friendly, cozy, etc." (*Webster's New Twentieth Century Unabridged Dictionary* 1977: 869). In contrast, home is "the abiding place of one's affections." As such, "homelike" connotes more than a shelter; yet it does not imply the emotional attachment that the more abstract idea of "home" does. How do assisted living practitioners go about making residential care and services "homelike" for the elderly?

Creating a homelike environment involves a definite design aspect. Architecture can do a great deal to lessen the institutional character of a building. Design features such as smaller buildings, private rooms, cozy spaces, and outdoor courtyards all contribute to a more homelike environment because they create a residential setting. Some assisted living communities (such as those designed by Sunrise Assisted Living) are actually built to resemble mansions or country homes, further adding to the homelike ambiance. Privacy and individuality are central concerns when designing a homelike environment. "Creating small private apartments with kitchens, baths and locking doors was only the first step in normalizing the environment, in making a home. Just as important was actively encouraging residents to furnish their apartments completely . . . having the use of one's own things in a space which approximates the features of home was assumed to be comforting, stimulating, and orienting" (Wilson 1990a:4). Assisted living supporters clearly seek to involve residents in creating a homelike environment by encouraging them to bring their own furniture and belongings (in most cases) so that they may personalize their dwellings. But, as with the notion of home, a homelike environment goes beyond the physical design or personal belongings. It also involves lifestyle and social structure (Wilson 1990a). This point will become clear through the voices of assisted living residents.

Supporting independence is another important dimension of a homelike environment. But how does one define "independence"? In a study conducted by Andrew Sixsmith (1986) a number of community-dwelling elderly were questioned about what being independent meant to them. Several themes emerged including the ability to take care of one's self and the ability to make personal choices and decisions. Sixsmith points out that older adults place an even greater value on maintaining their independence as long as possible since they realize that they are likely to become less independent with age. One primary way that elderly people believe they maintain their independence is by remaining in their own home. "Overwhelmingly, people felt that their own home helped to keep them independent" (Andrew Sixsmith 1986:342). Respondents in the study felt that they were content at home, that they could do what they wanted there, that they could "do things for themselves," and that they did not have to answer to anyone. Fearing a loss of home can amount to fearing a loss of independence. Loss of independence can then lead to loss of a sense of control.

The extent to which we believe that "what happens to us is a matter of fate, luck or our own powerlessness versus a belief that we are the master of our own destinies" is known as a sense of control (Howell 1985:58). This feeling is certainly connected to our living environments. If people know that they can control when they eat, how high the thermostat is set, and who is allowed into their domain, they are likely to feel much more comfortable and at home. Assisted living has certainly attempted to foster control and independence in a number of ways. Personalizing the environment has done a great deal to promote independence and control. If residents are free to decorate their own apartments, set their own thermostats, and lock their own doors, they will have more of a sense of control.

THE MEANING OF HOME

One prominent definition of "home" states that a home is "a dwelling place . . . the seat of domestic life and interests" (*Webster's New Twentieth Century Unabridged Dictionary* 1977:869). In this definition home is revealed to be a physical structure where people live and carry out their daily lives. This definition is the most basic in that it is directly rooted in place. Yet, even the physical level of home is multidimensional because the home is not only a material structure but also "a shelter for those things that make life meaningful" (Csikszentmihalyi and Rochberg-Halton 1989:139). People usually keep items closest to their hearts and memories in their homes. Photographs, furniture, art, and books are all cherished objects with which we choose to fill our dwellings. In effect, our homes embody the material history of our lives.

Because home describes a physical structure where activity takes place, it is easy to confuse it with the word *house*. Yet, many scholars in the field of environment-behavior studies find vast differences between these two terms. According to architect Dovey (1985), house and home mean two different things. People develop relationships with their physical dwellings that lead them to view their houses in symbolic ways. While they see a house as merely a structure, they also experience the deeper, more emotional meaning of home. A house may be a physical unit but home is "a complex entity that defines and is defined by cultural, socio-demographic, psychological, political, and economic factors" (Lawrence 1987:155). Homes are psychologically as well as physically involved in the process of our daily lives. This process is known as "dwelling." "Home is ... part of the experience of dwelling—something we do, a way of weaving up a life in particular geographic spaces" (Saegert 1985: 287). Saegert also emphasizes that "dwelling highlights the contrast between house and home" (p. 287). The reason is because here "dwelling" is used as a verb and it connotes a relationship between person and place. Many scholars support the idea that any definition of "home" should include a discussion of this relationship. Interestingly, the residents at Kramer and Wood Glen also experienced this house/home contrast. According to Kramer resident Zelda Arnold, "A home is if you have a kitchen and a dining room ... I always had 'open house' at my house, I always had something I could serve ... now my children come here and sit down and I can't even offer them a cup of coffee ... I always used to have company, here I just sit by myself, no one here, nothing to do" (interview by author, tape recording, Chicago, Illinois, 11 November 1992). Zelda senses the difference between the physical space she lives in and the relationship of home. Wood Glen resident Sandy Anderson makes the idea of home clear as well. "Home is a nice place to stay where I can invite my friends and enjoy myself by myself. Where it is peaceful and quiet the majority of the time" (interview by author, tape recording, Chicago, Illinois, 8 January 1993). Both Zelda and Sandy allude to the structural aspects of a home within their discussions.

A second definition of home cited at the beginning of this chapter explains home to be " a place of one's affections ... where the heart is." This definition highlights the emotional relationship between people and place as well as represents a host of ideas outside of the physical world. For instance, in the United States, homes function in many important ways and involve several aspects of our lives. Our dwellings represent social structure, cultural order, and personal identity.

Homes can symbolize social structure through either physical or cultural means. Physically, the decoration of the home can reflect the status, class, or political affiliation of the people living in it. For example, New England colonists who were loyal to the king of England painted a black stripe around the top of their chimneys as a symbolic gesture. There are several other examples. Jewish families place a mezuza (a small decorated case holding parchment with a Hebrew prayer on it) on their door post to symbolize adherence to their religion and to bless those who enter their home. Another example is the practice of setting aside a dwelling for use by a politically or culturally prominent figure. A governor's mansion, a king's palace, or a president's house all serve to mark the importance of the inhabitant.

Apart from the outer design, rituals can be used to help establish and reinforce home as a symbol of social structure. Saile (1985) points out that almost all societies practice some form of ritual either during the construction of a house or immediately upon its completion. In America this ritual takes the form of a house-warming party. By welcoming friends and neighbors into the new home a family reaffirms its connection to the wider social values and norms of society. An interesting point is the fact that this ritual is called a *house*-warming party rather than a home-warming party. Perhaps naming the ritual a house-warming party is significant in itself because after construction, the house is merely a physical structure. Not until friends and family share in welcoming the residents to their new dwelling does it truly become a home.

Beyond the initial construction and occupation rituals of the home, people reinforce the importance of their dwellings through recurrent ceremonies. These ceremonies not only support societal values and social norms but they also strengthen the meaning of home by taking place in the home. "There are many festivals, anniversaries, and celebrations that are meant to be enacted in the home" (Saile 1985:2). Wood Glen resident Sara Vernon highlights the importance of these ceremonial activities in her description of home:

It is where the heart is, to be cliché-ish. But it is where your children are, where you are loved and where you love. Where people care about each other and share their lives whether it is painful or not. You share and that is all that matters. And, having a lot of meals. I was thinking of all the turkeys I prepared for Thanksgiving. We always had twelve at my table. My dad would always carve . . . now I look back and say, "Thank God I did it." I was so happy that everybody came to my house. I loved that. (interview by author, tape recording, Chicago, Illinois, 18 November 1992)

As Sara's discussion shows, the home and the ritual conducted within it mutually act upon one another to validate the social values and rules of society.

On a broader scale, people practice rituals in relation to homes. When entering a church, synagogue, mosque, or temple, one is expected to perform certain rituals such as taking off one's shoes, bowing, or covering one's head. All of these rituals are done in deference to the "house of worship" that the person has entered.[1]

Ordering our lives is another abstract function of homes. We perceive homes as providing both spatial and social order because they help us to establish behavioral patterns that give us a feeling of security. Dwellings provide spatial order because they demarcate physical boundaries between inside and outside (inside being the home environment and outside being everything else beyond the home). Sociocultural order is created by the constant interaction between the physical structure and its inhabitants. A great deal of this sociocultural order is achieved through the temporal qualities that dwellings possess. Homes have linear temporal qualities that encompass events from the past, present, and future (Werner 1987). A sense of linear order results from the memories these events leave with us. Homes also embody cyclical temporal qualities that help us to order events and seasons in a cyclical fashion. An annual Thanksgiving dinner, such as the one Sara Vernon mentioned, or a yearly birthday celebration in the home marks the passage of time in a predictable pattern that people often find reassuring. Because homes help their residents to pattern their lives through time, they are often regarded as "agents of stability and change" (Lawrence 1985:118). Wood Glen resident Wendy James perhaps sums it up best in her definition of home.

Home? *That's where the heart is* [chuckles]. Home is one or two people that are congenial and like [the same] things—but not always—you don't always have to like everything that the other party does. It is nice to have a companion but if you don't then you have yourself and you have something that means something to you whether it's expensive or not it's up to you. *And you've got that around you and it is like a coat.* (interview by author, tape recording, Chicago, Illinois, 9 November 1992)

HOME AS IDENTITY

A crucial feature of home is that it serves as a symbol of identity. Our homes allow us to show others how we see ourselves and how we wish to present ourselves to outsiders. One aspect of this identification is that it is reflexive. We give our home an identity and it gives its identity back to us. As Winston Churchill put it, "We shape our buildings and afterwards our buildings shape us."

According to Rybczynski (1986) the notion of home as a symbol of personal identity first appeared in the Middle Ages. Homes were personified by assigning them names, many of which are still used today. For example, Hitler called his country home "The Eagle's Nest," Winston Churchill named his dwelling "The Cozy Pig," and Thomas Jefferson named his Virginia home "Monticello." We also decorate the interior of our homes to represent the image we wish to project to others, thus giving them identity through our individual tastes and design. Over time this identity becomes quite reflexive. "Identity implies a certain bonding or mergence of person and place such that the place takes its identity from the dweller and the dweller takes his or her identity from the place" (Dovey 1985:40). This bond results in the home being viewed as "a symbolic extension of one's self" (Schorr 1970:320). The perception of this extension of one's self is most clearly evidenced in the case of burglary. Korosec-Serfaty (1985) conducted a series of interviews to determine the effects of a break-in on residents. Residents' main response was that being burglarized is thought of as "being defiled" (Korosec-Serfaty 1985:77). The respondents further emphasized this impact with their repeated use of the word "rape" to describe the act of burglary. People who suffered from a burglary often felt a temporary loss of identity through the violation of their homes.

The home as a symbol of personal identity creates a setting for the acting out and displaying of the different sides of our personality and feelings. The home serves as the stage for a play of objects that tell stories about who we think we are. "Within the home environment . . . certain basic minimal cultural conceptions of personhood are expressed" (Rubinstein 1989:52). A person who fills her home with electronic gadgets, exercise equipment, and books is saying something very different about herself than someone who fills his with plants, sculptures, and antiques. And this is the real significance of home: each is different because each personality is unique. "A home is much more than a shelter; it is a world in which a person can create a material environment that embodies what he or she considers significant. In this sense the home becomes the most powerful sign of the self of the inhabitant who dwells within" (Csikszentmihalyi and Rochberg-Halton 1989:123).

This discussion of the symbolic properties of home is significant because "symbols serve a culture by making concrete its ideas and feelings" (Rapoport 1969:47). There can be no doubt that homes in their capacities to shape order, social structure, and identity fill important psychological functions. It is also evident that the emotional qualities of homes develop via the relationship between person and place. Scholars agree that these relationships must be present in order for a home to mean more than a "dwelling place" or "the place in which one resides." It is the human factor that transforms the first definition or meaning of home into something more emotionally and psychologically complex: "the abiding place of one's affections" or "the idea of who you are." For example, Kramer resident Katie Jacobs vividly meshes her personal identity with that of the identity of her home. "I think a home is somebody who had a good marriage and a couple of nice children" (interview by author, tape recording, Chicago, Illinois, 27 October 1992).

All of these definitions of home combine to create something called a *sense of home*. This sense of home is basically independent of the physical structure and develops once we have established a complex and fulfilling relationship with our homes. If our dwellings contribute to and reflect our positive sense of self, create order in our daily lives, and symbolize security, protection, and especially personal identity then we have acquired a sense of home. This sense of home is independent of place and remains with us for a lifetime.

If a positive relationship between person and place fails to develop, the resulting condition can often be "homelessness" (Dovey 1985). Here the word "homelessness" is not being used to represent a lack of shelter or dwelling but rather homelessness in an emotional sense. An inability to establish a personal relationship with one's dwelling or to express one's personal identity results in a gap between the definition of home as a place and of home as something more significant.

People who never experienced home as a restful or congenial place, or did not feel that home is where the heart is, are "home"-less. This sense of homelessness may be experienced when people have no choice or control over their living environment and feel inhibited. The case of older adults leaving their homes is one extremely relevant example.

The most complex set of relationships to the home is found in the generation of the grandparents. Some ... had to move to a retirement home bereft of memories and individuality. A number of others had to move in with their children or relatives, again becoming dependent on the moods of other people. Still others had to resettle in smaller quarters after their children had all moved out. Often the descriptions have a tone of grim resignation or of small expectations barely met: "it's a place to live and that's all." (Csikszentmihalyi and Rochberg-Halton 1989:133)

As will be shown later, assisted living residents expressed similar feelings about their residential environment.

It is important to contrast homelessness as it is used here with its more conventional usage. When we refer to someone as homeless we generally mean that he or she has no place to live. Homelessness is usually a place-rooted concept. However, a homeless person may still possess a sense of home if he or she still feels a sense of self-determination and independence in this situation. For example, a man who lost his home in the 1991 Oakland, California, fires emotionally expressed that even though his house was gone, "home is something you carry inside of you."[2] In other words, a person can be homeless but still have a home—a sense of home. A person who has no place to live is not necessarily homeless in the way the word will be used in this book, that is, to lack a sense of home.

THE PERSON-PLACE LINK

Any discussion of home would not be complete without a more in-depth look at the relationship between people and the actual homes in which they live. It is through the relationship with their dwellings that humans develop the more abstract, internal meanings of home explicated in the previous discussion. Psychiatrist Barry S. Fogel has researched the psychological relationships between people, their homes, and their desire to stay put. He compiled a list of what he calls the six basic benefits of home. These include benefits related to independence; benefits related to familiarity of a particular home environment; benefits related to residence in a specific neighborhood, including the social network of friends and neighbors; benefits related to activities of home maintenance; benefits related to the home as a place to entertain friends and family; and benefits related to the home as locus of meaning, "the site of important and memorable life events" (Fogel 1992:15–16).

Fogel adds to these six benefits by saying that "over and above these considerations, some people appear to feel attached to their homes much as they would feel attached to a significant person—their love transcends any rational calculation of benefit" (pp. 15–16). Fogel's observations draw on older adults' reasons for staying in their homes and indicate that there are a number of variables involved in elderly persons' attachment to their homes. He discovered that gender, socioeconomic status, health status, and marital status all play significant roles in both the meaning of home and the desire to stay there. In regard to gender he observed that women in general are more likely to be concerned with keeping their social networks and neighborhood intact and that the potential loss of proximity to friends may be the major concern with moving. Also, since women often spend more time at home than men, women "may be more affected by their home environments" (pp. 15–16).

The health status of older persons can have a great impact on both their reasons for moving as well as their meaning of home. A 1987 study by Litwak and Longino found that older people who were healthy and functional tended to move in order to pursue interests they may have such as golf. By contrast, unhealthy or functionally impaired elderly are more likely to move in order to be near services or family members who serve as care givers. Health status also contributes to differences in the psychological meaning of home. Very healthy and functional older adults' attachment to home will often stress the physical and social characteristics of their neighborhood. Conversely, elderly people with lower functional levels and lower health status are more attached to the autonomy and independence that their home offers. In addition, for more impaired elderly, holding on to their home may be "the one constant in an emotional world threatened by losses" (Fogel 1992:16).

Marital status is a third variable associated with the significance of home. For many people, home is where their spouse is, as in Katie Jacobs's earlier comments about home. The presence of a living spouse often can make a change in location less stressful for older adults.

The main point that Fogel seeks to make is that attachment to one's home is critically important in regard to decisions about whether or not to move. The psychological and emotional reasons for attachment to one's home can also be very helpful when a move is necessary. Fogel argues that "understanding what aspect of a person's current home means the most to him or her will help in finding the best residential alternative when living at home is no longer feasible" (Fogel 1992:18). For the older adult, an understanding of home affects not only the decision to move or stay, but also decisions about where to move (and when).

Kramer resident Fannie Isaacs poignantly brings Fogel's and Andrew Sixsmith's arguments down to a personal level in her discussions about home. Ninety-six-year-old Fannie feels a strong emotional and sentimental attachment to the notion of home as part of her own life story. Yet, she realizes that, presently, she feels "homeless" in assisted living. When asked what home means to her, Fannie responded: "You cannot say 'your four walls and a table?' Small things make home. And, if I say the coffee pot here [at Kramer] is not the same as mine [was], that's a small thing, but it is not. It belongs to my life. It [home] is everything together" (interview by author, tape recording, Chicago, Illinois, 5 November 1992). Fannie goes on to offer a more in-depth explanation.

Oh home? Everything. That is my trouble. For a long time I had a home, I had everything. I had a salt shaker and I had a pot and I had a dish that I could bake and cook in. Now I own two drinking cups and four plates—nothing else. I sleep in a rented bed . . . I had two televisions, I don't know where they are—gone with the wind. I had furniture, *I had a life for at least seventy years!* Everything I put together is gone. [She points to her room.] That's not my home!

Fannie also knows that for her a relationship to both people and place is necessary to feel that someplace is home. "Home is everything. It is in *you*. Every place could be a home. When I [used to] come home, I was sitting in *my home*, not in a *borrowed home*. And people are very nice here but I have no connection" (interview by author, tape recording, Chicago, Illinois, 18 January 1993).

Fannie's description of home, along with Fogel's explanation of older adults' attachment to their dwellings illustrate just how complex the idea of home really is. How does this emotion-laden notion relate to assisted living? Designers and developers of assisted living have endeavored to establish a home*like* environment, not a home. Why? Perhaps because in a larger scope "homelike" is a word that combines both the ideal *and* the reality of living in a residential setting such as assisted living. Ideally, the setting will be *like* home in that it will be comfortable, cozy, and familiar. At the same time, homelike embraces the reality that assisted living is not the resident's true home. It has characteristics that make it similar, but it cannot, at present, truly be home, for reasons such as those expressed by Fannie Isaacs. Assisted living proponents may actually have been very insightful when they included a "homelike" environment in the principles of assisted living. Maybe they realized that residents would not view this new setting as home. As the residents of Kramer and Wood Glen illustrate, home means several different things to different people. What these descriptions have in common is that they are personal, emotional, and difficult to put into words. These definitions and descriptions are also frequently idealized because they depict memories from residents' pasts. In order to comprehend the significance of these ideal definitions, it is necessary to compare them to the current reality that these same residents face in the "homelike" environment of assisted living.

THIS IS NOT HOME TO ME

The elderly residents of assisted living hold lifelong notions of home based on their past experiences. These elders' memories are idealized because they symbolize a time when they were younger and more independent. These older adults realize this fact and clearly understand the differences between the ideal of the past and the reality of the present. Unfortunately, for almost all of the respondents, the present reality of assisted living is negative. For residents such as Sara Vernon, assisted living does not feel like home because she is living with people she hardly knows. "Well you see home is where you are with your own people and I am—these are all strangers to me and they will forever be strangers. I have only one good friend here and I am very lucky to have her" (interview by author, tape recording, Chicago, Illinois, 18 November 1992). Kramer resident Zelda Arnold does not feel at home without her family around her. "You know, I've had a home with children around and everything, and of course this [assisted living] is difficult . . . but I adjust, I can get along you know. . . . A home is where you have your family together. You have your kitchen and you can do everything you want, we don't have that here" (interview by author, tape recording, Chicago, Illinois, 23 October 1992). A few residents voiced resignation about their present living arrangements. When asked if assisted living is home, resident Helen Finks responded: "It has to be! What choice do I have?" (interview by author, Chicago, Illinois, 16 March 1993). Fellow Kramer resident Wilma Rose agreed. "I have to call it home," she said. "I have no other home now. I gave up my home. . . . This is my home, I decided that and then made it my home. I have my children and family [nearby] so I am ok" (interview by author, tape recording, Chicago, Illinois, 5 November 1992). Resident Clara Martin had a more philosophical perspective on the reality of home. "I think home is something that we grow into, but we have to leave it for other parts of our life. It is a foundation" (interview by author, tape recording, Chicago, Illinois, 23 November 1992).

For some assisted living residents the ideal of home versus the reality of home is dramatized in their present housing options or their perceived lack of options. Several residents were asked if they would feel more at home in a living arrangement other than assisted living. The answers show their comprehension of their true level of independence and present life situation. Wood Glen resident Sandy Anderson was asked if she would feel more at home if she still lived in her old apartment in Chicago. "Not necessarily," she responded. "I've lived in so many different circumstances that I adjust to anything pretty much" (interview by author, tape recording, Chicago, Illinois, 8 January 1993). Ninety-year-old Gertrude Farmer realizes that the blindness that befell her a few years earlier prevents her from living the way she used to. When asked if she would prefer living in her own apartment, she said: "Yes, if I could see. If I could see I'd rather live the way I used to, but that is not possible. There is no cure" (interview by author, tape recording, Chicago, Illinois, 15 December 1992). For Wendy James, a physical malady did not lead her to assisted living. Rather it was difficulty getting food into her apartment that caused her to move from her community dwelling. "I thought for a while maybe I could go back and take a small apartment [in Chicago]. But my girlfriend says to me, 'Wendy, you came in because you weren't cooking. You know you'd have to cook and get out and shop—don't talk silly!' I says, 'ok' " (interview by author, tape recording, Chicago, Illinois, 19 November 1992). Fellow Wood Glen resident Tillie Von Deurst said that loneliness prevented her from considering an apartment as a "homier" alternative to assisted living. Tillie said that since her husband died she would feel too lonely in an apartment by herself. Other residents such as Yvonne Diamond just simply miss their old homes and the comfort they provided. When asked if there would be any type of living environment that would give her a stronger sense of home, Yvonne quietly said, "If I lived in my own house, where I came from" (interview by author, tape recording, Chicago, Illinois, 3 November 1992).

These assisted living residents are well aware that they cannot go back to the way they used to live their lives either because of activities of daily living (ADLs) or medial needs. However, the residents expected more from their present accommodations. Residents hoped that assisted living would feel like home. They were disappointed. "They [the staff] say, 'But it's your home.' It's not our home" (Katie Jacobs, interview by author, tape recording, Chicago, Illinois, 27 October 1992).

The passing of time also plays a role in their perceptions of home. "Well, if you ask 100 different women about home . . . are you talking about home as it was, the one we left? Or the home that we had thirty-five years ago?" Tillie Von

Deurst tried to explain how her concept of home has changed from thirty-five years ago. "It is so difficult. I was thirty-five years younger! That was when I had the book shop, my life was very interesting, very exciting" (interview by author, tape recording, Chicago, Illinois, 17 November 1992).

Zelda Arnold felt that she was not at home at Kramer because she did not truly belong there. At age ninety, she was not too sure where she did belong. The following is an excerpt from one of our tape-recorded interviews:

JF: Is there a feeling of belonging here? Because you said that at your son's house you felt awkward.

ZA: Well sure, I don't belong there.

JF: Do you feel like you belong here?

ZA: Well, I don't know where I belong [laughs]. I've got to live somewhere.

JF: Are you more comfortable here than you would be at your son's house?

ZA: No . . . my children don't feel that I am an obligation, they don't feel that way about me at all. But I just feel like I don't belong there.

JF: Do you feel any more like you belong here than at your son's house?

ZA: [laughs] I don't really know where I belong. When you get to be my age, you don't know where you belong [chuckles]. (interview by author, tape recording, Chicago, Illinois, 11 November 1992)

Feeling lost or out of place was common at both assisted living sites where fieldwork took place. The disturbing part of this issue is that the residents frequently expressed guilt or responsibility for feeling out of place, thus keying into the elderly mystique. Yvonne Diamond verbalized her thoughts this way: "I don't know. I just don't like it [Kramer] and I don't know why, I really don't. Everybody who visits here says, 'Oh it's beautiful.' I think . . . my own interpretation of why I don't like it is because *it's not my home. I miss being in my home*" (interview by author, tape recording, Chicago, Illinois, 9 October 1992). In a later interview, Yvonne came up with another reason why Kramer is not home. According to her, the fact that her fellow residents are becoming more frail and impaired makes assisted living less homelike. "As I said before, I've seen more people get sicker and I feel sorry for these people. And the thought of their having to go to a nursing home—that alone disturbs me" (interview by author, tape recording, Chicago, Illinois, 3 November 1992).

For many residents in assisted living it is a combination of factors that prevents them from seeing assisted living as "home." Changes in marital status, the passage of time, and the loss of friends can all merge to prevent a sense of home from developing in their new residential environment. Resident Bertha Edmonds's statements reveal multiple reasons why Wood Glen is not home.

"I'd *never* call this place home. . . . Well, take New Jersey—that was my home—my hubbie and I built it up to what it was for us. We made it a home, we made it something we enjoyed coming to at night—where we enjoyed having our friends come. Oh no, I can't call this [Wood Glen] home" (interview by author, tape recording, Chicago, Illinois, 20 November 1992).

Some residents have decided to *make* assisted living their home, however forced it might be. As Kramer resident Helen Finks exclaimed earlier, "It has to be! What choice do I have?" Perhaps such exclamations are simply the residents' way of coping with their present reality, brought on by changes in their lives. Wendy James was suffering from extreme malnourishment when she entered Wood Glen. It was during her recovery that Wendy determined that she would *make* assisted living her home. "I just laid here [from malnutrition]. But then, afterwards, like I say, I looked around and said, 'It's home,' and that's it! . . . It's all I've got!" (interview by author, tape recording, Chicago, Illinois, 19 November 1992). Wendy is not exactly enthralled with her living arrangement but realizes that she is at Wood Glen for a reason and believes that she might as well make the best of it instead of complaining about her losses.

Most residents at Kramer and Wood Glen are not looking "on the bright side" as Wendy tries to do. In reality, several residents at both sites are bitter about their present living situation. Fannie Isaacs, always outspoken, was vocal in her opinion. "I live with borrowed things. I don't know. You cannot understand what it [home] means. It is small—it is things you can buy but you cannot buy. Sometimes I sit and I say, 'I had this stool but I haven't [got it] anymore'" (interview by author, tape recording, Chicago, Illinois, 18 January 1993). Fannie is an extremely independent and active ninety-six-year-old woman who takes long walks every day and until the age of ninety-five lived on her own in South Carolina. The move to assisted living was a very difficult one for her and she claims it will never be home. Fannie might have summed up the emotions and reality of many of her fellow residents when she explained to me why assisted living is not truly home and why outsiders cannot understand their situation. "How can it [Kramer] be home? It is a station before you go there [points upward toward the sky]. In between we are here. But it is very hard to understand, you are young, you see the world differently. You might say, 'Oh that old woman.' Yeah, we are old but I don't *feel* old. I am old in years but I don't feel old you know?" (interview by author, tape recording, Chicago, Illinois, 5 November 1992).

Family also plays a key role in making a place feel like home. Almost every resident mentioned family in his or her definition of home or in his or her explanation of what home means: "home is a good marriage and a couple of children," "home is where your children are, where you love and where you are loved," and "home is a place you live in comfort with people that you love."

These definitions are based on the older adults' memories of their old homes and their former lives. But families play different roles for these residents through time. These changing roles affect their present feelings about home. The loss of a spouse seems to be the most devastating change affecting the way most of these seniors perceive home. Wendy James said, "My home—after my husband died, it wasn't a home any more. It was just a place to live, you know? Too many memories. Here, I am on my own, I made my mind up to it and that's it. Oh, there's a lot of things in my life that would be wonderful but I am not that young woman. I am an old lady now" (interview by author, tape recording, Chicago, Illinois, 19 November 1992). Wendy's comments confirm Fogel's statement that "for many people, home is where their spouse is" (Fogel 1992:16).

There are of course residents in assisted living who never married. Some of these single seniors speak of family as critical to their sense of home. Wood Glen resident Clara Martin never married but still connects home to family and relationships. "A home is a place where you live in comfort with people that you love . . . that was the way I was brought up. I was brought up in the old days when you are all sharing and loving each other" (interview by author, tape recording, Chicago, Illinois, 23 November 1992). Gertrude Farmer, also single, said that home "means protection, [being] cared for, if you have problems you know where to take them" (interview by author, tape recording, Chicago, Illinois, 15 December 1992).

Prior to moving into assisted living, many residents faced conflicting emotions about their families. Knowing that their past roles had changed these older adults were still not content to give up their independence and oblige their children (by moving out of their homes). They love their children and they want to know their children care, but they do not want to be cottled. One day in her suite, Yvonne Diamond perceptively observed the following:

I heard an interesting thing. . . . The other day I was talking to one of my suite mates. And she says, "I don't care to live with my children. I wouldn't want to live with my children"—I don't believe that. But, this woman said, "My son lives in Wilmette. He has four bedrooms and lives there with his wife and no one else—no one else lives there, they have four bedrooms, they have a big swimming pool, and they have *no room for me!*" And that's all that was said. I did not respond. But you see, *the inner wish is to be with family.* And maybe people don't want to [be with family] because it doesn't always work out. But, in times gone by, somehow it worked out. (interview by author, tape recording, Chicago, Illinois, 9 October 1992)

The older adults living at Kramer and Wood Glen understand that their lives have changed; yet, they do not necessarily want to live with family members. The paradox is that the home used to be centered around family, and presently, those same family members may have unknowingly been partially responsible for taking away their parents' sense of home.

After people move into assisted living the role of the family changes yet again. Almost all of the residents at the two Chicago sites expressed their present reliance on their families. These family connections are often the lifeline for the assisted living resident, their only tangible link to their former way of life. For residents like Sara Vernon, the situation is clear. "I think I would feel it more [the isolation] if I didn't see my daughters. I *know* I would feel it more" (interview by author, tape recording, Chicago, Illinois, 18 November 1992). Conflicting feelings about family members remain for the elderly resident after moving into assisted living. Often the very people who moved them into assisted living (their children) become the older adult's refuge from isolation. When the respondents talk about their families they are usually happy, relating stories from their past, being away from assisted living, and interacting with others. Residents speak fondly of going to their children's homes for holidays and special occasions. Residents seem most happy when they talk about visiting their relatives, being away from assisted living. They now appear to live vicariously through the lives of their children. If the residents of assisted living do not feel comfortable enough to live with their children, can they make assisted living into a home for themselves? Before this question can be answered, it is necessary to understand how our relationship to the physical environment can affect our ability to call a place home.

THE IMPORTANCE OF THE PHYSICAL ENVIRONMENT

Our residential environments may or may not be perceived as home depending on a variety of factors. We have seen Wood Glen and Kramer residents' explanations of what the concept of home means to them and why. Residents' feelings and perceptions help us to understand the personal reasons behind feeling at home and how one develops a personal sense of home. There are broader, theoretical issues to be addressed in order to illuminate why assisted living residents are not "at home" in this setting. These broader issues revolve around the nature of the physical environment: what it means and how human beings communicate with it.

Approximately thirty-five years ago, the multi-disciplinary interest in human-environment relations spawned a new academic field: human-environment studies. Many disciplines came together to discuss the question of how people and environments affect each other. Scholars in this field sought answers from a variety of perspectives, some of which are highlighted here.

A critical early link between social and physical environments is the notion of the built structure as a form of communication. "The built environment, in addition to providing shelter, serves as a medium of communication because encoded within it are elements of the social structure" (Duncan 1985:148). The environment communicates primarily through what are called "codes" and "cues." "A code is defined as the structure of a general set of possibilities for communicating and understanding particular characteristics of human culture. In this sense, architecture has a cultural as well as pragmatic meaning; architecture therefore encodes cultural and social rules and conventions" (Lawrence 1989:89). Lawrence further states that there are four primary codes that symbolize the relationship between the "design, meaning and use of domestic space" (Lawrence 1989:93). These four codes include a code that classifies space and activities, a code that differentiates space and its activities, a code for how we position our activities in space, and a code for "domestic activities that indicates the meaning of one activity in the total range of domestic activities" (p. 93). Such codes can be problematic for people in a group-living situation because of conflicting views of how activities and space should be demarcated. Sometimes it can be difficult for residents to understand exactly what activities and behaviors will be "allowed" by staff and other residents.

Along with codes, cues help to convey social meaning in the physical environment. "Cues have the purpose of letting people know in which kind of domain or setting they are" (Rapoport 1982:56). In other words, codes determine a variety of settings and cues suggest how one could or should act in a given setting. Ultimately, codes and cues work together to help people function in their surroundings, residential or otherwise. However, codes and cues can only communicate well when they are "socially and culturally valid" (Rapoport 1969:129). For structures to be socially and culturally valid, they must "speak the same language" as the user. For housing, this language can only be communicated if the dwelling truly represents the residents' sense of order, identity, social rules, and values. If this does not occur, then a "language barrier" exists between the user and his or her living space. "If the design of the environment is seen as a process of encoding information, then the users can be seen as decoding it. If the code is not shared, not understood, or inappropriate, the environment does not communicate" (Rapoport 1977:3). Many residents at Kramer and Wood Glen clearly expressed their feeling that the environment does not communicate to them as positively as they would like. The residents do not share the "codes" of their physical surroundings. For example, sometimes codes are negatively communicated to residents through objects provided by the residence. Kramer resident Fannie Isaacs said it best: "I live with borrowed things" (interview by author, tape recording, Chicago, Illinois, 18 January 1993).

Proshansky, Ittleson, and Rivelin (1970) outline a list of assumptions in environmental psychology regarding the influence of the physical environment on behavior. One of the suggestions is that "human behavior in relation to a physical setting is enduring and consistent over time and situation; therefore, the characteristic patterns of behavior for that setting can be identified" (p. 29). They point out that behaviors witnessed over time in different settings remain fairly consistent within each individual setting. Therefore, one can assume that the cues available to us help us to sort out how to behave in different environments. However, the behaviors deemed "appropriate" in different settings can vary greatly across segments of a single society.

The weakness in Proshansky et al.'s assumption is the fact that physical environments may actually change their character over time. How are inhabitants supposed to react then? Assisted living is an example of one such environment. The initial purpose of assisted living may be to house semi-independent elderly in a homelike setting. However, if residents are truly allowed to age in place, the assisted living setting will certainly change over time. Residents may see more walkers and medical equipment present and this could give them a different message about what the environment is and what it is for. In such cases it is difficult to imagine that human behavior in relation to physical settings will be "enduring or consistent over time and situation" (p. 29).

The question becomes how to reduce if not close the gap between elderly residents and their group-housing environments. The answer may be found in the understanding of both residents' and providers' expectations for the environment.

When approaching the issue of housing for the elderly, it is essential to include three different perspectives: (1) the residents' view of and actions in the environment; (2) the providers' perspective and expectations of the environment; and (3) the meeting of these two viewpoints. These distinct perspectives represent differing concerns.

The first group to be discussed are the residents. One concern for residents is that of the notion of competence. Psychologist Robert White (1959, 1971) first proposed the idea of competence as a useful tool for the process of psychoanalysis and later applied it to children's play. He said, "[C]ompetence is the cumulative result of the history of interaction with the environment. Sense of competence is suggested as a suitable term for the subjective side of this, signifying one's consciously or unconsciously felt competence—one's confidence in dealing with the various aspects of the environment" (White 1963:185–86). In a later work he added, "[A] sense of competence is a vital aspect to self-esteem" (White 1971:271). Constance Perin (1970) further expanded the idea of competence by pointing out that "there is a useful and crucial difference between *being* in an environment and *doing things in it*" (Perin 1970:48). Perin states that people in their homes want to be able to accomplish their daily tasks competently and with a sense of control over their surroundings. She adds that individuals want to feel competent not only when dealing with physical chores but also when they are involved in interpersonal interactions. More plainly—competence involves fully living in a home, not just residing in a house.

Competence is a skill that can only be measured by residents themselves. Only they know their daily routines and how aspects of their built structures facilitate or inhibit the completion of social and physical tasks. The major argument presented here is that residents of all different sorts of environments are active participants in their environment *not* passive objects that are totally influenced by their structures. Any influence is mutual. People see their experience in their particular environment as something that only they can fully comprehend. This critical point is often overlooked in housing settings for the elderly. Residents are perceived as passive recipients of care and socialization rather than actively struggling to maintain their independence. "Residents' interactions with the environment represent personal and collective struggles, accomplishments, responsibilities, and changes, and these become associated with the physical settings in which they occur and charge them with purely local meaning" (Brower 1989:194). This point will be raised again in chapter 6 when I pursue a discussion of the marketing of assisted living.

It might be argued that only residents have the experience of "dwelling" in their surroundings. Saegert (1985) claims that in order for outsiders to understand the insiders' dwelling experience, several questions must be answered. These questions closely parallel those raised in the discussion of competence. Saegert asks, "[H]ow does housing fit the lives of the population? How do the processes of producing, distributing, and consuming housing and the integration of housing into the experience of dwelling relate to the opportunities, constraints, and meanings of neighborhoods, towns, and cities, as well as larger geographical units?" (Saegert 1985:306).

The residents of a setting see their environment from an insider perspective because they live there. Conversely, in the case of assisted living, the provider sees the environment from an outsider perspective. In housing for the elderly, both perspectives must be examined jointly.

The "outsider's trap," to exaggerate a bit, is that one looks at places, as it were, from an abstract sky. He/she tries to read the texts of landscapes and overt behavior in the picture language of maps and models and is therefore inevitably drawn toward finding in places what he or she intends to find in them. The "insider's trap," on the other hand, is that one lives in places and may be so immersed in the particulars of everyday life and action that he or she may see no point in questioning the taken-for-granted or in seeing home in its wider spatial or social context. (Buttimer 1980:171–72)

Taken together, these two perspectives can both be useful for creating a more encompassing understanding of the environment.

The insider/outsider positions can be successfully merged through the creation of a "congruent environment." Perin (1970) claims, "[A] building can be congruent with the kind of life to go on in it" (Perin 1970:44). Congruence with the environment can be accomplished by designing structures that are not too physically and socially restricting to the user's sense of competence. "The fact that people act and behave differently in different settings suggest another important point, which is that people act appropriately in different settings because they make congruent their behavior with the norms for the behavior appropriate to the setting" (Rapoport 1977:3). If settings actually help to shape our behavior then there can be a very positive effect in what are referred to as enabling environments. However, this congruence of behavior can have disastrous consequences in a "disabling environment." If people do indeed attempt to make their behavior congruent with "the norms and behaviors appropriate to the setting" and the setting is a nursing home, then behavior modifications can have serious consequences for the elderly person. To older people, nursing homes, and even assisted living at times, may symbolize illness, helplessness, and decline. Accordingly, if residents "read" these behaviors as expectations from their environment then they may respond with learned dependency or passive, "giving up" behaviors, thus turning assisted living into the perfect setting to reinforce the elderly mystique.

Not only can the physical environment change through time, but so can its inhabitants. This is certainly the case with many housing environments for seniors. It would be nice to pretend that the population living in an environment would remain the same over time; however, such assumptions would never be realistic, especially when talking about older adults. As Lawton et al. (1980) point out, the population will always change. "People do not stay the same, and as the people change the character of the environment may change. Specifically, people have frequently observed that no matter how healthy the original population of tenants in a housing environment may be, those tenants will age and their service needs may change in a major way" (Lawton, Greenbaum, and Leibowitz 1980:57). At its extreme, an incongruent environment can result in a total institution.

A Far Cry from Home: The Total Institution

We have seen thus far that assisted living does not feel like home for many of the residents of Kramer and Wood Glen. Residents at Kramer and Wood Glen express their lack of positive congruence with their assisted living environments and their sense that their residential communities do not foster positive and independent behaviors. An explanation for why many residents at Kramer and Wood Glen feel dependent and frustrated in their environments is that assisted living may very well represent the antithesis of home: the total institution. According to Erving Goffman, a total institution may be defined as "a place of residence and work where a large number of like-situated individuals, cut off from the wider society for an appreciable period of time, together, lead an enclosed formally administered round of life" (Goffman 1961:xiii). Goffman outlines five types of total institutions represented by environments such as mental hospitals, penitentiaries, army barracks, and monasteries. The fifth type of total institution, Goffman explains, is exemplified by "places organized to care for persons felt to be both incapable and harmless" (pp. 4–5). Included in this category are homes for the blind, indigent, and the aged. This final group is of interest for my analysis because it includes nursing homes. Although assisted living is technically *not* a nursing home and indeed the industry strives to prevent assisted living settings from displaying an institutional atmosphere, upon closer inspection assisted living appears to embody many characteristics of a total institution.

The behaviors that occur inside of total institutions help to define them. In our society individuals tend to work, play, and sleep in separate places. This is not the case in total institutions where these three behaviors all occur in the same place: "[A]ll aspects of life are conducted in the same place and under the same single authority" (Goffman 1961:6). Residents of total institutions are compelled to carry out most or all of their activities in the company of virtual strangers. Life in total institutions is very scheduled: meals occur at a certain time, different activities take place at a certain time, and staff leave at a certain time.

Goffman notes that in total institutions there is a strong division between the residents and the staff. This is partially due to the fact that residents may have limited or no contact with the outside world whereas staff can go home at the end of their work shifts. Occupants often end up feeling trapped in the institution and disconnected from the wider community. Residents' feelings can turn into resentment toward staff members who are able to leave whenever they wish. Those who inhabit total institutions know what they are missing. They know they lack the freedom they had previous to entering their present situation. According to Goffman, this is a goal of total institutions that "create[s] and sustain[s] a particular kind of tension between the home world and the institutional world and use[s] this persistent tension as leverage" (Goffman 1961:13). In short, "the total institution is a social hybrid, part residential community, part formal organization" (p. 12).

Assisted living possesses many components of a total institution. It is both a place of work and a residence. There are a number of similarly situated people who are frequently cut off from the wider society for an appreciable period of time and who lead formally administered lives. As I will illustrate later, the majority of assisted living residents did not choose their living arrangements, just as "inmates" of total institutions often do not choose their living arrangements. Residents are forced to sleep, work, and play in the same place with the same people, none of whom they chose to live with. As Wood Glen resident Sara Vernon expressed earlier, she did not choose the people she lives with and therefore cannot see assisted living as her home.

Unlike home, which reflects our sense of self and identity, total institutions reflect the exact opposite. Goffman argues that total institutions place a barrier between the resident and the wider world, marking the "curtailment of self" (p. 14). Importantly, if we cannot express ourselves in our living environments, we will not develop a sense of home.

Assisted living can indeed be seen as a total institution. The question remains whether or not all assisted living settings inevitably become total institutions. There are also questions about the relationship between the nature of total institutions and the continuum of care. These issues will be explored further in later chapters. Before this, though, a relevant question to pose is why assisted living is experienced by residents as a total institution when many have fought so hard to prevent this from occurring. The reasons are many and have to do with a combination of issues. The first of these issues to be explored is the nature of assisted living: the ideals versus the realities.

NOTES

1. An interesting point to note here is the fact that places of worship are called "houses of worship" rather than homes of worship. If a church or a synagogue is supposed to be emotionally enriching and spiritually fulfilling for its users why are these places called houses rather than homes? As demonstrated earlier, house is a word devoid of the emotional connection and personal relationship of home. Home of worship would seem to be more representative of the strong relationship a person has with his or her religion. Perhaps it is up to the members and congregants, the human factor, to fill the house of worship and make it a home.

2. This anonymous quote came from a television newscast of interviews with victims of the 1991 Oakland, California, fires shortly after their homes burned down.

CHAPTER 3

The Nature of Assisted Living:
Ideals versus Realities

In the 1980s a new housing alternative appeared that helped elderly people preserve their independence by providing them with a number of supportive services in a homelike setting. This type of housing has been known by a number of different names in different parts of the country, including sheltered care, personal care, adult congregate living, and enriched housing (Hendrickson 1988:22). It is also known as assisted living.

In the United States assisted living serves three separate populations: the frail elderly, people with dementia, and people with AIDS. While these groups have diverse needs, assisted living is flexible enough to accommodate people in each of these categories. Assisted living sites usually serve these populations in different settings. For the purposes of this book, I will focus on assisted living for the frail elderly. A useful way to begin a discussion of assisted living is to explain its origins and history.

ORIGINS AND HISTORY

Assisted living has its origins in European models of long-term care in which elderly persons can age in place in a residential setting. In the United States assisted living arrangements began appearing in the early 1980s both as a form of board and care residences and as part of continuing care retirement communities. By the mid-1980s freestanding assisted living residences were being developed in many states and were evolving both as a housing alternative and as a health care alternative. By 2001, the majority of states will have enacted some sort of federal regulations for assisted living. The regulations show great variation among states, with twenty-nine states using the term "assisted living" as their licensure category (Mollica 2001).

According to architect and assisted living expert Victor Regnier, there are several factors affecting the evolution of this housing option. These factors include increasing numbers of older frail persons; availability of community-based long-term care; increasing costs of nursing home care, questioning the inevitability of institutionalization; new alternatives evolving between congregate housing and skilled nursing care; phasing out of intermediate care; greater consumer demand for alternatives to institutionalization; and corporate America's interest in creative housing alternatives for older frail people (Regnier, Hamilton, and Yatabe 1991).

As part of its history, assisted living has come to be seen as both an option that fits along the continuum of care and as an option that is separate from the entire continuum of care. The continuum of care represents the traditional model of care for older adults. Elderly residents move in a linear trajectory from one setting to another. Each move represents an increase in need for medical care and assistance with daily activities. The majority of developers and scholars have felt compelled to place assisted living along the continuum of care with many citing the following reason: "[S]ince the purpose of assisted living is to meet the needs of the frail elderly in order to avoid premature institutionalization, it can be safely assumed that the location of it in an established continuum of care framework immediately precedes intermediate care" (Kalymun 1990:100). Simultaneously, assisted living scholars such as Rosalie Kane and Keren Wilson highlight the importance of viewing assisted living as an alternative to the continuum of care rather than being part of it. These scholars criticize the continuum because of its rigidity in dealing with housing and health care options such as assisted living. "The continuum model has been challenged because it seems to require that older people be slotted along the continuum at just the right level of care for their level of disability and that any deviance from the expected pattern be considered an inappropriate level of care (either too much or too little)" (Kane and Wilson 1993:8). The continuum of care model also poses other questions for the development of assisted living. How much disability can/does it serve? What are the limits of this nursing home alternative? Since there are no national regulations for assisted living, individual states have had to decide for themselves how to answer these two important questions. Depending on what type of state licensure is present, assisted living may serve either a very broad or a very narrow population. However, if assisted living is approached as an alternative to the continuum of care rather than as a part of it, then this option may have a chance to serve a much larger population and allow older adults to age in place until they die. I will return to this issue in later chapters.

Whether or not assisted living is conceptualized along the continuum or as an alternative to it, complications still arise. First, assisted living is known by a number of names in different parts of the country, including residential care, adult congregate living, personal care, catered living, board and care, community residences, and domiciliary care (ALFAA 1992). Second, states license and regulate these housing/health care options differently, making it even more difficult to define exactly what assisted living is. A positive outcome of such ambiguity is the flexibility of this housing option. Presently, the lack of federal oversight creates freedom to develop this housing alternative so that it may best meet the specific needs of the elderly populations in individual states. If the future of assisted living is indeed headed toward national regulation, then policymakers will have to be cautious to avoid transforming it into a nursing home clone. They must also be aware of the ideals and realities of this housing option. To begin tracing the ideals and realities of assisted living, one must first dissect its definition.

ANATOMY OF A DEFINITION

One of the most challenging features of assisted living is its definition, or rather its plethora of definitions. Assisted living has been known by a number of different terms in different states. These terms are not necessarily equivalent in what they offer as a housing option or what they mean from state to state. But, in order to discuss what assisted living is we must analyze how it is defined. The Assisted Living Federation of America (ALFA), established in 1991, is the principal association in the United States promoting the interests of the assisted living industry and trying to enhance the quality of life for residents (ALFA 1994). ALFA is regarded as the leading assisted living organization in the country, offering information, representation, public education, and guidance to operators of assisted living from every state. Quite significantly then, it is interesting to see ALFA acknowledge that "defining assisted living can be the biggest obstacle to the development of assisted living as well as its catalyst" (ALFA 1999:5). While acknowledging the difficulty of defining assisted living, this national trade association highlights the importance of understanding the key components of assisted living so that the best possible environments are created for residents.

A useful place to begin is with the definition of assisted living proposed by ALFA. The organization defines assisted living as

a special combination of housing, supportive services, personalized assistance and health care designed to respond to the individual needs of those who require help with activities of daily living [ADL] and instrumental activities of daily living [IADL]. Supportive services are available 24 hours a day to meet scheduled and unscheduled needs in a way that promotes maximum dignity and independence for each resident and involves the resident's family, neighbors, and friends. (ALFA 1999:6)

In addition, Mollica, Wilson, and Ryther (1992) insightfully noted that "conceptually at least, assisted living can be described from four perspectives: the philosophy of the model, the environment or setting, the services available and the residents who live there" (p. 9). This conceptual division serves as a useful guide for the different definitions presented in this chapter.

The best way to begin an analysis of assisted living is to build upon the definition presented by ALFA with definitions offered by well-known scholars in the field. "Assisted living is any group residential program that is *not* licensed as a nursing home, that provides personal care to persons with need for assistance in the activities of daily living, and that can respond to any unscheduled need for assistance that might arise" (Kane and Wilson 1993:xi). Kane and Wilson refer to this definition as an operational definition because assisted living is still developing and expanding.

Experts in the field have sometimes defined assisted living differently in their own separate publications in order to focus on the different aspects of this residential option. Victor Regnier has defined assisted living in several ways. First, he sees assisted living "as both a description of a housing type for older, frail people and a philosophy of care which emphasizes independence, restorative health, choice and control, privacy, autonomy and share responsibility in a residential 'home-like' environment" (Regnier 1991:1). In the same publication Regnier states that

assisted living housing represents a model of *residential* long-term care. It is a housing alternative based on the concept of outfitting a residential environment with professionally delivered personal care services, in a way that avoids institutionalization and keeps older frail individuals independent for as long as possible. Care can consist of supervision with minor medical problems, assistance with bladder or bowel control and or management of behavioral problems as a result of early stages of dementia. In an assisted living environment all of these problems are managed within a residential context. As a housing type, assisted living fits between congregate housing and skilled nursing care. (p. 1)

Finally, Regnier offers a third definition that focuses on the support that such services can offer residents. "Assisted living is a model of residential long term care where professionally managed and administered services are provided in an effort to keep residents physically and psychologically independent in a residential home-like environment" (Regnier 1992:4).

Regnier's three definitions are similar in that they emphasize a residential rather than a medical model of care. Regnier's definitions differ from each other in their focus. For instance, the first definition highlights the philosophy of care while the second definition concentrates on the details of medical and behavioral problems that can be supervised in these settings. His third definition focuses on resident independence (both physical and psychological) and highlights the importance of a homelike milieu.

Other scholars have also attempted to define assisted living by focusing on residents. "Assisted living emphasizes 'home-like' living units, privacy, resident choice, independence, shared risk, and shared responsibility in which residents actively participate in the accomplishment of regular tasks and activities" (Mollica et al. 1992:ii). Resident involvement and empowerment in their daily lives is seen by many as a central feature of assisted living. However, such a definition does not offer many details regarding the various health problems that assisted living residents may need help with.

When looking over the various definitions of assisted living, ALFA's earlier definition is perhaps the broadest because it encompasses family, neighbors, and friends as well as the health and housing services that the setting offers. AFLA believes these three groups of people play a crucial role in the happiness of residents who live in assisted living. While definitions of assisted living vary, it is evident that this housing/health care option is explained differently by different interest groups. "The current assisted living situation can be likened to the proverbial blind men trying to describe an elephant. The one who felt the tail described an entirely different animal than the person who touched the ears" (Namazi and Chafetz 2001a:1). Further, Namazi and Chafetz state that while writing their 2001 book on assisted living "the authors located some fifty different definitions of assisted living facilities" (p. 3).

Through the past decade two separate categories of assisted living definitions have emerged. The first type of definition is "Senior Housing with Non-Health Care Services" and the second is "Senior Housing with Health Care Services" (ALFA 1999). Under the first category, housing is provided along with the following types of services: meals, transportation, housekeeping services, security, concierge services, and limited assistance with activities of daily living (ALFA 1999:7). As ALFA points out, "[T]his model is generally not regulated as a health care residence and is not licensed. It focuses on maintaining a strong residential characteristic with little emphasis on health services" (p. 7). This model can be quite problematic because if resident frailty increases and need for assistance with activities of daily living increases then "residents often must move out quicker, resulting in a high turnover" (p. 7). Often, assisted living providers whose sites fall into this category seek to admit older adults who are at a very high functioning level. Settings under this definition are also often very residential in nature because the site does not fall under health care codes and regulations.

Perhaps the biggest problem with the Senior Housing with Non-Health Care Services model is that it prevents any real aging in place for residents. Residents can only stay if they can maintain the level of ability they had at the time of admission (or close to it). Often this translates for providers into focusing on the instrumental activities of daily living alone and ignoring ADL assistance. Providers holding to this definition see their purpose as offering assistance only with instrumental activities of daily living such as meal preparation, transportation, and laundry services.

The second category of assisted living is Senior Housing with Health Care Services. Under this model, the following services are usually provided: "transportation, meals, housekeeping, security, significant assistance with ADLs, health assessments, emergency call systems, nursing staff on site 24 hours a day, and health monitoring" (ALFA 1999:8). This model encompasses ADL *as well as* IADL needs and allows residents to stay longer. This model of assisted living is much more likely to require licensure because of the inclusion of health services. This can sometimes lead to architectural environments that appear less homelike and more institutional in nature. Assisted living sites under this model may have to struggle much more to provide a residential setting for the populations they serve. The major benefit of the Senior Housing with Health Care Services model is that it focuses on aging in place. Seniors can stay longer and have their health needs met as their health or abilities decline.

Underlying the issue of defining assisted living is the fact that many corporations that develop assisted living units continue to build assisted living sites at a rapid rate, even though they are not sure what it is or where their approach fits among these two categories. This trend is troubling because it means that some companies are building assisted living units for the sole purpose of making money, not to adhere to the philosophy of assisted living or to cater to resident needs. As recently as 1998, the national director for health and wellness for Marriott Senior Living Services said, "[N]obody knows what assisted living is . . . each provider almost has to define it for himself" (quoted in Tarlach 1998:72). Admittedly, defining assisted living is complicated. But, it is disturbing to note that Marriott Senior Living Services currently manages more than eighty assisted living sites across the country, yet their national director for health and wellness says, "[N]obody knows what assisted living is." Why do corporations continue to build assisted living unit if they do not know what they are building? Assisted living can be confusing but organizations such as ALFA have certainly helped to create a general outline for explaining what assisted living is. Companies and organizations interested in building and expanding assisted living need to research and understand the depth of this housing option before constructing more and more sites. Some developers only see the potential for huge profits and quick moneymaking, rather than having the residents' best interests at heart. Such an approach also shows a lack of adherence to the philosophy of assisted living.

PHILOSOPHY OF CARE AND ASSISTED LIVING PRINCIPLES: THE IDEAL

The philosophy of care is the cornerstone of assisted living. There are several components to this philosophy and understanding them can help us understand the ideal that assisted living providers and residences strive to fulfill. Embedded within assisted living's philosophy of care are six principles: privacy, dignity, choice, independence, individuality, and a homelike environment (Wilson 1990; Regnier 1991; Mollica et al. 1992). These principles make assisted living unique among other residential options for the elderly because they focus on the residents.

Assisted living experts Victor Regnier and Jon Pynoos expand on the six assisted living principles by suggesting twelve principles geared toward the environment-behavior side of assisted living. "These principles combine and expand the six categories to identify a broad range of considerations for judging the responsiveness of the environment to the needs of very old, frail people" (Regnier, Hamilton, and Yatabe 1991:18). Pynoos and Regnier believe that a comprehensive model of assisted living should entail all twelve of the following principles: privacy, social interaction, control/choice/autonomy, orientation/ wayfinding, safety/security, accessibility and functioning, stimulation/challenge, sensory aspects, familiarity, aesthetics/appearance, personalization, and adaptability. Combining these twelve environment-behavior principles with the six general principles goes beyond abstract philosophy. Assisted living providers need an avenue where they can translate the goals of these ideal concepts into actions that will improve residents' quality of life. For providers, the most basic facilitator for such translation is the physical environment of the assisted living setting. The physical setting plays an important role in accomplishing these assisted living goals and therefore warrants further investigation.

The Physical Setting

The physical milieu informs us about how assisted living models are put into practice both during and after the individual community is planned and constructed. Since it is the physical environment that residents first experience, it is important to thoroughly understand this component of assisted living.

One of the distinguishing characteristics of assisted living housing is its physical design. Assisted living is heralded as the bearer of a homelike environment to an overly institutionalized population. Assisted living proponents believe that the settings should be residential in appearance, be flexible, and promote privacy, dignity, choice, independence, and individuality. The reality of many assisted living sites is that, even when allowing for a great deal of heterogeneity, many places are still very inconsistent in their attempts to lessen any institutional appearance and atmosphere. The first point to consider is the terminology used to describe the physical environment. "The term 'setting' or 'environment' is more descriptive of assisted living than 'facility.' The term facility has become linked emotionally (for consumers) and operationally (for providers) with undesirable, institutional qualities. . . . As a consumer-driven option which meshes housing and services, the setting feels more 'homelike' " (Mollica et al. 1992:12). The problem is that many published articles written about assisted living refer to the structure as a facility (Hawes, Phillips, and Rose 2000; Blankenheim 2001; Rosenblatt 2001). This helps to reinforce the notion that assisted living is not "home" for residents but rather a building in which to treat their ailments. Mollica attributes the homelike ambiance to the physical design of most assisted living structures; however, by referring to assisted living as another "facility" for older adults, the description of the environment undermines the residential design goals. This issue will be discussed in greater depth in chapter 6.

Much thought and attention have gone into planning assisted living structures to fit a residential model of care. Many assisted living scholars (Wilson 1993, 1996; Mollica et al. 1995; Regnier 1995, 1996; Brummett 1997; Marsden 1997; Frank 1999) believe that certain design elements should always be present in assisted living settings. Each individual apartment should include private sleeping spaces, a full bathroom, kitchen space that has storage capacity and food preparation areas, lockable doors, personal furnishings, and individual temperature controls. Of course, how many of these design elements are actually in place differs from state to state and program to program. Specific regulations can also influence the presence of these design elements.

According to architect Victor Regnier (1991), there are five aspects of assisted living that influence the degree to which a building will take a residential or institutional form. These aspects include the size of the structure, the level of service autonomy for residents, the scale of the building, the original purpose for the structure (was the building once a school or hotel?), and finally, appearance. How assisted living appears can greatly affect residents' reactions to the building and whether or not they feel comfortable there.

These five aspects combine in a number of ways to create a variety of assisted living settings. The major factor influencing how residential or institutional an individual setting becomes is usually the type of group/organization that is developing the site. "Due to the heterogeneous nature of the existing groups representing the assisted living industry, the product currently reflects a wide range of environments—tending to easily identify the biases of the sponsor. The floors in residents' rooms which also contain crank beds and an institutional line of furnishing creates the stereotype of the assisted living facility owned by a sponsor whose background is in nursing" (Seip 1987:34). One must be careful, however, to avoid over-generalizing. Simply because one assisted living environment is operated under the auspices of a nursing home does not necessarily mean that it adheres to a medical or more institutional model. Further, simply because the sponsor is coming from a retirement housing background does not mean that the assisted living site will be more homelike.

The Kitchen

More than any other physical design feature, kitchens offer residents a level of choice and autonomy not experienced via other aspects of the physical environment. If residents do not like what is offered in the main dining room and have access to a kitchen, they can exercise their right to choose as well as their independence. However, many assisted living developers do not install full kitchens or even kitchenettes in resident apartments. Often, the reasons cited for the exclusion of kitchens are marketing based. Seip (1991) claims that "kitchens for free-standing assisted living facilities are never an advantage to the service program or the marketing program" (p. 95). Apparently, Seip is not marketing to potential residents but rather to some other group because, in my research, I found that the majority of elderly residents want access to a kitchen. Seip also claims that "the widest segment of the resident profile cannot and should not attempt to cook for him or herself" (p. 95). While this statement may be true for cognitively impaired residents, for those who are not cognitively impaired it is patronizing. Further, this statement directly contradicts his own national survey results that show the majority of residents are physically and mentally competent enough to at least prepare simple meals for themselves. It appears as though many developers agree with Seip's stance on kitchens. Of the ten assisted living settings I visited, only five had any sort of kitchen, and only two of the ten sites had any cooking facilities in the kitchen. These findings raise two important questions: what exactly constitutes a "kitchen" and why should it matter to residents when meals are provided for them?

In assisted living the components that make for an adequate kitchen seem to be interpreted in several ways. Does the presence of a small refrigerator actually constitute kitchen facilities? Or do there need to be cooking capabilities for a true kitchen? The number of refrigerators in assisted living communities is on the rise. According to its 1998 survey of 178 assisted living sites, the National Investment Conference (NIC) found that 57 percent of the assisted living units surveyed contained a refrigerator. This contrasts somewhat to findings from a 1998 study by the Assisted Living Federation of America (ALFA) of over 400 assisted living communities. In the ALFA survey, providers said that 69.5 percent of apartments contained refrigerators. The discrepancy between these two percentages may be due to differences in the date of construction of the assisted living community. The NIC survey shows that only 30.8 percent of apartments constructed between 1982 and 1986 contained refrigerators while 66.7 percent of units constructed after 1997 included kitchens. Therefore, it may be that the ALFA survey contained a larger number of sites that were more recently constructed, so their overall numbers were higher. Both surveys do show the trend for more and more apartments to include refrigerators as a residential amenity. A curious question to raise here is, why *wouldn't* an assisted living community allow or include a refrigerator in a resident's apartment? Perhaps they think it is too dangerous for residents or perhaps they do not trust the residents to adequately take care of their refrigerators. Or perhaps operators believe having refrigerators in rooms may cause the appearance of roaches. Whatever the reason, a portion of a resident's choice and autonomy is lost without a refrigerator. Food storage capability is certainly appreciated by residents who do have it, but a refrigerator is still not the same as having cooking capacity.

According to the NIC survey, the number of two-burner and four-burner stoves in resident units is actually on the decline in assisted living. As of 1998, merely 18.8 percent of the 178 sites surveyed contained *any* stovetop capacity for residents. This number shows a downward movement from sites constructed a few years earlier. Communities built between 1987 and 1991 had stoves in 24 percent of the units. Construction after 1997, however, shows only 8.3 percent of units containing a stove.

Microwave ovens and toaster ovens are both more prevalent than stoves in assisted living apartments. Forty-three percent of all 178 communities allowed toaster ovens in their units (NIC 1998). This number is also on the decline from a high of 53 percent for assisted living sites constructed between 1992 and 1996. Finally, microwave ovens can be found in 30 percent of the 178 communities surveyed. This number compares to 39.1 percent found in the ALFA survey of more than 400 sites. It is interesting to note that ovens were not even included in either the NIC survey or the ALFA survey.

Many would define a true kitchen by the presence of cooking facilities. Regardless of the cooking method used (oven, stove, microwave, or toaster oven) less than one-half of assisted living sites appear to have any cooking capacity. The question is, why does it matter?

The true importance of kitchens goes far beyond choosing one's food, controlling the way it is cooked, and eating when, where, and with whom one desires. Consider the fact that approximately 80 percent of assisted living occupants are women whose average age is eighty-four. The majority of these women were housewives for at least a good part of their adult lives. A kitchen may very well serve as an important symbol of identity, competence, and home. If these women positively identify with the meaning that a kitchen embodies, they will have a stronger foundation for attributing a sense of home to their new environment if it has a kitchen.

Therefore, it is quite remarkable that only half of the communities I visited have *any* sort of kitchen. Within the five assisted living sites that have so-called kitchens, only two of the five sites with kitchen access offer a "full" kitchen: sink, refrigerator, stove, and oven. The remaining three sites offer either limited or no cooking facilities for their residents. In sum, of the original ten sites I visited in the Chicago area, only two offer access to a private, fully operational kitchen.

The connection female residents have with their kitchens is likely to be restricted in a kitchen space that offers them little chance to practice their skills and ability to choose what they eat and how it is prepared. A study conducted by Kane and Wilson (1993) supports the fact that kitchens are either overlooked or downplayed nationally in assisted living settings. In their study, Kane and Wilson surveyed sixty-three assisted living sites from across the United States. One of their survey questions dealt with "autonomy-enhancing features of individual units." Providers were asked to list whether or not a unit "must have," "can't have," or "does have" a number of features, including refrigerators and stoves. Of the sixty-three settings surveyed, only three *require* each apartment to have a refrigerator, while at fourteen sites residents were *not allowed* to have a personal refrigerator. With stoves the situation is even worse. Only two of the sixty-three settings *require* each unit to have a stove, while forty-four sites prohibit stoves all together. These numbers can translate into diminished autonomy and options for residents.

Several of the Kramer residents from my study expressed their opinions on both the importance of kitchens and the lack of a full kitchen (there are no ovens). According to resident Yvonne Diamond, "There have been times when I have skipped a meal [served in the dining room]. I decided to eat in my own room and what I did was make some cereal or something. There have also been times when I couldn't eat what they were serving so I go upstairs and have some bread with something to drink" (interview by author, tape recording, Chicago, Illinois, 9 October 1992). Zelda Arnold expressed frustration because the kitchens at Kramer do not include ovens:

I'm used to cooking and baking for myself. . . . I never walked into a bakery in all the years I was married, I always baked my own cake and cookies and bread. Here I have to eat all this bakery stuff. . . . I was angry because they [Kramer administrators] promised my son [that] "your mother can do anything she wants here, she can cook, she can bake, she can work in the greenhouse." . . . Maybe they did that [exclude kitchens] for a reason. You know, everyone isn't particular in how they keep their appliances and it would make a mess. This way when you just have a burner you don't bake so you don't have a problem. (interview by author, tape recording, Chicago, Illinois, 11 November 1992)

These resident remarks vividly illustrate how important kitchens are to them. Even the absence of an oven in an otherwise complete kitchen does not go unnoticed. Further, Zelda is perplexed about why the ovens are not included. She recalls being told she could bake when she came to Kramer, only to be disappointed when she arrived. This contradiction is not necessarily that unusual. "Some argue that assisted living facilities purporting to offer a social model of care should contain single-occupancy apartments and private bathrooms and kitchen areas, to distinguish them from board-and-care facilities. In practice, group housing accommodations identified as assisted living may not offer these features" (Golant 1999:37).

Because a large number of assisted living communities provide meals, some residents never use their kitchens for cooking and baking. However, residents still see the freedom of choice to skip a meal or make a snack when they choose as very important to them. Unfortunately, some providers and developers overlook this point, saying that full kitchens are a waste of money and are too dangerous for residents to use.

Several of the most prominent assisted living scholars believe that kitchens are a necessity, not a luxury. Regnier says that assisted living dwelling units "should be private, have at least a kitchenette for food storage and preparation. . . . A stove top or microwave oven can provide the resident with food preparation options. . . . It is important that the unit appear to be a complete housing unit and not a hospital room" (Regnier 1999:10). Scholar Keren Brown Wilson (1993) takes this idea further by linking it to the concept of home. Part of our notion of what makes a place a home is a setting where we can control our daily lives and have some autonomy. The presence of a functioning kitchen makes assisted living more homelike for residents because it personifies a residential environment and offers residents options.

Personal Belongings and Furnishings

The concept of assisted living is supposed to change the institution-like quality of residences for the elderly. The lack of a clear definition of this housing type, however, creates much confusion in terms of design changes, or rather lack thereof. Among the ten assisted living communities I visited as part of my research, only three offer residents their own separate multiroom apartments. The other seven are simply one- or two-room units, usually with a private bathroom attached, but not always. These seven settings would not even qualify as assisted living in states like Oregon, which have incorporated design standards into their regulations (one part of the Oregon regulations state that assisted living units must be a separate apartment that includes a kitchen and a full bathroom). In several of the Chicago area sites there was little if any discernible difference between assisted living rooms and regular licensed skilled care nursing home rooms. The situation gives rise to questions regarding the social climate in these places: are the assisted living residents treated the same as nursing home residents because they are housed in the same institutional rooms as nursing home residents?

Another critical factor associated with the assisted living environment is personal furniture. Seven of the ten sites I visited allow residents the option of bringing their own furniture. Based on feedback gathered from residents, it is clear that settings where people bring their own furniture seem to have a less institutional feel because every room is unique and truly reflects individual styles and tastes. Residents express individuality and personal autonomy in their decorating choices, and their personal belongings are instrumental in helping residents establish a sense of home. Disallowing the use of personal furnishings is antithetical to the very purpose and philosophy of assisted living.

Kramer and Wood Glen residents showed me objects and mementos that have the most significance for their lives. While describing these items and their history, residents became visibly delighted or enthusiastic as they retold a favorite story. Without exception every resident displayed family photos in his or her room/apartment. The importance of these photos is almost immeasurable. Pictures of children, grandchildren, great-grandchildren, the residents themselves as children, and wedding photos were the most common types of pictures displayed. Photographs are fascinating because even though everyone has these items exhibited, no two photos are alike and no two stories behind the photos are the same. More than any other item, photos seem to give the resident a sense of home because the pictures connect the elderly person to a network of people and past events that are central in his or her own lifelong experience.

The assisted living rooms at Wood Glen were much more diverse than those at Kramer. Since Wood Glen residents can bring their own furniture and Kramer residents are not allowed to do so, Wood Glen residents are better able to make a personal statement about their own tastes. They literally surround themselves with pieces of their past. Every Wood Glen resident I asked had some story to tell about the furniture or how important a particular piece was to him or her. For example, Sandy Anderson felt that her furniture made her room more homelike. "Well, everything here came from my home—nothing really belongs to the Wood Glen Home except the carpet on the floor! Everything else, all the furniture belongs to me so I feel very much at home this way. The kinds of wood in the things doesn't always match but I don't care as long as it holds the things that I want to keep close to me" (interview by author, tape recording, Chicago, Illinois, 8 January 1993).

The situation is somewhat different for the residents at Kramer. Since all of the residents have the *same* furniture, it is difficult to escape from the dormitory feel of the suites. The smaller details are what distinguish one room from the next at Kramer. Since Kramer is a very modern building with many large windows, the residence gets much sunlight. Many tenants choose to fill their rooms with plants or flowers to take advantage of the natural light and to make their rooms more "homey." They also personalize their shared suite living rooms with paintings, homemade afghans, and heirloom rugs. They like to have some of their personal touches "spill over" into the living room areas that they share with five other residents. However, decorating of common areas only occurred with some of the suites at Kramer. Clearly those suite mates who had closer relationships with each other felt more comfortable about sharing personal items with others. For instance, in Zelda Arnold's suite she proudly displays posters in the living room that were drawn by her grandson, a famous illustrator of children's books. Residents of course decorate their own rooms as well. Katie Jacobs, a resident of a different suite, has a tall bureau where she prominently displays a large doll that she was given as a small child in Russia. Larry Harris, a former U.S. postal worker, has hung a large framed drawing of his face on a postage stamp on the wall in his room.

The physical space and interior decoration of different assisted living sites create social impressions for visitors and potential residents. The decor, colors used, type of furniture, and lighting all contribute to one's perception of the social environment in the assisted living setting. For example, Kramer is decorated with light colors, vases full of flowers, a grand piano, and colorful paintings. Good words to describe Kramer's ambiance are bright and crisp. Since Kramer appears cheerful to the visitor's eye isn't it likely that his or her impression of the social climate will be similar? By comparison, the Wood Glen Home has a much more solemn, formal air. The assisted living floor contains heavy dark wood, stained glass, and rooms with smaller windows and less light overall. The rooms and the assisted living floor emanate a somber, fairly serious impression to some visitors. Would it then be more difficult to escape the feeling that one is in an institution and that the residents are more frail and dependent? It is impossible to generalize but it is worth noting that the physical environment can certainly leave a strong impression (whether accurate or false) about what the social environment may be.

THE RESIDENT PROFILE: WHO LIVES IN ASSISTED LIVING?

As with the assisted living setting itself, terminology is very important when discussing residents of assisted living. Appropriate nomenclature is significant if we are to view assisted living as something other than an institution.

We use the term "tenant" for those who rent assisted living settings. The terms "patient" or "client" are obviously inappropriate except in the narrow context of a tenant's experience as a patient or client of a particular professional. The word "resident" would be acceptable (though it has become identified with nursing homes). However, language is powerful, and the word "tenant" reinforces the theoretical separation of housing and services and keeps in the forefront the rights of people in their own homes. (Kane and Wilson 1993:12)

Kane and Wilson are quick to point out that many providers they spoke with did not employ these empowering terms. Rather, they used words like "patient" and "facility." This issue will be explored in much greater detail in chapter 6.

The typical resident in assisted living is female, eighty-four years old, and widowed (NIC 1998; ALFA 2000). Twenty-two percent of residents are male. The mean age of residents differs by gender with male residents being a bit younger at 83.2 years and female residents at 84.5 years (NIC 1998). According to a 1998 study by the National Center for Assisted Living (NCAL), residents need help with an average of 1.7 Activities of daily living (ADLs). However, it is important to examine the breakdown of the numbers in more detail. Twenty-six percent of residents allegedly required *no assistance* with any ADLs.[1] Twenty-two percent of residents required help with one ADL (usually bathing). The rest of the breakdown is as follows: 24 percent required help with two ADLs; 18 percent required help with three ADLs; 8 percent required help with four ADLs; and 6 percent required help with all five ADLs. Overall, the NCAL study showed that 27 percent of assisted living residents needed help with three or more activities of daily living. Hawes, Rose, and Phillips (1999) found similar results in their national study of 1,251 assisted living sites. In their survey, administrators estimated that 24 percent of their residents received help with three or more ADLs. In terms of cognitive impairment, Hawes et al. also found that approximately 34 percent of assisted living residents had moderate to severe levels of cognitive impairment.

The racial/ethnic makeup of the assisted living population overall is not very diverse. According to a 1998 survey by the National Investment Conference (NIC), 97 percent of residents are white, followed by 1.9 percent African-American, 0.8 percent Native American, and 0.1 percent Asian.

Marital status and geographical proximity to family were also examined by several studies. According to the National Investment Conference study of assisted living, the majority of residents (73%) are widowed. A total of 10 percent of residents are married, 9.4 percent are single, and 8.4 percent are divorced (NIC 1998). Many residents have family members in close proximity to their residence. According to a 1998 survey by ALFA, 22.7 percent of residents live within ten to twenty miles of their nearest family member and 11.2 percent of assisted living residents live within a distance of twenty to fifty miles to their nearest relative. The majority of residents appear to have frequent visitors. According to NIC's research findings, 95 percent of residents in assisted living communities in their survey were visited by a family member or friend in the last thirty days. Approximately 45 percent of residents had received four or more visits in the past month.

Seniors come to assisted living from a number of different living situations. Prior to moving into assisted living, the most common place of residence for these older adults was their own home. A total of 69 percent of seniors came to assisted living from their own homes (NIC 1998). Other residents moved to assisted living from nursing homes (10.5%), other assisted living communities (9.1%), or the hospital (5%) (NIC 1998).

Where do residents go when they leave their assisted living community? Forty-three percent of residents move from assisted living to a nursing home, while 11 percent are discharged to a hospital. A total of 9 percent of residents leave their assisted living community in order to move into a different assisted living community, and 13 percent of assisted living residents move back to their own homes. It is significant to note that only 22 percent of assisted living residents actually die in assisted living (NCAL 1998). This number illustrates that a high number of residents do not fully "age in place." Some of the numbers here are also attributable to discharge policies within assisted living communities. I will return to this issue in chapters 6 and 7.

WHAT DOES IT MEAN TO AGE IN PLACE?

Aging in place is defined in the *Dictionary of Gerontology* as "the effect of time on a non-mobile population; remaining in the same residence where one has spent his or her earlier years" (Harris 1988:18). This strict definition of aging in place refers only to changes that occur to the occupants over time; it does not address the changing nature of the environment itself. In fact, several definitions of aging in place offered by scholars in recent years focus almost exclusively on changes in the inhabitants, overlooking changes in the environment (Mangum 1994; Callahan 1993; Merrill and Hunt 1990). Nevertheless, housing is not static.

In contrast to these narrow definitions, Lawton (1990) describes aging in place as a much more multidimensional phenomenon for seniors. "Aging in place represents a transaction between an aging individual and his or her residential environment that is characterized by changes in both person and environment over time, with the physical location of the person being the only constant" (Lawton 1990:288). Lawton's definition clearly illustrates the dynamic nature of aging in place for both person and environment. Lawton also explains that three types of changes occur as aging in place happens. First, there are psychological changes in the individual over time. Next, the residential environment itself will change due to physical wear, the natural environment, and the behaviors of people in the environment. Third, changes occur in the process of aging in place based on alterations the resident may make to his or her housing in order to create a more supportive, private, and stimulating milieu. Change is thus a critical notion to bear in mind when discussing aging in place.

More recently, elders are wanting to age in place in environments other than their longtime homes. Many older adults who move to senior housing settings want to remain in these environments and avoid any subsequent moves. Residents hope that services and the physical environment can be altered to meet their changing health needs.

Housing providers have responded to elderly persons' desire to remain in senior housing in one of two ways. One response has been the "constant approach" and the other has been the "accommodating approach" (Lawton, Greenbaum, and Liebowitz 1980). The constant model tries to preserve the original character of both the tenant population and the physical environment, to have both remain constant over the years. Within this model, residents are forced to leave the housing settings as their health begins to decline. New, healthier residents who fit the original ideal proposed for the setting at its inception will then replace the ailing residents. The constant approach does not allow for aging in place as it attempts to keep the tenants and the setting static over time. When someone no longer fits the environment, he or she is asked to leave.

Conversely, the accommodating approach "accommodates administratively by tolerating an extended period of residence by tenants despite growing impairments and by relaxing admission requirements" (Lawton et al. 1980:62). The community may assist residents in staying longer by adding more services, but this is not necessarily the case. Accommodating environments can occur passively—if providers simply allow residents to stay. Accommodating environments can also occur actively, with providers integrating new services that declining residents need in order to remain.

The constant approach clearly inhibits aging in place. Accommodating environments, while more health care and resident centered, may not actually promote aging in place, but rather what I refer to as "prolonged residence." Again, prolonged residence means that a tenant can stay in assisted living until some undetermined point in time when he or she needs assistance with four or five activities of daily living (sometimes fewer) or suffers from an unspecified ailment. At this point in time, the liminal phase of prolonged residence is terminated and the older adult is discharged to a higher level of care. Older adults therefore do not know if their tenure in their present housing environment will be five months or five years. Prolonged residence certainly does not guarantee an older adult can remain in his or her residential environment until he or she dies. While prolonged residence is preferable to being evicted or discharged to a nursing home as soon as they no longer fit the image of an ideal resident, it still places a strain on residents. The reason for this anxiety surrounding prolonged residence can be understood through anthropological rites of passage mentioned in chapter 1. Residents end up residing in a liminal state, a "limbo" of sorts, not knowing how long they will be able to stay in their present housing situation. The danger then is that, though pleased to be accommodated, the resident is never certain when the accommodations will cease.

With more and more writings using the buzz phrase of "aging in place," it becomes difficult to know exactly what they mean by the term. In many instances, the marketing literature and trade journals that speak to "aging in place" in assisted living do not explain what they mean by this phrase. It is assumed that the reader knows how the phrase is being interpreted. In reality, most marketing literature uses aging in place to mean prolonged residence rather than staying until death (see chapter 6 for a further analysis of this issue).

Calkins (1995) explains that definitions of aging in place can be viewed on a continuum of sorts. First, there is the official dictionary definition of aging in place that has been mentioned above. The next point on this continuum of aging in place definitions would be what is called *a single move*. "In this situation, the elderly do not have to move *again* once they have left home and moved to the supportive residential setting" (Calkins 1995:569). The next step on the aging in place ladder would be a scenario of residents remaining within the same building, regardless of health needs. Using Wood Glen as an example, an assisted living resident may have to leave the assisted living floor because of increased impairment, but he or she could continue to live in the building at the higher level of care provided on a nursing floor. Finally, aging in place has been translated, in its broadest sense, to mean remaining on the same residential campus (such as is the case with Continuing Care Retirement Community). Here, providers refer to their residents as "aging in place" because they do not have to relocate outside of the organization, even though residents may have to move several times within the campus setting (for example, from independent housing to assisted living and then to the nursing home).

A critical question Calkins (1995) asks in relation to this continuum of aging in place is, how do *residents* interpret aging in place? Calkins points out that most scholars have not addressed this question and hence have not looked at the residents' point of view. If older adults fear that they will be forced to leave when they have greater medical needs (at the discretion of the administration of the residence) then their experience is going to be very different than what providers and scholars may think. However, before examining residents' thoughts on aging in place, I will first turn to providers' experiences. Since providers set the boundaries for aging in place in an assisted living community, understanding their point of view creates a framework with which to examine the residents' experiences.

NOTE

1. It seems unusual to have such a high number of seniors residing in assisted living who require *no assistance* with ADLs. After all, the expressed purpose of assisted living is to help residents with activities of daily living such as bathing, dressing, eating, toileting, and ambulating. A relevant question to ask is, why are these seniors moving into assisted living if they require absolutely no assistance with ADLs?

CHAPTER 4

Staff and Administrators' Views: The Ideal and the Real

Providers of assisted living have a unique perspective. They are present in the assisted living communities and they have the opportunity to have ongoing interaction with residents, family members, and regulators. It is important to understand the issues that providers face in assisted living. Throughout this chapter, the voices of providers from the Chicago area will be brought to the forefront. Their perspectives and opinions represent the full range of assisted living experience and illustrate how variable this housing option is. Administrators and staff reveal some of the dilemmas they face when trying to balance the ideals and realities of assisted living. This chapter will explore providers' experiences dealing with admission and discharge criteria, models of care, licensure and care, health status of residents, and finally the problems and benefits of assisted living. Each of these areas are important to explore because they inform us about critical issues that providers must deal with each day in assisted living.

ADMISSION AND DISCHARGE CRITERIA

All of the ten assisted living settings that I visited in the Chicago area contained some sort of criteria for acceptance into their assisted living program. Some providers were very strict about resident qualifications while others had only vague requirements for admission. Criteria at many communities seemed to be contradictory in nature. At one moment administrators were definite about minimum physical requirements for health status and activities of daily living (ADLs) ability but then quickly qualified or countered themselves.

Barbara Carns, administrator for Bartholomew Home, explained their entrance criteria to me in this manner:

We have certain criteria for assisted living. People must be alert and oriented—but "occasional forgetfulness is understood" is how we say it. They must be able to get dressed themselves—for the most part—although we might help them to do a button or shoelace or something. They must be continent of bowel and bladder—for the most part—unless there is some kind of stress that they can manage themselves. [They have to be] ambulatory without a wheelchair for the most part. I mean canes and walkers are OK. Our rooms are almost too small to try and do wheelchair transfers and move them around . . . we like to see them able to participate socially in some of the activities going on in assisted living. We provide supervision and administration of their medications by a registered nurse. (interview by author, tape recording, Chicago, Illinois, 6 May 1992)

Carns's statements show just how ambiguous entrance standards can be. Some of this vagueness is due to the nebulous definition of assisted living. Also, Bartholomew Home is licensed in Illinois for sheltered care. The licensure affects the level of care that can be provided as well as the site's definition of assisted living. The odd point here is that being licensed as sheltered care in Illinois gives Bartholomew Home more ability to offer higher levels of care and services. Therefore, it is interesting that Carns's description of assisted living criteria depicts a very independent senior with few ADL needs at time of entrance.

Other providers I spoke with were careful to point out that changes in their in-coming population over time have altered their admission standards.

The expectation would be that residents can take their own medications. They pick them up weekly from the nurses' station. The goal is to help the person remain independent. We do the shopping, the cooking, the cleaning, and the laundry so hopefully they can have fun. . . . They are ambulatory and able to maintain their own ADLs. However, with the change in age of the people coming in . . . they are more frail and we are providing more services. (interview by author, tape recording, Chicago, Illinois, 12 June 1992)

A problem associated with this change in resident frailty is the question of whom assisted living is supposed to serve. Every provider interviewed admitted that the health status of applicants has diminished significantly over time. Most providers find themselves altering the ideal of their programs so that residents may stay longer. They are wary, however, of turning assisted living into a nursing home. This raises the question of discharge policy.

Removing a resident from assisted living is a very delicate issue and most providers say they try to handle such situations on a case by case basis. Here are some examples of how different providers in the Chicago area decide upon an exit procedure. The social work liaison for Kramer explains the decision-making process this way:

It is always a case by case decision . . . we have so many meetings before we come to that final decision. We really try everything possible here at Kramer. We usually talk to the family about our concerns, maybe mom or dad needs more help, maybe they need a companion. . . . What we base that decision on is their cognitive ability—if they are no longer oriented to person, place, or time. If they are disruptive to the group. If they can't really meet their needs and Kramer cannot provide a safe environment. We really take into consideration safety and can we sustain it. (interview by author, tape recording, Chicago, Illinois, 26 October 1992)

I asked the social work liaison if there is a point with physical health problems when a resident will be asked to leave. "Bedridden—and needing a lot more nursing care than what we can provide. We have only a nurse liaison. We don't have nurses on staff. Oftentimes what we say is that they can hire a home health nurse to come in" (social work liaison interview).

Bartholomew Home administrator Barbara Carns stresses safety as a decisive factor for discharging a resident.

Usually it is a safety issue. Often it will be repeated falls . . . if there is a stroke or something or a problem that sends them to the hospital and when they return they are at a different level [of care]. Persistent incontinence—they will often try to hide that but then you begin to notice a very bad odor in their room, then you know. Sometimes confusion will get to the point where they are squirreling away food and they've got ants and cockroaches. (interview by author, tape recording, Chicago, Illinois, 6 June 1992)

Carns's response is interesting because it seems to challenge the very purpose and nature of assisted living. Assisted living is supposed to help with ADLs (including toileting ability), and according to some states, keeping food in one's apartment is considered a right that assisted living residents have. Further, questions of oversight and care may also be raised here. Why wouldn't someone be helping a resident with incontinence problems? Why wouldn't a staff person be checking on residents daily (or more often) thereby avoiding any "hiding" of incontinence problems? Clearly the Bartholomew Home follows the Senior Housing with Non-Health Care Services model of assisted living where residents are offered assistance with only instrumental activities of daily living such as cooking and cleaning.

Syndi Reis, director of housing and group living for the Committee for Elderly Jewish Affairs in Chicago, stressed the need for flexibility and compassion in the discharge decision-making process.

There isn't a written policy on that [discharge] at Kramer because how one person can cope with a problem does not necessarily mean that it is the same [for everyone]. If you said, "When you become blind then you can't live here anymore"—that's *ridiculous!* One person who is blind can get to meals, the washroom, and socialize. Another person who is blind is totally incapacitated. So, it is almost discriminatory to do that [have a set policy].

It is a process we deal with on a regular basis. Basically, we try to provide as much support to the individual as needed but we also have to take into account the group. People can have help at Kramer but if it becomes either a safety risk to them or somehow a disturbance to the group—like if somebody is confused and knocking on people's doors in the middle of the night and keeps waking up and things like that where it is a disruption and even with help it is *still* a disruption then that will be the way you know. We can make lots of individual accommodations. When it starts to affect the group and to be a serious risk in some way, I think those are two sort of hallmarks. . . . It puts a strain on the others [residents] and that is something that we take into account also. And the residents feel conflicted about it too. On the one hand, it is painful for them to see, they want it out of their face. On the other hand, there is a sense of "this could be me—don't kick them out." So it is a very tough one. It is something that we struggle with but I think that is the bottom line, when it becomes a real risk or disturbance. (interview by author, tape recording, Chicago, Illinois, 24 March 1993)

Clearly many providers try be compassionate and understanding when it comes to asking a resident to leave. Most respondents told me that they really want residents to age in place but they are afraid of "over-medicalizing" the environment, transforming it into a hospital ward. They are struggling to maintain at least some of the ideals of assisted living by having a residential environment that is noninstitutional. Beth Levinson, activities director for Kramer, had this to say about the difficulty of deciding when to ask a resident to leave assisted living:

There is no dividing line—there is no black and white. You are dealing with human beings. I will tell you this, I see Kramer bending over backwards to keep some people as long as possible and that is admirable. *However*, that plays havoc with the other residents. It plays havoc because it is a *constant* reminder of what could happen to them and it is a very real feeling. So, on the one hand, we are trying to keep a resident as long as possible and, on the other hand, we are hurting the healthier residents 'cause they are constantly reminded at the dinner table how this person's health is declining. (interview by author, tape recording, Chicago, Illinois, 4 November 1992)

Levinson points out a very critical detail that will be discussed in the next chapter: how conflicted residents are about staying in assisted living. Along this line I then asked Beth what seems to be more important: aging in place or saying, "Well it is time to go because this bothers other people." Her response was very revealing. "That is a tough one. I see sometimes *great intolerance* on the part of other residents toward the very ill. They don't want to be reminded. [They say,] 'Why is *she* here? This is not a nursing home!' And I always try to remind them that none of us knows what is going to happen to us tomorrow and that we must be more tolerant" (Levinson interview).

The gray area surrounding discharge procedure reflects the difficulty of trying to balance the ideals and realities of assisted living. It also shows the conflict surrounding the issue of aging in place for providers and residents. No matter how independent a resident may be at the time of entry, providers have to face the reality that this population will deteriorate over time. Negotiating policies that are fair for all parties involved is a difficult task.

MEDICAL AND RESIDENTIAL MODELS OF CARE

Assisted living has developed along two separate lines of care: a medical model and a residential model. The medical model is the one traditionally used for care of the elderly. It prioritizes medical service delivery and tends to view older adults as "patients." The residential model is relatively new to the realm of elderly care. It emphasizes independence for the elderly while de-emphasizing either the medical component of care, or the medicalization of the environment, or both. The residential model attempts to view older adults as residents rather than patients. The providers of assisted living clearly understand the fact that parts of both models are needed in order to best serve the needs of the elderly. Trying to balance the medical and residential models poses a serious dilemma for all of the providers I interviewed.

JF: Is a balance between medical and residential models of assisted living necessary? Or is it inevitable that we will be in a medical model?

GB: I hope not! [laughs] But I can see that happening more and more. We are getting more and more intervention with our medical director. Here [in assisted living] they are supposed to go out and see their own physician on a regular basis. We are finding out now that they are not able to go out as easily and our medical director is doing some of the follow-up here. [There is] more hands-on medical assistance to it. . . . It is such a fine line, and when you get nursing, it is hard to hold back and not be the nurse. You feel you really need to step in. (Genni Bonorelli, director of nursing, Ashmore Manor, interview by author, tape recording, Chicago, Illinois, 1 May 1992)

Providers such as Penny Morris from the Lenington Home found the issue of balancing the two models to be critical. She told me, "I think that what you have come up with is one of the major, major problems and it is sort of a real focus for all facilities, everyone is used to a medical model and in a long-term care/retirement living [setting] you need to have a holistic or social model" (interview by author, tape recording, Chicago, Illinois, 12 June 1992). Lisa Bond, director of nursing at the Wood Glen Home, felt the same way. "That is really probably going to be the hardest thing [balancing the social and medical aspects of assisted living] because [of] the regulations [for sheltered care]. They come in and dictate policy and sometimes you get so caught up in policy that you miss the person" (interview by author, tape recording, Chicago, Illinois, 6 August 1991).

Medications

Providers find that a residential/medical balance is very difficult to maintain because the health status of residents will be declining over time and because some state regulations in Illinois have made it impossible for an assisted living site not licensed as sheltered care to begin providing medical care. A clear example of this problem is the dispensation of medications. In Illinois, assisted living settings have not been able to administer medications to residents unless they are licensed as sheltered care. Even though licensure and regulations have changed (as of 2001), dispensation of medications is an ongoing concern in assisted living. Assistance with medication is a very common need among elderly persons, who may take an average of five or more medications a day. In other states as well as Illinois, if the assisted living site is not licensed as sheltered care (or some other level of care) then assisted living providers have to devise ways of helping residents with their medications without actually dispensing them. It will be useful to provide examples from Illinois to show how sites deal with medications.

Debra Santorini, administrator for Companion Hamlet and a former nurse, related an interesting story on the subject of medications. Santorini said that when Companion Hamlet initially opened its assisted living program in suburban Chicago, she asked a government regulator for the state of Illinois if it was permissible to have medical reminders. Santorini stated that the regulator told her that "medication reminders are all right, just like any other reminders as long as they are not too stringent. As long as you are not calling somebody four times a day and telling them *did you take your pill?* As long as you're not going into their apartment and making sure that they are taking the pill that was set out. A reminder should be only that: a reminder" (interview by author, tape recording, Chicago, Illinois, 7 April 1992). Santorini explained that this advice was difficult to put into practice. She cited the case of a resident who forgot to take an important pill before going to bed and the dilemma the nurse on duty faced about whether or not to administer the pill. Santorini advised the nurse to leave the pill alone because, as the state regulator had said, "a reminder should be only that: a reminder." Santorini told me that the difficulty with such situations is that

> so much of it is opinion, so much of it is your *own interpretation* of what you have heard, and that is my interpretation. I'm not saying that that's even right. I mean I just saw what happened with that one incident [in another state] and went "Oye!" [laughs]. I can't have this going on! You know you just have to start defining it [assisted living] until it gets black and white for you but I think that's why the government gets nervous. (interview by author, tape recording, Chicago, Illinois, 7 April 1992)

Communities that are licensed at a higher level of care have fewer disputes over medications because they are allowed by law to administer the drugs to the residents. However, the issues of resident dependence on staff and over-medicalizing the environment still linger. The Wood Glen Home's assisted living floor is licensed as sheltered care. When it was transformed into assisted living, the administration was unsure about how to deal with medications. Originally, the policy was that residents on the assisted living floor had to be able to self-medicate. Within a year after opening the assisted living floor, the ideal and the policy were altered. Luckily, their assisted living program was licensed as sheltered care so there were more options for dispensation of medications. Bess Coleman, activities director at Wood Glen, was asked if residents on the assisted living floor self-administer their medications.

> If they choose, and if we deem it not a danger. . . . When we were first talking about this concept of the first floor, nursing wasn't going to *touch* the meds, they [the residents] were all on their own for getting their meds, taking their meds, buying their meds—*whatever to the meds.* [We'd say] "Meds? We don't have anything to do with the meds, we're just giving them a room"—ha! And a lot of them [residents] go to the second floor for their meds and are under nurses' direct supervision for those medications and for those treatments. (interview by author, tape recording, Chicago, Illinois, 29 October 1992)

Sheltered care settings such as the Wood Glen Home have the leeway to change their medication policies because they are licensed. The licensing allows the dispensation of medication *directly* to residents. At Kramer, there is no flexibility because Kramer is not licensed as anything. In 1992–93 providers there told me they had to have a hands-off policy on medications. This leads to some questions regarding sheltered care licensing and how it affects assisted living. Even though assisted living in Illinois now has a separate licensure category, it is helpful to look back and consider how changing licensure can affect assisted living.

SHELTERED CARE VERSUS ASSISTED LIVING:
PROBLEMS AND CONSIDERATIONS

The issue of medications highlights the difficulty that providers often face in distinguishing between sheltered care and assisted living in the state of Illinois. Some communities market their sheltered care as assisted living while other places have a philosophy that the options are interchangeable, even though one is licensed to administer nursing care and the other is not. Many providers readily admit that the boundary is very blurred. Some providers even see one option as part of the other. Dr. Lester Marx, physician at the Centenarian Home in suburban Chicago, had this to say about assisted living and sheltered care:

The line between sheltered care and assisted living is not always easy to draw. You could probably get along just as well having sheltered care for these people except for the fact that they [residents] don't need their medications passed [to them]. You know, that's basically it. . . . I think it is in that area where I look upon assisted living as a subgroup of sheltered care, an offshoot of sheltered care if you will. (interview by author, tape recording, Chicago, Illinois, 14 April 1992)

Interestingly, another provider I interviewed, Debra Santorini, had the *opposite* perception from that of Marx: she believes that sheltered care is a subgroup of assisted living.

DS: Any licensed program can do *less*, they just can't do more.

JF: You can have someone [in sheltered care] who is really independent and really doesn't need this and that.

DS: Right. *I* could move to a sheltered care program today and live there if I chose to do that because you can always have less [services], you just cannot provide more [than licensing will allow]. I mean it's not incorrect in that way to say that sheltered care is assisted living.

JF: So, it is sort of like assisted living is the square in a rectangle [of sheltered care]?

DS: Well, I'd almost say the reverse. I would say assisted living is the bigger umbrella and maybe what we need to do is define the residential programs as something else. Maybe assisted living should be the catch-all title for all of these things, with a subcategory of sheltered or residential—you know? And you go from one place to another and you find them [providers] calling it everything. . . . If you looked at it [assisted living] as encompassing anything that offered that level of assistance, it really could take in sheltered care as well as other things. See, sheltered care is licensed so it would never take in the nonlicensed population. . . . You could say this: "we're an assisted living–sheltered licensed" or "we are an assisted living–nonlicensed residential" and that is pretty much how I define it. So, the problem is that the public doesn't know that part of it yet. (interview by author, tape recording, Chicago, Illinois, 7 April 1992)

Depending on which way one looks at assisted living, both Santorini and Marx could be correct. Marx claims that assisted living is a subgroup of sheltered care. This is true if one considers assisted living in terms of the medical model. The larger group would be licensed sheltered care where increased medical assistance is allowed by law. Since assisted living was not licensed as a separate category in Illinois, providers could do much less *medically* for their residents if they were not licensed as sheltered care. From Marx's perspective, assisted living is a subgroup of sheltered care because everything that is done in assisted living can be done under licensed sheltered care. However, much more can be done *medically* for a resident in sheltered care than can be done in assisted living in Illinois.

Santorini, on the other hand, sees sheltered care as part of assisted living because she is looking at the two options from a residential model. As she stated, any licensed program can deliver less in terms of medicine dispensing and service delivery but it cannot do more. Licensed sheltered care permits much more assistance medically for residents but all residents do not necessarily need that much care. Here, the bigger umbrella is assisted living; its basic services are providing meals, assistance with activities of daily living (ADLs), and social activities. Everything that can be done for residents in a nonmedical capacity in assisted living can be done for them in sheltered care. However, everything that can be done for residents medically in sheltered care cannot necessarily be done for them in assisted living.

These two perspectives highlight the confusion among providers in Illinois regarding where assisted living fits into the continuum of care. Perhaps, as several assisted living experts have suggested, this option should not be placed anywhere along the continuum of care but rather should be seen as an alternative to the continuum (Wilson 1993; Regnier 1992).

Removing assisted living from the continuum of care and developing it as a true alternative where residents can fully age in place might allow residents more opportunity to see assisted living as home. Providers could stop worrying about admission and discharge criteria and start treating assisted living as the residents' home. At the same time residents could overcome some of their own anxieties about their increasing frailty and about the prospect of being asked to leave. When these older adults lived out in the community, there were no policies forcing them from their homes at a designated time. If assisted living can allow aging in place until a resident dies, providers might be able to eliminate the sense of dread most elderly have about "being sent to the nursing home" and that the nursing home is their only real "last stop." The question is whether or not this idealistic alternative to the continuum of care will work in reality.

THE REAL BENEFITS OF ASSISTED LIVING

As part of every interview I conducted with providers, I asked them what they believed were the most beneficial aspects of assisted living. I was curious to find out whether their responses would focus on physical amenities, social activities, services, or a combination of these three areas. Bobbie Dawson, director of marketing at Wood Glen, had this to say:

Oh that's easy. Nobody wants to talk about nursing homes, retirement homes. "I am too young, I don't need it," but it happens. So, you go to a retirement home. Well, what's after a retirement home? You go to a nursing home. [Then residents think,] "I am in a nursing home, that's it, this is the end of my life, that's it, they've taken everything." . . . If you are in a retirement home and something happens you get kicked out, bottom line. . . . Today though, more people are aging in place, it is a resident right issue. They are letting people stay in these quote "retirement homes," which are no longer retirement homes. But it is an aging in place issue. If for some reason you are in a retirement home and maybe you are just getting a little dementia or you know you just can't really walk for long distances without being assisted—without an assistive device, then this [assisted living] is an alternative. Or, if you are in your own home and retired—I mean who wants to cook for one? Who wants to clean a five-room apartment when you are eighty-nine years old? Nobody. So, they can come here and it is a very nice alternative. (interview by author, tape recording, Chicago, Illinois, 2 August 1991)

Lisa Bond, director of nursing at the Wood Glen Home, focused more on the housing aspect of assisted living as being the most beneficial: "Security and stability because they [the residents] have been promised that they can stay in that area [assisted living] indefinitely, for a relatively low income. That, I think, is the best thing because older people sometimes have difficulty with housing" (interview by author, tape recording, Chicago, Illinois, 6 August 1991).

The activities director at the Wood Glen Home saw the major benefits of assisted living as resident independence, both its ideal and reality:

In general I think it will take some of the fear out of the aging process because people [residents] can still maintain some independence even if it is just a modicum of independence. In a lot of cases I think we might find that independence is really an *illusion* because of the support that we are giving, but that's OK, too. I don't have to be totally convinced that you have to be 100 percent [laughs]—you'd be out there in your own home if you could! But if we could give the illusion that—because of some support services that are in place—you [residents] are more independent or if you truly are more independent then it takes a bit of the fear out of aging. It gives you a chance to see that there is some means of transition to get you to a next level, if necessary. (interview by author, tape recording, Chicago, Illinois, 5 August 1991)

Hanna Jorge, a registered nurse at the Wood Glen Home, had a similar response:

Certainly for the resident . . .—the appropriate resident—I think it can be a way they can really maintain a high level of functioning and kind of a structured yet not overly so kind of environment. They can continue to come and go as they are able. They can use minimal assistance, being able to maintain their community contacts—having their friends come in for lunch, going out with people. Having, for a moderate monthly fee—really being free from worry about their day-to-day living environment. Having their basic needs [met], having opportunities for socialization, having trained professional staff available to them and alert to them and their needs. (interview by author, tape recording, Chicago, Illinois, 2 July 1991)

Thus far there have been three recurring themes in the respondents' answers: (1) the idea of relieving older adults from the stresses of living out in the community; (2) the transitional nature of assisted living; and (3) assisted living as part of the continuum of care.

Providers in Illinois have been conditioned to see assisted living as transitional because they have been told that assisted living falls along the continuum of care, just after independent living and right before a nursing home. Therefore, providers in Illinois have historically thought of assisted living only in terms of a bridge between two other options and that a resident's stay is only temporary. The role of assisted living along the continuum of care also highlights providers' conflicts regarding the ideal and the reality of assisted living.

Providers in most states have the idea that residents will only live in assisted living for a finite period of time. This is the reality that most providers see. However, the length of stay can range from a month to ten years. The ideal situation would be for a resident to die in assisted living and not progress along the continuum into a nursing home. If residents are going to die in assisted living, there are only two possible scenarios: (1) "the ideal" where residents die when they are still relatively healthy and somewhat independent; or (2) "the potential reality" where residents are allowed to fully age in place, deteriorating over time, and eventually dying. The aging in place/continuum of care controversy is indicative of the many problems that providers face in assisted living.

PROBLEMS WITH ASSISTED LIVING

In addition to inquiring about the many benefits of assisted living, I also asked providers in the Chicago area about the problems they perceive with assisted living. Dr. Lester Marx is a physician at the Centenarian Home, a continuing care retirement community in north suburban Chicago. He explains the dilemma he faces in his community. "Problems in a continuing care retirement community (CCRC) are always the same. People deny their own frailty by and large and they always feel that they can continue to live and maintain themselves in an area that is really above and beyond their abilities. . . . They don't want to go from independent living to the health care center. They don't want to go to assisted living. . . . People seem very unrealistic about what their abilities are" (interview by author, tape recording, Chicago, Illinois, 14 April 1992). While Marx's observations are certainly common among many assisted living providers, it is also a viewpoint indicative of the continuum of care model. Marx believes that residents need to "move on" when they are no longer able to perform certain tasks. Rather than moving people around to different levels of care, why not move the different levels of care around to meet the person's needs?

Penny Morris, administrator for the Lenington Home, saw the conflict between residence policies and resident rights to be the major drawback for their assisted living program.

Sure. I think as we get older we are used to a lot of choices and even though we promote resident rights and try to promote choices, you have to have meals at a certain time [in the dining room]. You have to have set menus. Breakfast is at 7:30. If you want to sleep till 9:00 and miss breakfast that's OK. But there will be no one there to give you your breakfast. Probably the only shortcoming I see [for assisted living] is the need to have specific hours. I mean you have to make an appointment for your shower or your bath. That is one of the losses, not being able to decide when you are going to have breakfast or lunch. (interview by author, tape recording, Chicago, Illinois, 12 June 1992)

Clearly Morris is concerned about the constraints that are placed on her assisted living residents. They are supposed to see assisted living as "home"; yet, they cannot choose what to eat or when to take a bath. The food issue might at least be solved if residents each had a kitchenette where they could store food. This would then offer residents much more choice and flexibility.

Barbara Carns, an administrator from the Bartholomew Home, alluded to the continuum of care itself as a large problem with assisted living. "I think it is often hard when they [residents] reach the point where they can't stay there [in assisted living] and you have to change their care to a higher level, the cost immediately doubles and that is a big hit to people. I think it picks up psychologically the fact that 'now I can't continue to function the way I did before' " (interview by author, tape recording, Chicago, Illinois, 6 May 1992). Again, the central problem that Carns seems to be expressing is one related to aging in place in assisted living.

Other providers I spoke with saw the residents' loss of control as a major drawback to assisted living. Laura Himelstein is the site coordinator for Kramer and she has seen many residents deal with losses as part of their lives in assisted living. "A loss of independence, loss of control—there is something that everybody gives up to come here. For some people it is a bigger loss than for others. . . . Everyone has left something important behind and that, on an individual basis, is what counts" (interview by author, tape recording, Chicago, Illinois, 4 November 1992).

Although the providers' answers to my question about the negative aspects of assisted living differed in their specifics, a major theme emerged. The providers' primary concerns focused on the residents: their decline in health and their loss of control and choice in the assisted living environment. Since health, control, and choice are key factors contributing to an elderly person's independence, it is important to pursue these issues further.

CONTROL AND INDEPENDENCE

I asked providers two related questions about resident control and independence in their assisted living communities. First, I asked what aspect of their assisted living environment they believe contributes most to residents' sense of control and independence. Second, I asked administrators how they could best create and maintain independence and control among their residents. Dr. Lester Marx had an interesting perspective on these two questions.

JF: Are there any particularly important aspects to the living environment that really contribute to their [residents'] sense of control and independence?

LM: I think very much so. I think first of all, the décor, which is very traditional. We feel very strongly . . . that it should be traditional. These people [residents] feel much more comfortable with tradition, old wood, with Chippendale and Duncan Fife than they do with chrome and glass and glitz. So, it is as homey an environment as we can possibly produce. I think the caring nature of the staff—they are able to . . . assist people in making adaptations.

JF: How do you feel the Centenarian Home can best create and maintain an environment that promotes independence and control among residents?

LM: Well, we try to do that by self-governance. There are resident councils throughout [the CCRC]. We try and have activities that keep people young. We are constantly trying to be innovative—to look for new activities. We present patients with a full menu of activities, whether they partake or not is up to them.[1] (interview by author, tape recording, Chicago, Illinois, 14 April 1992)

Barbara Carns believes that choice is an important factor in residents' control and independence at the Bartholomew Home. "Well, keys to their rooms is a *big thing*. They can lock their rooms and when you get into skilled care they don't lock their own doors. I think that helps them maintain a sense of control. You know, they do lose a lot of that when they come in because just for practical

reasons you have to schedule meals at a certain time, etc. . . . I think [we need]
to give them as much say so as they can have, give them choices about activities,
try to schedule more than one thing going on at once so that they can have a
choice" (interview by author, tape recording, Chicago, Illinois, 6 May 1992).

Physical design and medical care can also be keys to residents' control and
independence. At Ashmore Manor, administrator William Eckstrom believes
that the rooms themselves are important. "Their [residents'] rooms are very individualized. We do *not* have a bed and a couch and a chair, they bring all their
own furniture. . . . I think as people become more ill what helps independence
is the access to nursing care, to doctors" (interview by author, tape recording,
Chicago, Illinois, 1 May 1992). The administrators at Ashmore agree that personalizing one's environment can be very important in assisted living.

Wood Glen Home administrator Karen Abrams believes that privacy contributes to residents' sense of independence and control. "Well, they are not being monitored constantly and I think there is some positive in that. They don't
have to feel like staff is watching them. They have as much privacy as you can
expect. . . . They can close their door and get away from it all" (interview by author, tape recording, Chicago, Illinois, 8 April 1992). Other providers at Wood
Glen said that the attitude of staff can make a big difference. Bess Coleman, activities director, stressed that staff attitudes toward both the residents *and* the
assisted living program can help promote resident independence.

Well, [what helps with independence] is whether you approach it [the Wood Glen
Home] as an institution plain and simple or . . . you know. To me, any time you are in a
communal living situation it does not necessarily have to be institutional but there is a
certain amount of you [the person] that you give up, that you sacrifice because of that
[coming into a communal living situation] no matter how independent you are. Ask
anybody who has ever lived in a dorm. There wasn't anybody who did not think that
they were their own person and independent if they were asked. But, you did give up an
awful lot, sacrificed it for communal living purposes. You know, you didn't always have
the bathroom when you wanted it. . . . So, maybe it is just a matter of saying, "Look,
this is a communal situation and there are 100 other people living here and as a result
there is a certain amount of give and take," . . . that is still not the same as saying, "You're
in an institution, here are the rules and regulations, take it or leave it." So, it is how you
[the provider] are presenting it. Are you going to lean on somebody because they want
to play the piano at 10:00 at night? (interview by author, tape recording, Chicago, Illinois, 5 August 1991)

Dara Kander is the director of housing for Kramer Group Living Residence. In
her experience it is the open communication between residents and staff that is
most helpful to residents for promoting independence and control. "Having
them in the group meetings, being able to have that avenue to express their

needs as well as having an individual structure so if they don't feel like they want to express their opinions with the group, you know having the social worker here or Laura here to be available for them to talk to" (interview by author, tape recording, Chicago, Illinois, 6 May 1992).

Independence and control are two central issues to consider when analyzing assisted living. The providers' responses show that they see a number of different things as contributing to residents' independence and control. Some Chicago area providers thought that the physical decor and furniture were most important for contributing to residents' sense of control and independence while other providers focused on different details such as locking doors and staff awareness. Still, other administrators stressed more abstract issues such as the freedom to come and go without monitoring or having the opportunity to voice concerns as encouraging residents' independence and control.

Many administrators pinpointed the importance of resident autonomy and trying to foster it. They see residents themselves as having an important role in preserving their own independence. Key words providers used in reference to the residents' part in preserving independence were "self-governance," "say so," "doing more for themselves," and "resident responsibility." The administrators also saw themselves as playing a major role in resident independence. They describe their own roles with key phrases such as "staff working closely together," "giving residents more choices," "avenues where residents can reach staff," "whether or not you approach the facility as an institution," and "giving access to nursing care." Clearly all of the respondents believe that both residents and providers have important roles to play in the preservation and promotion of resident control and independence.

An important point related to these issues is how independent the providers actually think their residents *are*. According to Laura Himelstein,

Our population is definitely aging and I think it is changing. Some of our residents were more independent when they came in than they are now. We have some [residents] that could probably function in their own apartment in the community with some type of assistance and there is a small number that could probably function quite well in a nursing home. And, in between we've got those who fluctuate. (interview by author, tape recording, Chicago, Illinois, 4 November 1992)

Kramer nurse liaison Francine Key thinks that age is a major factor in residents' independence. When asked how independent the residents seem to her, Key replied, "Well, I think it depends on their age. You know so many start at seventy, seventy-five, and they can still function independently fairly well. But as they age in place their vision declines and the hearing declines so they are not as independent. If they are arthritic they can't ambulate as well and yet you see people who at ninety-five can still go walk around the block" (interview by author, tape recording, Chicago, Illinois, 19 November 1992).

Several providers in the Chicago area did not see their residents as independent at all. I asked Karen Abrams of Wood Glen if she thinks the assisted living residents are fairly independent. She replied, "No, I do not. Some may be independent in certain basic daily activities" (interview by author, tape recording, Chicago, Illinois, 8 April 1992). Syndi Reis, head of housing for the Committee on Jewish Elderly Affairs, agreed with Abrams.

JF: Do you think the assisted living residents are fairly independent?

SR: No, I don't. I think there are those with physical frailties and then there are those with emotional dependencies who are there [at Kramer] not because they need it physically, but because they can't manage alone. They get too lonely, they get too depressed, they don't eat you know? I don't think it is an independent population. I think the independent population is in their homes. Do we try to maintain their independence as much as possible by giving them choices and by involving them in things? Absolutely. But I don't think it is an independent group. (interview by author, tape recording, Chicago, Illinois, 24 March 1993)

Some of the responses to the question of resident independence may be based on how the provider defines independence. I asked providers at all ten sites to define the word "independence" in relation to their residents. The following responses raise some interesting concerns regarding the assisted living population. Dr. Richard Arsk is the physician at the Wood Glen Home. I asked him how he would define "independent." "Able to—to do everything for themselves, such as dress, groom, take medicines, eat, socialize. Pretty much I think the only thing that they [assisted living residents] don't generally do on their own is take their medicines. I think the nurses are sort of in charge of making sure that they [residents] get them appropriately, but independent in activities of daily living . . . independent in their day to day living" (interview by author, tape recording, Chicago, Illinois, 9 April 1992). Arsk's response to the question is somewhat troubling. He defines independence in assisted living as able to do everything for one's self. And, he perceives that the only thing that residents of assisted living get help with is taking their medications. If residents were independent in all of their ADLs, why would they be living in assisted living? As we will hear from Wood Glen residents later, they perceive their fellow residents as far from able to perform daily tasks on their own.

I asked Nancy Simpson, social work liaison for Kramer, how she would define "independence," and her answer was very similar to Arsk's. "For Kramer? I think if a person is able to meet their basic needs, meaning able to feed themselves, um . . . if a person is able to meet their basic needs—clothe themselves, feed themselves. I don't think you need to define it as somebody who goes out on all the trips, or who is very sociable" (interview by author, tape recording, Chicago, Illinois, 26 October 1992). Simpson is defining independence for Kramer residents based on ADL ability, just like Arsk did. She does not believe that one needs to be socially active to be considered independent at Kramer, just that one must be able to take care of his or her basic needs.

Beth Levinson, activities director at Kramer, still believes there are some independent residents there. "It [independence] is still here. People here still have to take their own medication. Laura and I are not even allowed to give them a Tylenol if they ask for it. We are not permitted to put eye drops in after they come home from cataract surgery. That is a very difficult decision to make for us to say 'no'"(interview by author, tape recording, Chicago, Illinois, 4 November 1992).

All of the previous responses show that providers define independence among their residents in relation to the continuum of care. In 1992 and 1993, most providers expected residents, upon entry, to be able to take care of their activities of daily living. This expectation reflects the placement of assisted living along the continuum of care because providers think that the needs of in-coming residents should not overlap with those of nursing home residents. If these providers viewed assisted living as *separate from* the continuum of care they would not be as concerned about residents' independence with their activities of daily living (ADLs).

The responses are also troubling on some level because they illustrate the overwhelming ignorance on the part of providers regarding the definition and purpose of assisted living. Assisted living is supposed to provide *assistance* with activities of daily living. The population assisted living is supposed to serve consists of those older adults who need support with their ADLs. Even in 1992, the average assisted living resident needed help with 1.5 to 2 ADLs. The responses in this chapter show that many providers in Illinois were envisioning new residents as being self-reliant in their eating, dressing, bathing, toileting, and ambulating needs.

Some assisted living settings, especially those which are free-standing, do not even have on-site help available for any kind of ADL assistance. There are no services present except for meals and housekeeping. Yet, assuming that residents will be independent at their time of entry goes against the very principles and philosophy of assisted living.

As a housing/health care option, assisted living was created to aid older adults with their daily needs so that they can maintain their autonomy. Why then are so many providers thinking that in-coming residents will *not* require any assistance? It seems that many providers are adhering to the Housing with Non-Health Care Services model that was described earlier (ALFA 1999).

They think that the objective of assisted living is to provide meals, prevent loneliness, and plan activities for residents rather than to assist them with activities of daily living. Following this model, when residents reach the point where they need help with three or four ADLs, a number of providers decide that residents are too impaired to remain in assisted living. Residents are then transferred to the next level on the continuum of care. A number of administrators seem confused about the very nature of assisted living. However, some of their opinions may be based on state regulations. At the time of my research, Kramer was not licensed as sheltered care and, therefore, it was impossible for administrators to provide care for residents, even if they wanted to. Providers at Kramer were put into a position where they must evict a resident who required health care or risk legal consequences.

If assisted living was operated through the true aging in place model, then it could absorb older adults on all levels of the continuum of care, rather than being one step on the ladder. There can be little doubt that, in many states, most providers and developers perceive assisted living as part of the continuum of care and not as an alternative to it. As I will discuss later, an important question becomes whether or not this alternative model can work in reality.

HEALTH STATUS

Closely tied to independence is health status. I questioned providers in the Chicago area about the health of their residents. Did they think that the health status of residents turned out to be better, worse, or the same as they expected? I also asked about the health status of residents at the time of their entrance into assisted living. The answers I received spanned the gamut from complete surprise about residents' health to calm resignation about their level of impairment. Dr. Lester Marx of the Centenarian Home was not surprised by the level of impairment of the residents.

I would say we were pretty much on target. We had started this [assisted living] primarily for those individuals who were living independently but who were physically too compromised to maintain their living independently. And this has allowed us to give them a place where they can live satisfactorily without having to go into the health care center, which indeed is a much more restrictive lifestyle. So, they still maintain independence and a sense of dignity while receiving a little bit of assistance. *It is a way station.* We don't anticipate people will spend protracted periods of time living in assisted living. It is a *way station.* Their abilities are waning. And they are quote "failing." Because of that we don't think that they will stay here for a protracted period of time. (interview by author, tape recording, Chicago, Illinois, 14 April 1992)

Other providers said they noticed distinct changes in residents' health status. Lenington Home administrator Penny Morris has seen residents decline with time.

I would say it has always been ambulatory [upon entrance], able to maintain their own ADLs. However, with the change of age of the people coming in we are looking at the people coming in to be in their late eighties and around nineties. They are more frail and we are providing more services. So, if they do need assistance with ambulation for long distances—in other words if the distance is very large like if they need to come from sheltered care to the clinic to see the doctor, there is an aide to take them. (interview by author, tape recording, Chicago, Illinois, 12 June 1992)

In the view of many providers, the anticipated level of health for new residents is closely connected to their perceived level of independence. As time passes, providers are realizing that they must abandon their notions that assisted living residents will be self-sufficient in their activities of daily living. All of the providers I spoke with are aware that the health status of new residents has deteriorated and that their assisted living programs will have to adjust to meet changing needs if they are to stay in business.

JF: What would you say is the general health status of people who come in [to assisted living]? Is it better or worse than you expected?

GB: In my opinion, worse.

JF: Do you think that is changing through time?

GB: I believe that they [residents] are trying to hold out and be independent longer and [are] really resisting sheltered care. I think the connotation of sheltered care/assisted living is almost going into the nursing home. Instead of being over here, independent—more independent requiring minimal assist—I think they are requiring more assistance when they come into assisted living. (Genni Bonorelli, administrator, Ashmore Manor, interview by author, tape recording, Chicago, Illinois, 1 May 1992)

Providers such as Debra Santorini found questions regarding health status quite difficult to answer. Assisted living residents at Companion Hamlet can be quite borderline.

Actually, well, it is kind of hard to answer a health question because I always think in medical terms like their diagnoses. Most of them fare pretty well. They actually do better than I would have predicted. We knew that we were sending people up there [to assisted living] on a marginal basis and if they are physically marginal or mentally marginal it usually means that health-wise they tend to be marginal just because their health habits have not been really good. And what happens when they get up there is that there is someone who is providing some oversight making sure that if they have a cold that they get to the doctor. . . . Health-wise they tend to hold on longer than I predicted but there are some people who are marginal and most of those health problems are ones that we can't deal with so you know when someone does get into a lot of health problems it is pretty hard for them to stay up there [in assisted living]. (interview by author, tape recording, Chicago, Illinois, 7 April 1992)

Bess Coleman, activities director for the Wood Glen Home, said she was not surprised by the level of impairment experienced by some residents. However, some of the other administrators were disillusioned with the health status of residents. "I would say for [other staff members] there was some disappoint[ment] that they did not get the Bob Hopes of the world coming in to play golf every day! They missed the point that nobody who is *that* active needs us" (interview by author, tape recording, Chicago, Illinois, 2 April 1992).

At Kramer, nurse liaison Francine Key stressed that concerns from family members *about* the resident's health were just as prominent as any health problems actually experienced by residents.

Well, I think that you know—I don't think if they were physically capable of doing everything that many of them would be here. There are some that can still get around. For many of them I think [the reason why they are here] is *the family's anxiety*. You know that they [the family] want [to know] if something should happen, someone will be able to call them. It is their [the family's] lifeline. (interview by author, tape recording, Chicago, Illinois, 19 November 1992)

Laura Himelstein stressed the differences in Kramer residents' ability to maintain their health over time: "We have people who have gotten better in the sense that they are getting three meals a day and they are getting socialization and they are getting that little TLC. We also have residents that age in place and are just getting older and staying right where they are. We have others that grow out of us. Their needs become more than what we can provide" (interview by author, tape recording, Chicago, Illinois, 4 November 1992).

Syndi Reis spoke for the experience of every provider I interviewed when she described the changes in residents' health at Kramer. She seemed to echo the sentiments of all the other respondents.

When you look at the whole group living thing and where it was and where it has come, then I think you can see some trends. We've got a resident [at Kramer] who is part of hospice, we've never had that before. We had a resident die at Kramer, we never had that before—they usually die in the hospital. We have people with dementia. There are more medical problems and I think that's a result of age. The average age is going up in terms of the people coming into the program. (interview by author, tape recording, Chicago, Illinois, 24 March 1993)

Residents' health status covers a fairly wide range in assisted living. Some seniors are healthy physically but need social contact and companionship while other residents are quite frail. Most providers agree that the overall health of residents is changing and that the need for a medical component in assisted living is increasing with time. Staff and administrators' comments on health status highlight one aspect of their viewpoint on residents. A way to probe deeper into administrators' perspective is to examine some quantitative data on the subject.

STAFF AND ADMINISTRATORS' PERCEPTIONS OF RESIDENTS: A COMPARISON OF KRAMER AND WOOD GLEN

Policies and procedures are an important part of any assisted living setting. How a site operates influences staffs' and residents' ideas of fairness, responsibility, leniency, and reliability. Because policies are so divergent from one assisted living location to another, a comparison of Kramer and the Wood Glen Home is useful for indicating the broad spectrum of assisted living practices. To be sure, assisted living settings vary a great deal in their design, organization, administration, and policies. Therefore, it might appear pointless to compare two sites that are obviously quite different in their layout, size, and programs. However, such comparisons are relevant because Wood Glen and Kramer represent the reality of assisted living: it is very diverse. Kramer is a suburban, free-standing assisted living residence, arranged in suites, that houses up to twenty-nine individuals. In contrast, Wood Glen Home is a nursing home that has set aside one floor as assisted living. Up to seventeen people can live on this floor.

The results of the Multiphasic Environmental Assessment Procedure (MEAP) will be used to aid in the comparison and contrast of these two sites. The MEAP was originally developed by Moos and Lemke (1988, 1980) to evaluate sheltered care settings for older adults. The procedure used to administer the MEAP is discussed extensively in Appendix I.

Resident Diversity and Staff Richness

The Resident and Staff Information Form (RESIF) is a sixty-five item questionnaire measuring "those aspects of the overall environment of a facility that derive from the characteristics of its residents and staff" (Moos and Lemke 1996:29). The elements of the RESIF are illustrated in Table 4.1. These nine dimensions have been grouped into larger categories that are as follows: characteristics of staff, sociodemographic background of residents, residents' functioning and activity, and residents' use of services and activities. Staff at both sites answered these questions.

Table 4.1
Resident and Staff Information Form (RESIF): Subscale Descriptions
and Item Examples

1. Staff Richness—Reflects the resources that are available from the staff in terms of experience, training, and variety of backgrounds. (Is there a doctor and an occupational or physical therapist? Is there an in-service training program? How many of the staff are over fifty-one years of age?)

2. Resident Social Resources—Assesses the current status of residents with respect to demographic variables that facilitate social competence. (How many of the residents are married? How many of the residents have had some high school education?)

3. Resident Heterogeneity—Measures the extent to which residents are a diverse group of individuals. (How many residents are men? How many residents come from various religious backgrounds?)

4. Resident Functional Abilities—Measures residents' independence in performing daily functions and the extent of handicaps in functioning. (How many residents can take care of their own appearance? How many residents do not know what day or year this is?)

5. Resident Activity Level—Measures the extent to which residents are involved in activities that they initiate themselves. (How many residents have read a newspaper or book in the past week? How many residents took a walk in the past week?)

6. Resident Integration in the Community—Measures the rate of residents' participation in activities that take them outside the facility. (How many residents go out to attend a concert or play? How many residents engage in volunteer or paid work?)

7. Utilization of Health Services—Reflects the extent to which residents utilize the health services that are provided by the facility. (How many residents receive physical therapy in a typical week?)

8. Utilization of Daily Living Assistance—Measures residents' use of the daily living services available within the facility. (How many residents use the barber or beauty service in a typical week? How many residents eat dinner [provided by the facility] on a typical day?)

9. Utilization of Social/Recreational Activities—Assesses resident participation in activities offered within the facility. (How many residents participate in discussion groups? How many residents attend parties?)

Source: Rudolf H. Moos and Sonne Lemke. *Evaluating Residential Facilities: The Multiphastic Environment Assessment Procedures,* p. 30, copyright © 1996 Sage Publications, Inc. Reprinted by permission of Sage Publications, Inc. and Sonne Lemke.

For this particular section of the MEAP there are differences between the dimensions shown in Table 4.1 and those used in Figure 4.1. As Appendix I explains, I did not use three of the nine elements of the RESIF because providers at both sites had a difficult time accurately completing all nine dimensions and

Figure 4.1
Resident and Staff Resources Dimensions

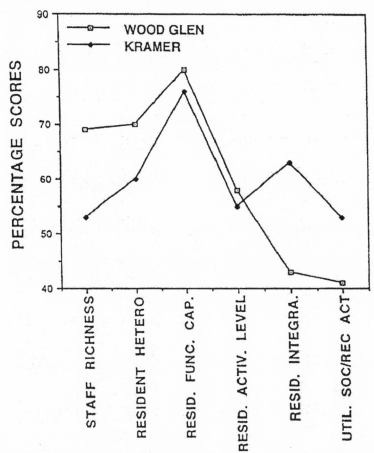

left many answers blank. This caused me to eliminate several of the dimensions because of lack of data. Therefore, Figure 4.1 shows a comparison of Wood Glen and Kramer using six of the nine dimensions for the RESIF. Excluded dimensions include resident social resources, utilization of daily living assistance, and utilization of health services. Looking at Figure 4.1, clear differences between Kramer and Wood Glen emerge. First, however, I would like to call attention to the similarities.

The staff at Kramer and Wood Glen scored residents very similarly on the dimensions of resident functional abilities and resident activity level. The percentage scores between the two sites differed only slightly on both of these dimensions. The score for resident functional ability was 80 percent for Wood Glen and 76 percent for Kramer. These results are noteworthy because they show that despite differences in assisted living policies regarding resident functioning and independence, the resident populations are basically perceived as identical at the two sites. In fact, the Wood Glen residents actually scored slightly higher in their level of functioning. These numbers support Kane and Wilson's 1993 findings that residents in free-standing assisted living settings tend to be more frail than residents in other forms of assisted living. More than this, these scores reveal that despite the fact that free-standing assisted living sites tend to target more independent elderly persons as potential residents, over time the profile for residents living in the assisted living community is the same, if not more impaired, than that of residents living in assisted living next to higher levels of care.

Community Integration

Resident integration into the community is the dimension showing the most deviation between Kramer and Wood Glen. Kramer staff scored their residents at 63 percent for integration into the community while Wood Glen staff scored their residents at 43 percent. These figures suggest that Kramer residents are much more active than their Wood Glen counterparts even though they scored lower than Wood Glen residents for both functional abilities and activity level. But, what exactly does "integration in the community" mean?

Moos and Lemke developed fourteen questions on the RESIF to measure how many residents leave an assisted living community to participate in outside activities. Providers were asked to answer the following question: "About what percent of the residents leave the facility for the following activities at least a few times a year?" Some of the activities listed include visiting friends or relatives, going on a ride or tour somewhere, going to a sports event, attending religious services, attending a funeral, going shopping, dining in a restaurant, attending a concert or play, going to the movies, engaging in volunteer work, or going on an overnight trip. The scores for Wood Glen and Kramer residents suggest that Kramer residents are more active in the wider community. However, there are reasons other than activity level that may account for these scores.

I would like to note that, based on my own observations at the two sites, I agree that Kramer residents do participate in community-based activities more often than Wood Glen residents. Kramer residents dine out more frequently, attend more plays and concerts, and definitely visit friends and relatives more frequently than Wood Glen residents. I suggest three reasons for this difference. First, at Kramer, I found that 100 percent of the residents have at least one immediate family member living in the Chicago area (usually a son or daughter but sometimes a sibling, grandchild, or spouse). This is not the case at Wood Glen. Although no documentation exists on this issue, I learned from my interviews that at least four of the fifteen assisted living residents at Wood Glen have no relatives in the Chicago area. This fact could certainly account for some of the difference between Kramer and Wood Glen scores. As is the case with many older adults living in life care settings, Kramer residents who participate in community-based activities often do so with family members. They go to restaurants, shop, attend concerts, and visit overnight with relatives. Since several assisted living residents at Wood Glen have no relatives in the Chicago metropolitan area, it is understandable that their overall activity score would be lower.

The second reason for the difference in scores is availability of transportation. Both Wood Glen and Kramer have vans to take residents shopping, to doctor's appointments, or to special events. Nevertheless, the availability of transportation differs at the two sites. First, the van at Wood Glen serves the entire nursing home population (115 residents). Therefore, it is much more difficult to schedule a time to take the shuttle somewhere unless it is a planned group event. At Kramer, the van also serves a second assisted living site with twenty-five residents. This means the van that comes to Kramer serves a total of fifty-four residents, less than half the number of the Wood Glen Home shuttle. In addition, since residents attend many outside activities with family members, the family is frequently the source of transportation. And, since Wood Glen residents have far fewer relatives in the Chicago area, it is reasonable to conclude they would go out less.

Finally, the third possible reason why Kramer residents go out more is finances. In general, Kramer residents have higher incomes than those at Wood Glen, or Kramer residents have relatives with higher incomes than those of Wood Glen residents' relatives. Having more money means that Kramer residents can afford to go out more often for lunches, concerts, or special events.

If we accept the presence of family, transportation, and money differences as explanations for the higher integration of Kramer residents into the broader Chicago community, we may also account for the curious gap between the low resident activity/functional level at Kramer and their higher community integration level. The residents at Kramer are equally impaired, if not more so, than the residents at Wood Glen. Yet, they seem to be more active in the community. Why? Kramer residents have more family members close by who provide companionship, transportation, and sometimes financial assistance for many outside activities. In effect, the family is the link to the wider community and the "outside world." Older adults residing at Wood Glen may have a slightly higher functional ability and activity level but they lack this critical link to the community. The RESIF provides some important information about resident characteristics at Wood Glen and Kramer (as seen through the eyes of administrators). Nonetheless, we must also understand how residents perceive their living environment.

This chapter has shown some of the various perspectives Illinois providers have regarding assisted living and its residents. Assuredly, administrators are very concerned about how to care for residents as they age in assisted living. Some providers are conflicted about what residents' health status should be upon entrance, when to ask a resident to leave, and even what assisted living is. The biggest source of conflict seems to be whether or not to abandon the continuum of care model (closely aligned with the Housing with Non-Health Services model) in favor of a model that allows residents to fully age in place. The populations served by the two models can be vastly different. Still, it is evident that providers are committed to the notion of assisted living as a housing and health care option that will improve the quality of life for older adults.

As part of the continuum of care, assisted living is often seen as temporary—a "way station" or a "bridge" to the next level of care. The problem with such perceptions is that residents may also be seen as "temporary" because they are progressing along the continuum of care with only a brief stop at assisted living. If providers view their setting as a temporary arrangement, a mere link between two other stops on the continuum, how can they treat assisted living as "home" for their residents? Further, how can residents themselves treat assisted living as their home if they are told from the first day, "When you decline you will have to leave." Who would be comfortable calling such a place home if they do not know how long they will be able to stay? Placing assisted living along the continuum of care quite possibly undermines one of the most basic principles of assisted living: the creation of a homelike environment.

Providers thoughts about assisted living are crucial to consider as policies and regulations continue to develop across the United States. Equally important are the reflections of assisted living residents. How do they experience their assisted living environment? How are their thoughts and feelings different than those of providers? How do they see aging in place? The next chapter will present unique insights from residents living at Kramer and Wood Glen. The residents' perspective can offer the assisted living industry and policymakers some important wisdom.

NOTE

1. It is quite interesting to note that Dr. Marx refers to assisted living residents as "patients." The importance of the language surrounding assisted living is discussed in greater depth in chapter 6.

CHAPTER 5

The Residents' Reality

Assisted living residents possess a completely separate perspective from that of providers. Residents *live* in the assisted living setting twenty-four hours a day while providers only work there during business hours. Residents are usually of a different generation than the administrators and this can certainly influence their perceptions, but of even greater importance are the variety of health problems in their current lives and unknown future manifestations that residents often face while in this collective living arrangement.

This chapter presents residents' experiences in assisted living: their attitudes toward other residents, staff, and themselves. How do their beliefs about health status, control, autonomy, independence, usefulness, and friendship influence their daily lives in assisted living? Residents demonstrate how the incomplete rite of passage of moving into assisted living leaves them in a type of limbo. This limbo is further enhanced by an adherence to the elderly mystique. I begin this discussion with brief residential histories of several Kramer and Wood Glen residents. To understand what meaning residents give to their assisted living arrangements, it is important to hear seniors describe their lives before they moved into assisted living.

WHERE I USED TO LIVE

Residents offer vivid stories about their lives and experiences before moving into assisted living. Many of the respondents' life histories were intertwined with their dwelling experiences and "home life." The following excerpt is from an interview with Wendy James, chronicling different points in her life. All of the segments, from birth onward, include references to her residential setting.

Well, I was born in Bathgate, Scotland, 1912, January 9. My mother had to stop putting dinner on the table and go into the bedroom and have me—and then come back to the kitchen again! Can you imagine? Well, anyhow, from there we moved. We lived in two or three towns in Scotland. My father was a railroad man so we moved from one place to another. . . . I met George, my third husband, and he was a Chicagoan. It was right after the war . . . we lived on the south side near the stockyards and when the wind blew hard you could smell it. . . . When we first came here [to Chicago], you could not get an apartment. We had to take a room, a big room with a family on the south side. (interview by author, tape recording, Chicago, Illinois, 19 November 1992)

Another Wood Glen Home resident, Sara Vernon, expressed her strong connection to her home through her positive memories.

I lived in a two-flat originally until I was married. Then I had my own two-flat and home [with my husband] after that. Then when I moved to Florida, I bought a condo. . . . I loved the two-flat best of all. Those were the ten best years of my life because my mother and father lived upstairs. I did not see them that much, but I knew they were there. And my husband traveled so, at night at least I knew [they were close by]—and my husband liked that too. My family was very close. (interview by author, tape recording, Chicago, Illinois, 18 November 1992)

Some residents talked more about their childhood memories. These, too, involved their residential environment. Yvonne Diamond, a Kramer resident, expressed her thoughts this way:

We were always in an apartment—my mother and father and my sister, who is thirteen years younger than I am. Most of my life . . . I can recall my grandmother, well, a lot of the time my grandmother lived with us. That was typical of years ago. Many years ago there was always a maid, someone who came from Europe. There was always room for somebody. Now these people have tremendous homes and there's no room for an old relative. (interview by author, tape recording, Chicago, Illinois, 9 October 1992)

Childhood memories of home and community can also be very frightening, when accompanied by traumatic circumstances. This was the case of ninety-year-old Katie Jacobs, a post–World War I emigrant from Russia.

The First World War started, and it was not too far away from home. One day the town—small towns were taken by the Russian soldiers. Well, a bunch of soldiers came to my house and asked my mother for kerosene. Everybody then had kerosene because that's what you burned for light. We didn't have electricity. So she [my mother] gave them a bottle of kerosene. They poured it over the house and lit a match and put it on fire! We started screaming and running away because of the flames, it was something else. In our town people were screaming and running out of the city . . . our town was burned and the people went away. I was about nine or ten years old. . . . After two or more years living away [from the town]—we waited until the war ended to go back home. So finally it did end, and we were told we could go back home. When we came home [after much traveling] it was about four o'clock in the afternoon and my mother and father went to where the house had been. And the house was gone, burned. Where our house was, potatoes now grew. (interview by author, tape recording, Chicago, Illinois, 27 October 1992).

For some of these older women, their adult memories also centered on the home and their activities in them. Zelda Arnold offered the following story: "After I got married I lived in a twelve-room house in Portish Park. I had three children, three sons. I lived in this house for seventeen years and my children grew up there. . . . I stayed home and kept house and raised my children. My husband supplied everything. I had everything on God's green earth that any woman would ever want" (interview by author, tape recording, Chicago, Illinois, 23 October 1992).

All of these personal memories illustrate how important our residential histories are to our life history. Various dwelling experiences influence how we view each successive home environment throughout our lives. This is true for older adults entering assisted living. Their past residential history plays a role in shaping their perceptions about their new environment. Another important factor affecting assisted living residents' perceptions about their milieu is the circumstance surrounding their move to assisted living.

HOW I ENDED UP HERE

Each resident at Kramer and Wood Glen has a different story to tell about his or her entrance into assisted living. These narratives are important because they allow access to underlying and unspoken issues not evident from most straight interview questions and answers. These personal narratives also point to discrepancies between the ideal versus real reasons why older adults come to assisted living.

Several residents I interviewed came to assisted living because of the illness or death of a spouse. Gary Davidson, a resident of the Wood Glen Home, came to the assisted living floor because his wife was ill and had been moved to the skilled care portion of the nursing home. Soon after his wife went to the nursing home, Gary realized that he was having difficulty trying to get to Wood Glen to see his wife every day *and* take care of his own daily routines. Gary decided to move to the assisted living floor at Wood Glen so that he could be near his wife and have his daily needs taken care of. Now Gary can see his wife every day regardless of the Chicago weather.

Bertha Edmonds first discovered the Wood Glen Home when her husband became very ill. She could no longer take care of her husband, so she moved him into Wood Glen. After he died, Bertha felt overwhelmed with the loneliness and the burden of a house. In addition, her own health was beginning to decline. The administrators at Wood Glen suggested that Bertha move to their assisted living floor.

Yvonne Diamond came to Kramer after her husband died. She told me she was feeling very depressed and lonely, and believed that living with other people might help. Yvonne is young for an assisted living resident (late seventies) and extremely active. She still volunteers at a nursing home and tries to maintain as many activities as she can from her life in her former home.

Wilma Rose, fellow Kramer resident, experienced similar depression and loneliness after her husband passed away. She explained it this way: "After my husband passed away, I came to this place. I couldn't sleep; I couldn't stay alone anymore. Too lonely" (interview by author, tape recording, Chicago, Illinois, 5 November 1992). Ideally, many of the residents who come to assisted living believe that loneliness is the sole reason for their move. Realistically, the emotional reasons for moving are also accompanied by health factors.

Gertrude Farmer is a ninety-one-year-old Wood Glen resident who entered assisted living because of vision problems. Gertrude's eyesight degenerated to a point where it was impossible for her to care for herself in her own home. She was quite unhappy with the move and told me so during our interview.

GF: Well, I just console myself, this was very very difficult because I gave up so much. I wasn't really ready and this was [supposedly] just an overnight deal. You just have to console yourself 'cause it's going to come sooner or later.

JF: So the adjustment was pretty difficult when you came in?

GF: Very, very, very. I cried and cried and cried.

Although Gertrude longed to be back in her own apartment, she clearly understood the reality of her situation.

JF: Do you think that you would prefer living out in the community in an apartment?

GF: Yes, if I could see. If I could see, I'd rather live the way I used to. *But that is not possible.* There is no cure.

JF: What would you like best if you could live out in the community? Why would you be so anxious to go?

GF: Well, *it's freedom of choice in every way!*

Wendy James, fellow Wood Glen resident, also came to assisted living for health reasons. However, Wendy did not express the distress that Gertrude did. Wendy said:

My doctor chose it [Wood Glen]. He had me come here because he was scared to leave me alone anymore. See, I had a pacemaker put in and I [have] this Meniere's disease [where she gets dizzy]. He said, "You can't be alone, Wendy. I will find you [a place]." I wasn't eating a drop of food—I had malnutrition then. So, the doctor said, "You've got to go," and he recommended this place. . . . I was so sick. I was malnourished. I remember I lay here and—I don't even—I vaguely remember going down to dinner to eat, vaguely the first little while. (interview by author, tape recording, Chicago, Illinois, 19 November 1992)

Malnutrition was also the major reason for Tillie Von Deurst's move to Wood Glen.

I like it [the Wood Glen Home]. For me it is good, it is what I needed evidently. The reason [I came] was because I was so underweight and emaciated. Consequently, from being so terribly thin I had all kinds of infections. So, I wanted a place where I would have good food. So we started [looking] on the south side, I was at the University of Chicago hospital for a while. Then we [my daughter and I] stopped at various homes, and I noticed the menus they put on the board and I was not particularly impressed. When I walked in here the first thing I did was walk into the dining room and I talked to the residents who were sitting at the table eating—find out straight from the horse's mouth. They said the food was very good. (interview by author, tape recording, Chicago, Illinois, 31 March 1992)

The third and most complex reason cited for relocating to assisted living was family persuasion. Most often an adult child decides that "mom" or "dad" is not safe at home anymore and so they coax the elderly parent into assisted living. Many other factors go into a move, and it should be noted that many elderly residents who feel "forced to move" have accompanying health problems. Nevertheless, if these problems were manageable in their own homes even with some outside assistance, and the elderly parents preferred to stay in their own homes, why and how were they convinced to move? It should be pointed out that this discussion specifically refers to elderly persons who are *not* cognitively impaired at the time of relocation. In the two extensive examples given here, the residents were not only cognitively intact but also quite opinionated about their move. Although a number of residents at the two sites commented on their family coercing them to move, very few would elaborate on their feelings or situation. The stories that follow are notable exceptions.

Zelda Arnold is a ninety-year-old resident at Kramer. At the time she moved in, Zelda was eighty-nine, had a cane and a hearing aid, but was in otherwise good health. She is also the only Kramer resident who still has a car—and she sometimes uses it. Zelda lived most of her life in Chicago, but spent the last twenty or more years in Hollywood, Florida. The following conversation traces Zelda's move to Kramer from Florida.

JF: Did you like Florida?

ZA: I loved it. How can you not like it? I would sit in my kitchen, it had a window like this, and I'm lookin' at the ocean. It [the ocean] was across the street. Gorgeous place. I used to come here [Chicago] for the summer months 'cause I have two sons here.

JF: So why did you end up coming back here? You were starting to say earlier that it was their [your sons'] doing?

ZA: Yeah, I didn't want to come here. . . . After my husband died, my children did not want me so far away. Of course we used to communicate all the time but . . . I didn't know [I was coming here]. I came to Chicago for a birthday party in October, and my daughter-in-law took me through this place. It was empty; it was all completed but no furniture or anything. So she [my daughter-in-law] says, "What apartment would you like if you lived here?" I said, "Well, I think I'd like this one if I were to live here." . . . So anyway, then I went back home [to Florida] and I didn't know they rented this place—I didn't even know they were *thinking about it*. . . . So, anyway, then I got this letter with an airline ticket, April 6th. So that's when I came here, I've been here practically since they opened up. And my son kept saying, "Why don't you come earlier, then you can get in on the ground floor." I said, "No, I'm not coming if it is cold there."

JF: So, there was no discussion involved? They [your family] just kind of decided?

ZA: [laughs] They decided, yes. They decided that I couldn't do it [live on my own anymore] that it would be too much. I don't know—I lived in Florida and I got along fine. I never had any problems.

JF: Did you have anyone living with you then?

ZA: No, no, no. I was on my own. But I didn't mind, I could be on my own. You know I did not have to do all the work. I had a girl come in once a week and do all the cleaning and everything so I just had the daily work. I didn't mind.

JF: Do you think you would be happier if you were out in your own apartment?

ZA: I think so. Well, I don't know. It all depends where you live in an apartment. Here in the city? No. But in Florida it was different you know? We had a pool there, and you are just all together, but everybody had their own apartment. (interview by author, tape recording, Chicago, Illinois, 11 November 1992)

Interestingly, this was not Zelda's first experience with elderly housing in Chicago. A year before she came to Kramer, her family moved her into a different place on the North Shore of the city.

ZA: I came here [Chicago] the year before I moved [back here full time]. They [the family] picked me up and took me to the Bay Front [a retirement residence]. They had rented a studio apartment for me. I did not have a [private] bathroom. My daughter-in-law decorated the place, I was there for two months. I could do what I wanted but . . .

JF: So why did you decide to leave the Bay Front?

ZA: I didn't like it at all. I was going back to Florida anyway, I came here for the summer months.

JF: So that was a trial run to see how you would do [in elderly housing]?

ZA: That's what my children did, I wasn't expecting that but that's what they did. But I didn't like it because it was up in Evanston and they had no place to park my car. There wasn't even a spot in the garage!

For all of Zelda's disappointment with her move and her longing to remain in Florida, she, like Gertrude Farmer, has a clear understanding of the differences between the ideal and the reality of her situation.

JF: You had mentioned to me the last time we talked—you said you would prefer being in your own apartment out in the community. Could you talk about that? I mean what would be the ideal living set-up for you now?

ZA: Well, what *I think*—my children say I would not be able to do. I don't know. They say I would not be able to be on my own. I said if we rented an apartment and set up housekeeping and hired a woman to live with me I would—I could do whatever I wanted. It would not even cost me as much as it costs me to live here and I could do *what I want*. I don't have an oven here [at Kramer]. I can't bake, I can't do anything. I would like to set up a kitchen where I can work in a kitchen! I would do my own cooking, and I would not have to put up with whatever they served!

JF: Do you think that type of living set-up would give you more freedom?

ZA: I think so but my children say, "You wouldn't be able to handle it." So, I don't know. It is a lot of extra work. They [my family] say I would have to stand on my feet too much, and they think I ought to stay off my feet so I don't know. (interview by author, tape recording, Chicago, Illinois, 11 November 1992)

Clearly, the opinions of Zelda's family influenced her a great deal. When talking about her situation, Zelda's tone of voice reflected signs of resignation to her situation. Although it was evident that she resented living at Kramer, her verbal expressions always had a tone of passive resignation, probably because she was so dedicated to her family and did not want to let them down. I would personally have to say that Zelda was one of the most independent and active residents whom I encountered in assisted living. My impression was that she certainly could have lived in the community with some assistance and Zelda definitely could have afforded it.

There was one more option for Zelda, that of moving in with one of her two sons. Zelda had well-defined feelings about this alternative as well.

ZA: I could have lived with any one of my boys, they have the room for me, but I don't want to impose on them. I know when I used to come in from Florida just for the summer months, they would have opera tickets and theater tickets for the season, and when I came in, they would have to get an extra ticket for me. And I didn't feel like [bothering them].

JF: You don't like the idea of living with them because it . . .

ZA: No. I *could* live with them, I wouldn't have any problem but I don't feel like I would *like to*—like I say, when I am there they always feel like I have to go with them. And I don't feel like I should intrude on their life. (Arnold interview, 11 November 1992)

Perhaps this is one of the reasons why Zelda allowed herself to be placed in assisted living: she did not want to burden her family. Many residents at Kramer and Wood Glen voiced similar opinions. This issue of "not intruding" on family members (especially adult children) in relation to entering assisted living will be analyzed on a national level in the following chapter.

Fannie Isaacs is a very independent ninety-six-year-old woman who moved to Kramer from her home in Charleston, South Carolina. Originally from Germany, Fannie immigrated to the United States before World War II at the age of forty-two. Fannie's daughter, grandchildren, and great-grandchildren all live in the Chicago area. They wanted Fannie to move north so she would be closer to them. Fannie wanted to stay in South Carolina where she had spent the last fifty-three years. She entered Kramer just prior to her ninety-sixth birthday.

In the span of three months I conducted three tape-recorded interviews with Fannie. The first of these interviews took place early in November, only two weeks after Fannie moved into Kramer. I was finishing an interview with fellow resident Wilma Rose when Fannie sat down and joined the conversation. The exchange was very lively, especially between the two residents.

FI: I was by my daughter [stayed with my daughter] two weeks before I came here. But I dreaded it [coming here]. I fought ten years not to come here. But I don't want to interfere in the life of my daughter.

JF: Has adjusting been hard for you?

FI: I am not adjusted here—in ten days?! At my age I do my best, I walk, I wear winter clothes, I eat, I sleep. But adjust? That is not so easy. I don't know if I will ever adjust.

WR: You have to!

FI: No, I don't *have to!*

WR: I did it and it wasn't easy . . .

FI: No, you didn't, you didn't [adjust]!

WR: Yes, I did and it wasn't easy.

FI: You *think that you did* but you still think about yesterday, I can feel it.

WR: The only time I am sad is when I think of my [late] husband. If I don't think of him. . . . When I think of the children I'm OK but when I think of him I am not OK.

FI: So you see, *you cannot be adjusted.* You try very hard for the children . . .

JF: What about for you? You said, "Well for my children I come and try to be OK with it," well, what about for *you*?

FI: For my children I play. I'm a very good actress . . .

JF: But what about for yourself? How do *you* feel?

FI: Myself is not important, my surrounding is important, I am not important . . .

JF: Why?

FI: I have nothing to see [do] anymore. I am here. They say, "You can't be alone"; they say, "it is very good for you" [to be here]. They say, "That is the only thing you can do," so here I am.

JF: How would you be happiest right now?

FI: I don't think I can be happy anymore . . .

JF: Would you be happier in South Carolina?

FI: I don't know, I don't know. . . . Here I am so careful, I walk [in the ice and snow] and tell myself, "Don't fall down." I don't want my children to think, "Oh now mother is here and we still have the trouble."

JF: Earlier you said that happy is sort of a loaded word, which it is. Would you maybe at least feel more at home if you were in South Carolina?

FI: In South Carolina *I was home!* I came from Europe fifty-three years ago without money, without language, and I made it. I never undersell myself and I never let anybody push me . . . but here I am!

JF: Why was South Carolina home?

FI: I lived there fifty-three years, in the good and the bad. (interview by author, tape recording, Chicago, Illinois, 5 November 1992)

From our first meeting it was evident that Fannie had some strong opinions about her move and her new surroundings. In our second interview, I was very interested in pursuing the point she had raised about Kramer residents pretending that everything is all right. This issue highlights the contrast between the ideal and the reality of residing in assisted living.

JF: You and I talked last time about the issue of elderly people "giving in" to their families and moving to places that they don't want to move and then pretending they are happy.

FI: My conscience tells me if I don't do what they [my family] want me to do, maybe I will make them think I am not well. [Then] I have the feeling that it is my fault, so I give in. I fought ten years and I told my daughter and I told everybody, "Don't ever let them put me in a house"—and here I am! So I have nothing to say. Life did it to me.

JF: Do you think that a lot of elderly people have that same perspective?

FI: Every one! Every one! If you listen right. . . . I talk [to older people] and everyone is in the same situation but people don't come out [and say it]. Or, they don't want to come out—or they are so unhappy that they say, "The hell with everything!"

JF: Yeah, you and I had talked about what is said versus *what is not said*. [I hear from residents] "oh yeah, it is fine, I am happy," and I think to myself "no, you're not!"

FI: No. You see, people *say* they are happy. I am *not* happy. It happened to me too [coming here]. I don't know why and where my furniture is but here I am. They [other residents] sit and they "do" but they don't do. *They are done!* I don't know if that's the right word, you know? They make the situation with a tear in their eye.

JF: They sort of resign themselves to the situation?

FI: Yeah. Resign themselves [to the situation] and then resign to the world.

JF: Do you think any of these people, yourself included, any of these people here—that their children understand how they feel?

FI: I tell you, if you are young and you think you will never be old and you cannot understand how old people [feel], you will say, "Oh, she always complains"—so I don't say anything, why should I?

JF: When do you think somebody [an older person] decides to give up fighting?

FI: Look at me! Look at me! I stopped fighting. Otherwise I still fight—I fight for my life—but I don't fight my family. She [my daughter] wants me here, she feels better, I don't want to interfere. Her life—she feels if I were here she would be OK. I did her the favor [by coming here], not to worry them. I am here. The children are looking after me. I have no trouble, I have only to call and five minutes later she is here.

JF: So why is it that you wound up coming here? Because it helps them [your family] and it makes them feel secure that you're OK?

FI: I don't want to feel guilty that I make people unhappy. All right, you want me here? I come here. [Do I] want it? No. But I don't want to disturb my children. I don't want to do anything that would interfere [with their lives] so here I am, want it or not. Sometimes I get mad in the night. I say [to myself], "I should have"—I was not able [to]. I had been sick in the hospital. I was yesterday [figuratively] in the hospital and tomorrow I was in Chicago. I did not [have] my fight back yet. . . . I am here. (interview by author, tape recording, Chicago, Illinois, 18 January 1993)

Fannie's feelings show the distinction between her own desires and those of her children. She wanted to remain in Charleston and live independently. Notwithstanding, she also did not want to be an increasing burden for her family. Fannie's husband had died over forty years ago, so she was quite accustomed to living on her own. Her ideal living arrangement for herself was in direct con-flict with that of her family's. In the end, the ideal living arrangement envi-sioned by her family became Fannie's reality. "You don't get used to life here, you take it—but you cannot have it. You're pushed into a situation and here you are. You do this favor, you [do] the children a favor, it's not your life any-more. *You're the child, and your children are the parents*" (Isaacs interview, 18 January 1993). Fannie Isaacs's narrative was the only one that explicitly showed the divergence between the family's and the older adult's view of the ideal living situation. The final result of Fannie's move is that she lives the *reality* of assisted living while her family sees it as the ideal situation for everyone. Because she knows her family wanted this "ideal," she pretends to live up to their ideal ex-pectations. Her family sees it as home, while Fannie experiences it as a total in-stitution. Fannie tells her family she is content, when she is really angry and depressed. Many residents I spoke with reflected this same inner conflict be-tween doing what their families wanted and what they themselves wanted.

The residents' narratives have demonstrated that a number of intertwined factors contributed to their decisions to move into assisted living. These narra-tives also show us how difficult it can be for older adults to adjust to their new living environment and to their new social familial roles.

Personal Control, Choice, and Independence in Assisted Living

Assisted living purports to give residents a sense of choice and control that they may not have in other housing options for the elderly. In fact, choice and control are part of assisted living's basic philosophy of care. Since these princi-ples represent the ideal for assisted living providers, it is important to find out what the residents themselves think. Does the reality match the ideal? Opin-ions were fairly mixed.

Sara Vernon came to assisted living at Wood Glen because she had suffered a stroke, leaving her at least semidependent upon a wheelchair. At seventy-three, Sara is among the youngest residents in assisted living, and she is very inde-pendent in her daily activities. Her opinions about choice and control are very succinct.

JF: Do you feel you have a lot of choices regarding where you go and what you do?

SV: No, but they [staff] do ask you what you want.

JF: Do you feel like you have control over your life in terms of what you do?

SV: At times yes, and at times no.

JF: When yes?

SV: Well, there are times that the evening meals are very poor and if I find that they are going to be poor, I have canned tuna fish in my room. I take that downstairs and ask them to make me a sandwich, so therein I have control over my supper. (interview by author, tape recording, Chicago, Illinois, 18 November 1992)

As Sara's statements exhibit, the terms "choice" and "control" are closely associated in assisted living. Providers emphasize both concepts in order to give residents more independence in assisted living. Although control and choice are strongly correlated, they are not synonymous. It is crucial to distinguish the differences between these terms in order to show their relationship to residents' independence.

Ronald Abeles defines a sense of control as "people's interrelated beliefs and expectations about their abilities to perform behaviors aimed at obtaining desired outcomes and about the responsiveness of the environment, both physical and social, to their behaviors" (Abeles 1991:298). The need for control, however, may greatly increase when the older adult is living in a setting that is not his or her own home. This is because "a sense of control and quality of life are intimately interrelated" (Abeles 1991:297). A sense of control is just as important as the notion of control itself because a sense of control deals with perceptions the individual has about his or her *own ability.* For instance, residents at Kramer and Wood Glen may feel old or useless because they have lost a sense of control over their lives.

This concept is crucial because it is subjective rather than objective. This point is very important for assisted living housing because one of its basic principles is offering control to residents. Such control is objective in the sense that it is the ability to have control. A sense of control is how residents perceive their ability to take charge of situations.

Earlier, several residents voiced their frustration about not having full kitchens at Kramer and not having kitchens at all at Wood Glen. Part of a sense of control is "a sense of whether they [residents] could successfully perform the behaviors needed to achieve the particular desired outcome" (Abeles 1991:301). Zelda Arnold gets frustrated living at Kramer because the kitchens have no ovens and she can no longer bake for her family or guests. In this example, Zelda realizes that she "cannot successfully perform the behaviors needed to achieve the particular, desired outcome." Zelda does not have control. The loss of control is motivated by external factors rather than internal ones because the reason Zelda cannot exercise control is that Kramer did not install ovens. On a daily basis, the absence of an oven reinforces Zelda's liminality at Kramer. She cannot fulfill her old role as a baker and a cook, yet she has not been presented with an alternative role that will allow her to feel useful. She is suspended between roles.

Internal factors can affect a person's sense of control. These factors are believed to be more influential in old age. "It is hypothesized that with aging, forces within and without the person lead to a diminishing sense of control. The physical changes accompanying old age (e.g., worsening eyesight and diminishing stamina) and the internalization of negative age stereotypes are believed to attack the older person's self-beliefs and self-efficacy expectations" (Abeles 1991:304).

For many residents at Kramer and Wood Glen, the internal factors are linked to physical ability or disability. Wood Glen resident Clara Martin is one such resident. When asked if she believes she has a sense of control at Wood Glen, Clara replied, "Yes, yes. My drawback is that I can't walk out. When I came here I was walking [on my own] and I knew that eventually I would not be able to. But I didn't know it would come so quickly. I miss getting out. I should expect that at eighty-three. I forget because I have a young mind. I forget that I am eighty-three—but I still want to be active. I love the outdoors" (interview by author, tape recording, Chicago, Illinois, 23 November 1992). Abeles found that adolescents and children develop a positive sense of control when the setting offers choice rather than constraints and when it is sensitive to one's goals and desires. He said that same is true for the elderly. If this is the case, then choice actually serves as a catalyst for control. If residents can choose whether or not to do something, then this choice will increase their sense of control. A clear example of the relationship between control and choice is offered by Wood Glen resident Wendy James. "I go downstairs and have my cigarettes. . . . I could do without the cigarettes, but it's the idea that it is *my prerogative* to do or not to do—and I will hold on to it" (interview by author, tape recording, Chicago, Illinois, 19 November 1992). Wendy feels that she has control because she can choose whether or not she wants to smoke.

Choice facilitates a sense of control. But, how do control and choice interact in the daily lives of the majority of assisted living residents? Control and choice do not always fit the simple equation outlined by Abeles.

Residents at Wood Glen and Kramer often have emotional conflicts over issues involving choice and control. On the one hand, these older adults understand *the ideal* that they do have at least some choice and control in assisted living. But, the reality is that residents often feel obligated to do certain things and participate in certain activities even though they do not want to. Or, they feel bad about asking for assistance in order to get things done.

Gertrude Farmer faces physical limitations that make her question her control and choice. She is blind. I asked Gertrude if she thinks she has experienced a loss of control over her life since she has been at Wood Glen. She said, "Yes, because I can't—I don't have the freedom to go out when I want to because I couldn't cross the street by myself. I can't see whether the pavement is cracked or something like that" (interview by author, tape recording, Chicago, Illinois, 15 December 1992). Gertrude is sometimes offered the choice of whether or not to go out for a walk (with a companion); yet because of internal factors she does not possess the capacity to transform choice into control.

In theory, issues of choice and control confront all assisted living residents. Some residents do not always feel comfortable exercising this control because of various pressures they perceive from the assisted living environment. In terms of daily life, Tillie Von Deurst offered the following thoughts about choice at Wood Glen. "Sure, nobody puts any fences around me at all you know? [However,] there are a very few [residents] who can go out, I mean by themselves. In fact, I think it is only a couple of us who do" (interview by author, tape recording, Chicago, Illinois, 31 March 1992). She had more to say about the organized activities at Wood Glen. "Well, you can either join the activities or you don't have to. My problem is that I feel like I *should* [participate] . . . so that is the way I feel about most of the activities. See, I have my own activities. If I didn't have those, I would certainly feel very, very unhappy" (interview by author, tape recording, Chicago, Illinois, 19 November 1992).

In the wider scope, policies are a daily test of residents' choice and control in the assisted living milieu. How do providers negotiate policies with residents, especially when those policies impinge on the boundaries of resident rights and personal control? Perhaps no issue is more delicate for testing residents' freedom of choice and sense of control than that of personal rights to smoke and drink. In these contested areas, providers' policies and residents' rights can clash dramatically in assisted living.

Every assisted living provider must grapple with the issue of residents' rights to smoke. I had the opportunity to attend a series of meetings at Wood Glen when the assisted living unit was in its planning stages. The planning committee, consisting of the director of nursing, a social worker, an activities coordinator, a doctor, a dietitian, and two administrators went back and forth on the issue of allowing residents to smoke in their rooms. The situation was frustrating because the committee was trying to ensure residents' rights to smoke in their rooms but, by allowing smokers the right, the committee might be placing the rest of the nursing home residents in jeopardy. After all, the committee's argument went, this is an elderly population, eighty-five years or older, some of whom might fall asleep in bed with a cigarette, and then what? The committee was strongly divided on what to do. Finally, they decided to allow residents to smoke in their rooms on a trial basis.

Since most people moving into Wood Glen did not smoke and the administrators could not get past their apprehension, they decided to change the policy. After a heated debate, the planning committee decided to adopt a no-smoking policy in the rooms at Wood Glen. Designated smoking areas were created for the residents' use. Ironically enough, one of these areas was next to the front door of the nursing home so, when visitors enter, they inhale cigarette smoke. Cigarette smoking has since been completely banned from the nursing home.

Kramer experienced a very similar progression of events. Initially, Kramer allowed residents to smoke in their own rooms. As time went on, however, nonsmoking residents in the suites said they resented coming out of their rooms and smelling smoke in the suite living rooms. The next step was to tell smoking residents to close their bedroom doors when smoking. Still, other residents complained. Finally, staff was pressured by residents to change the policy. One lounge upstairs was designated as the smoking lounge while the rest of the site remained smoke-free. This policy is still a source of conflict because the smoking lounge upstairs at Kramer has no door and occasionally the entire upstairs hall smells of cigarette smoke.

The smoking issue tends to blur the lines between the ideal versus the reality of policies in assisted living. Are administrators denying some residents their full rights by forcing them to smoke in designated areas, or is this compromise the only logical solution? Undoubtedly, this compromise has not pleased all residents. Yet, this seems to be the only way to merge the ideals of individual freedom with the realities of a group-living situation. There are, however, situations even more delicate than the ones cited above.

This narrative comes from Companion Hamlet, one of the ten Chicago area assisted living sites I visited, and it highlights the sensitive nature of personal control and choice for residents. Companion Hamlet is a continuing care retirement community that has an assisted living community as part of its site. The director of assisted living, Debra Santorini, told me the following story in order to illustrate how challenging and intriguing balancing policy issues and resident rights can be.

This is a story of a new resident, "Jane," who had moved into assisted living on a Friday afternoon, aided by her nephew. On Sunday morning, a nurses aide came by Jane's apartment to see how she was adjusting and opened the door to find Jane asleep on the floor of her apartment. The alarmed nurses aide phoned Santorini at home. Santorini asked the nurses on duty if they had any idea why Jane might have been on the floor. One nurse said that when Jane moved in she brought with her certain items to make her feel more "at home" and to help her establish her old routine. One of these items was alcohol. On Friday, Jane told a nurse that her ritual was to drink a highball every night before going to sleep. The conclusion staff made was that Jane, possibly a bit forgetful, thought she had one highball when in reality she might have had four or five. As the director of assisted living, Santorini realized that this situation should not become a habit, or else both Jane and Companion Hamlet would be in trouble. Yet, she refused to remove the liquor from Jane's room because that would be violating her resident rights. Instead, Monday morning Santorini called Jane's nephew and told him the situation. Jane's nephew was amused yet understandably concerned. He said that he would drive out to Companion Hamlet and talk to his Aunt Jane. Jane's nephew sat her down and said, "Jane, I want to talk to you. Listen darling, you were just 'blotto' on Saturday night! You can't have alcohol in your room anymore." The arrangement agreed upon was that Jane could still have her nightly highball but she would go to the nurses' station (where the liquor would be kept) and the nurse would pour Jane a nightcap. The director of assisted living wanted desperately to find a solution that was acceptable to all parties; and luckily she did. What Santorini stressed was that at all times the assisted living community has to be operating from the perspective that resident rights come first. She said, "It all goes back to the issue of individual control, you allow them to control as much as they can handle . . . but you *have to have* a staff that understands that, otherwise it will be really difficult" (interview by author, tape recording, Chicago, Illinois, 7 April 1992).

This story provides an excellent example of how challenging it is to mesh policy concerns with resident rights. Providers are in a difficult position because they want to give residents enough freedom and control that residents will feel "at home." On the other hand, providers are bound by laws and regulations to protect the rights of the group over those of the individual. This limits residents' sense of control.

Overall, residents at Kramer and Wood Glen do not possess a strong sense of control because they realize that in their old age both external and internal forces have limited their ability for a true sense of control. They also feel that the assisted living environment does not offer them the same extent of choice and sensitivity that their own homes did. Kramer resident Gail Young summed up the situation this way: "When you move in here, you have no more control" (interview by author, Chicago, Illinois, 25 March 1993). Related to a loss of a sense of control is reduced "personal economy of action" (Goffman 1961:38).

Goffman defines "personal economy of action" as our choice and ability to postpone, delay, or rearrange certain activities so that we may complete another one. For example, someone might postpone eating dinner for a few minutes in order to finish a task. Someone might also set aside a task early in order to do something else. However, in total institutions, personal economy of action is stripped away. There is "no opportunity to balance needs and objectives in a personally efficient way" (p. 38). Of course, the lives of residents in assisted living are not completely regimented. But, residents must eat meals at a specified time, attend activities they like at specified times, and wait for assistance with activities of daily living (ADLs) at certain times. Residents' sense of control is highly reduced because their personal economy of action is diminished.

Notions of independence have a good deal to do with residents' sense of control and choice. Residents perceive themselves as having varying degrees of independence, related to both physical and psychological reasons. All of the people interviewed fully comprehended the reality of being in assisted living in terms of their independence.

In one conversation, eighty-nine-year-old Kramer resident Helen Finks had this to say: "We [the residents of Kramer] are not independent people anymore." Helen perceives that much of her loss of independence is due to her loss of mobility. She uses a walker and believes that it hinders her independence both physically and mentally. Helen finds it harder to go on group trips because maneuvering is difficult. There are psychological reasons as well. Helen believes that her walker could cause complications for other residents because it would take longer for her to get in and out of the van and because her overall movement would be slower. She told me, "I don't want to bother anybody," so she chooses not to sign up for trips that she might really enjoy. Yet, even though she is physically restricted, she resents the portrayal of older adults as sick and frail. Helen says that people have to see places like Kramer for themselves in order to know that everyone there is not "decrepit" (interview by author, Chicago, Illinois, 16 March 1993).

Kramer resident Zelda Arnold stressed the contrast between the ideal and the reality of her own independence. Zelda spoke to me about her independence in one of our interviews.

JF: So it seems like you have a sense of independence here but maybe not as much control or choice as you would if you were out on your own?

ZA: I have just as much [of a sense] of independence but I actually have a lot less because, [in the past] I did all my book work and all my detail work. When I came here my children *decided* that it would be too much for me so they do all the work. But I did all my own book work, and that kept me busy. I could still do that but . . .

JF: Are there things that you would like to do that [would] make you feel more independent?

ZA: I don't know. I would like to do my own book work. I noticed that since I am here I can't add as quickly as I used to because [then] I was accustomed to doing it every day. (interview by author, tape recording, Chicago, Illinois, 11 November 1992)

Most residents who were interviewed did believe that they were fairly independent in their assisted living environments. Nevertheless, their level of control did not equal the amount of control they used to have in their own homes. Residents said that they were offered the maximum amount of independence possible in assisted living. Still, they feel they are no longer truly independent because they no longer perceive that they have total control over their lives. This situation can reinforce residents' liminality.

As part of any rite of passage, liminality brings with it a certain amount of dependency. The initiates feel helpless and suspended, waiting to be integrated into their new role. The dependency ends as soon as the initiates are taught and prepared for their new role. Reincorporation then takes place, and the rite of passage is complete.

The liminality and dependency for both nursing homes and assisted living is different. "Unlike other liminal states the dependency is not accompanied by teaching [and] preparation for the next stage is actively discouraged" (Shield 1988:184). Since assisted living residents are never prepared for a new role, they do not know how to redefine themselves in their setting. As we have seen, residents like Sara Vernon, Zelda Arnold, and Fannie Isaacs seek to hold on to their sense of control and independence but are not quite sure why. What do they actually have control over in their suspended state? Because assisted living residents are seeking to find a new role, they, like nursing home residents, are likely to experience learned dependency upon staff. Many residents assume, "If I am not an independent adult any more and I have no defined role here, I must, therefore, be dependent on staff to tell me how to act and what to do." Unfortunately, staff often respond to residents' liminality by treating them like children. I will return to this issue shortly. In struggling to find a sense of comfort in this liminal environment, many assisted living residents I spoke with tried to define themselves by comparing their health status to that of other residents.

FINDING A NEW ROLE

Feelings of uselessness among residents in assisted living can stem from many sources. Physical limitations, boredom, health problems, and the elderly mystique combine to affect how residents perceive themselves. Elderly people want to believe that they can still contribute to society. Most of the residents at Kramer and Wood Glen are convinced they no longer serve a purpose in other peoples' lives. Their candid discourses are illustrated in passing comments, such as, "I feel useless here." Looking over my transcriptions and field notes, I realized this was a serious underlying problem for residents. These statements also illustrate the strong contrast between their present feelings of uselessness and feelings of empowerment in the roles they previously held.

Before moving to Kramer, resident George Simon lived in a small group home for several years. When contrasting the two residences, George reveals considerable insight. He expresses his feelings toward his first group-living site as follows: "There was a family atmosphere. There were only twelve people living there, and everyone was responsible for something—like setting the table or washing dishes. It made you feel useful" (interview by author, tape recording, Chicago, Illinois, 9 February 1993). Wood Glen resident Wendy James says, "I like to try and keep busy and feel as though I am doing something useful. I don't want to sit around twiddling my thumbs" (interview by author, tape recording, Chicago, Illinois, 9 February 1993). For many residents, feeling useful relates to daily chores and caretaking activities. For example, Zelda Arnold is very frustrated since she came to Kramer because she says there is nothing for her to accomplish that *she* sees as purposeful. She has no new role to assume in her assisted living setting. Her thoughts reveal liminality combined with uselessness. "Since I am here I just got down in the dumps—*I don't do a thing!* I used to knit and crochet and do—my hands were always doing something, baking or something. Here I haven't done a thing, so I am just thinking I better get myself doing something or else *I will go out of my mind!*" (interview by author, tape recording, Chicago, Illinois, 23 October 1992).

On a separate occasion Zelda said,

I don't know. I just didn't have any project that I was working on and . . . you have to have something to do. This is no good just sitting around with nothing to do. When you have a house you always have something to do. It is either cleaning or cooking or baking. There is always something in a house and here there is really nothing.

Well, that's the way I feel about it, everybody doesn't feel that way. Some people like to just sit and do nothing. Even in their younger years, you have people like that. I was always active and did something. . . . There is always something to do in your own house, and here you go stark crazy! (interview by author, tape recording, Chicago, Illinois, 11 November 1992)

Zelda believes that the activities and responsibilities surrounding the maintenance of her house made her feel useful. Now she has no house to maintain and is bored. At Kramer she cannot cook or bake because the kitchens have no ovens. She cannot entertain because she has no private space except her bedroom. Zelda has not found a new role to assume at Kramer, so she feels trapped in her liminal state.

Kramer resident Gail Young maintains a more general view of her predicament. "The useful, productive part of our lives is over. Now I can best be productive by trying to keep myself healthy" (interview by author, tape recording, Chicago, Illinois, 15 March 1992). Gail has decided to focus on her health and mere survival and has chosen to reduce her outward activities. Gail's reference to productivity reaches a deeper level than just activities of daily living; Gail is alluding to instrumental activities such as shopping, cleaning, cooking, and driving, which are considered instrumental to the independence of older adults. Assisted living residents at Wood Glen and Kramer regard these tasks as pivotal to their sense of self-worth. These tasks go beyond merely existing or "trying to stay healthy." Residents claim that instrumental activities of daily living (IADLs), such as shopping or paying bills, make them active rather than passive participants in their lives. Cooking and cleaning are activities that most assisted living residents performed in their former homes; they were part of their daily routines during the "useful" and "productive" part of their lives. These activities also help to make one's environment a real "home."

Providers at Kramer and Wood Glen often underestimate the critical importance of *instrumental* activities of daily living in the residents' self-perceptions and are frequently oblivious to residents' desires to perform these tasks. Instead, providers are often proud of the fact that their assisted living community essentially takes responsibility for tasks such as shopping, financial management, cleaning, and laundry so that residents can "feel free to relax and enjoy themselves." Residents counter that the only thing they "feel free" to do is sit and be idle. Providers often view IADLs as burdens, while residents view them as blessings.

The most disturbing part of many residents' accounts is their hopelessness and resignation about their present purpose in life. They truly buy into the elderly mystique. Ninety-year-old Wood Glen resident Gertrude Farmer explains, "I can't say that I like anything here best. It is just that I have a roof over my head and I feel like my cares are taken care of. I am just biding my time and waiting for the day . . . that's all" (interview by author, tape recording, Chicago, Illinois, 15 December 1992). Gertrude sees herself as suspended in time and waiting to die. Comparing their current situation to that of their former lives is a constant source of anguish for residents. Memories of their younger years serve as catalysts for their present feelings of uselessness, loss, and liminality.

One day Kramer resident Gail Young turned to me and remarked, "You know, something we keep doing around here—in case you haven't noticed— we compare our lives now to how they were then. We don't have much to do now, so that's what we do" (interview by author, Chicago, Illinois, 15 March 1993). Another Kramer resident, Fannie Isaacs, a feisty and extremely independent ninety-six year old, declared,

All the people here are in the same shoes. We had houses, we *had lives*—they [other residents] made a living, and now they are sitting. Everyone I talk to, the same thing comes up. *Emptiness.* You eat, you drink, you sleep, *That's life? That's not life.*

You cannot do this [feel useful] here. You are here. This place is a trash can for mothers and fathers—*it is the trash can of the world.* You bring your mother and your father here. *You* feel better that she's in a surrounding that if something happened [to her] somebody is here. *It is for you, not for me!* (interview by author, tape recording, Chicago, Illinois, 19 January 1993)

The comments of these residents illustrate the fact that many Kramer and Wood Glen occupants do not believe they possess the sense of purpose and fulfillment that they so desperately want to maintain. They want to *live* their lives not just *be* alive. Moving into assisted living and discerning no useful roles for themselves amplifies their sense of loss of control over their lives.

PERCEPTIONS OF INDEPENDENCE

Residents at Wood Glen and Kramer tend to measure themselves against each other, most frequently in the domain of physical health. Residents do not like to see those around them ailing. Many residents informed me that they believe assisted living should be reserved for "able-bodied" older adults and contend that many residents at Kramer and Wood Glen are too frail to be there. Sara Vernon is one resident who holds the view that assisted living must not degenerate into a nursing home. Sara, paralyzed on her right side from a stroke, is partially dependent on a wheelchair. She can, however, transfer independently and can walk short distances with a handrail present. In terms of daily routine, Sara is almost completely self-sufficient. Sara holds very high standards of independence for all assisted living residents at Wood Glen. She vehemently explained her view of the first floor assisted living wing at Wood Glen.

I think this first floor is a *mockery!* Because, originally, they had said this was going to be independent. When I say independent, I thought they meant independent except for a little assisted help at times. I need to have my bed made and I need to have help with a shower, but other than that I need no [help]. . . . And the others. . . . They have a *diapered* person on this floor! And now we have someone who is . . . she is ailing all the time. (interview by author, tape recording, Chicago, Illinois, 18 November 1992)

Sara's response leads one to question what is meant by the term "independence." I tried to clarify Sara's definition of independence by telling her that I was interpreting her definition to mean trying to do things for oneself, to attempt to do as much as possible. She replied, "Wouldn't you *want to do it?* If you had to depend on someone to get a towel or toilet paper . . . I'll go get it! If I don't know where it is, then I will go find someone who will go and bring it to me. I can't see being waited on. . . . There are some people who like to be waited on. I just can't tolerate people who want to be waited on. I find that repulsive! *Me, me, me!*" (Vernon interview, 18 November 1992). Sara maintains a fiercely autonomous view of how functional assisted living residents should be at Wood Glen. There is little doubt that her passion is influenced by her own physical constraints as a result of her stroke. Sara wants to fight for independence, and she cannot understand why someone more mobile than herself would not want to do the same. Other Wood Glen residents agree. On one occasion when I was interviewing Wendy James, she lowered her voice, leaned toward me, and almost whispered: "They've got some people here that shouldn't be on the assisted living floor. This woman next door to me . . . it has upset us to a certain extent. I think the first floor should be as independent as possible. Like, I make my bed, I change my linens. I do everything myself except vacuum and clean the bathroom" (interview by author, tape recording, Chicago, Illinois, 19 November 1992). I asked Wendy if she likes performing these tasks for herself. She replied, "Yes, I want to feel independent. That way I am my own boss, you know?" Wendy, like Sara, is very self-reliant and very independent by Wood Glen standards. She is completely ambulatory and takes many trips to different places in Chicago, both on foot and by city bus.

The perception of being more independent in comparison to other residents is prevalent, even among those who have more serious limitations and ailments. For example, Gertrude Farmer is almost completely blind and repeatedly complains about how the staff at Wood Glen does not give her the individual attention and help she needs. However, she is quick to say that she is much better off than the majority of assisted living residents. The contrast is evident from the following interchange:

JF: Do you feel fairly independent at Wood Glen?

GF: Well, yes, considering I am ninety-one years old. I know that I am a whole lot better than many.

JF: In terms of the first floor [the assisted living floor], does it seem to you that people here are pretty independent?

GF: No, I think most people have problems.

JF: Do you think those problems are severe enough that maybe they are not independent enough to be here [on the first floor]?

GF: Yes, yes. But, I don't think they [the Wood Glen Home] have room [for these people] otherwise.

JF: Do the residents on the first floor seem pretty healthy to you?

GF: No, no, no.

JF: Do the residents here [on this floor] seem more healthy than those on the other floors?

GF: No. Well, of course I am not up on the Alzheimer's floor or anything like that but I certainly think that this [floor] is a far cry from healthy people. I don't even consider myself a healthy one because I have problems.

JF: Maybe healthy is the wrong word—how about independent?

GF: Well, they are *supposed* to be more independent on this floor. They are *supposed* to be on their own and help themselves. And I do everything myself. I do my washing and my ironing and tidy up and I don't ask for anything if I don't need it. (interview by author, tape recording, Chicago, Illinois, 15 December 1992)

Residents at Wood Glen and Kramer should not be viewed as totally uncaring. On the contrary, they care a great deal about their fellow residents and voice genuine compassion about the failing health of those around them. Kramer resident George Simon declared, "It kind of breaks my heart when I see people here with walkers and canes. But, we all have some sort of health problems, that's why we're here" (interview by author, tape recording, Chicago, Illinois, 9 February 1993). Yvonne Diamond's concern was clear when she spoke of a fellow resident who is suffering from dementia.

This woman here, this woman she can't see, she can't get around, who can't . . . she's got Alzheimer's. I pray every day that she does not get hurt on the stairs. Yesterday she got mixed up even on the elevator. Now it's time for her to leave, and they [the staff] know this. I'm sure that they are working on something for her. They want to do the best for her, which is good. . . . But, see this woman, well she's senile and [virtually] blind, she goes in and out of it. It is going to kill her when they tell her she has to leave. (interview by author, tape recording, Chicago, Illinois, 3 November 1992)

RESIDENTS' PERCEPTIONS OF STAFF

An important component in the lives of assisted living residents is their relationship with staff and administrators. Although providers try very hard to make assisted living homelike for the resident; the presence of staff can have a counterproductive effect. As Goffman (1961) points out, the presence of staff watching over residents is a feature of a total institution. In their own homes, these older adults did not have people overseeing them and dictating when to eat, bathe, and so forth. How do they feel about it in assisted living? For the most part, residents at Kramer and Wood Glen did not express a great deal of negative feelings toward staff. Residents believe that staff and administrators are doing a good job and treat them fairly.

Particular issues surfaced during interviews that reveal how residents discern staff in different situations. For example, residents believe that many of their co-habitants complain too much. I asked residents how staff handle these situations. The answers are interesting. In one of our conversations, Sara Vernon said she feels sympathetic toward beleaguered staff.

SV: I think people here [at Wood Glen] complain a lot.

JF: Does it seem that staff listens to complaints?

SV: They listen but then after a while they just don't hear. But it has to be that way because it is the same complainers over and over. (interview by author, tape recording, Chicago, Illinois, 18 November 1992)

Fellow resident Tillie Von Deurst is uncertain about the reasons behind residents' complaints. She claims at Wood Glen, "Complaining is the greatest indoor sport! [laughs] I don't know [why]. I think they get bored, you know?" Gertrude Farmer doubts that the staff really pays attention to residents' complaints. "Well, I don't know. When they [staff] are out the door, you don't know what that means. They might say they do [listen to you], but nine times out of ten nothing is done."

In general, assisted living residents are sympathetic toward staff. They realize that staff is barraged with resident complaints and that it is not always possible for staff to fill resident requests. Residents' true frustration lies in their frequent need to rely on staff for assistance with things they used to do for themselves.

Complaints that do occur about staff are varied and depend a great deal on the situation. A lack of attention from staff and not trusting staff are the two major reasons for resident complaints at Kramer and Wood Glen. Assisted living resident Gertrude Farmer does not trust staff because she believes that they have been stealing from her room because she is blind. "The thing of it is I never know who is at my door. . . . When I first came in here [to Wood Glen], we couldn't lock our doors and they [staff] stole so much. Where I used to live—I never missed a thing in twelve years. But here, they just robbed you" (interview by author, tape recording, Chicago, Illinois, 15 December 1992). It should be pointed out that Gertrude has no proof that it is staff who is stealing her belongings. However, it is noteworthy that she places the blame on staff.

Another arena where residents do not trust staff relates to resident policies. Sara Vernon is annoyed because staff at Wood Glen seemingly lied about what population of older adults would be allowed to live in assisted living. "Some of them [assisted living residents] are at the beginning of Alzheimer's and they [the staff] *knew that* to begin with [before the resident moved in] so why did they put them on this floor? They should have been put on another floor but they [staff] still put them on this floor and made a lot of promises" (interview by author, tape recording, Chicago, Illinois, 18 November 1992). It was Sara's and other residents' understanding that the people living on the assisted living floor would be fairly independent and able to take care of themselves with just a little assistance. As seen earlier in this chapter, residents at Kramer and Wood Glen are somewhat dismayed at the acuity level of some of their fellow residents. As a result, they feel betrayed by staff and administrators.

In addition to population issues, residents have mixed feelings about whether staff tries to stress individuality toward the residents. However, there is a Catch-22 for staff on this issue. Residents at Kramer and Wood Glen want their privacy to be respected and to be treated as independent adults (as much as possible); yet, many complain that they do not receive individual attention from staff or administrators. Sara Vernon believes that staff does not stress individuality for the assisted living residents. "Do they [staff] foster that kind of thing [individuality]? No, I don't think so. . . . No [particular reason] just an observation I have made" (interview by author, tape recording, Chicago, Illinois, 18 November 1992). Assisted living resident Sandy Anderson states that staff seem to have a "hands off" approach with most of the assisted living residents. "I think they [staff] kind of leave you on your own. Now I can see that [in some cases] where people aren't well or maybe they've never lived by themselves and they don't quite know how to act, they may need a little help. But the rest of us are used to living on our own and get[ting] around and everything so we are just sort of left on our own" (interview by author, tape recording, Chicago, Illinois, 8 January 1993).

A more subtle issue of resident concern centers on a distrust of staff's motives or allegiance. This issue tended to arise during casual discussions with residents and involves a fear of retribution or "getting into trouble" with staff if residents do certain things. The fear is that they might be evicted from assisted living if they anger staff or administrators. Recall that several residents would not agree to tape-recorded interviews because they were worried about who was going to hear the tape. Some residents who consented to an interview asked me during the taping if anyone was going to listen to the tape besides me. For example, when I interviewed Yvonne Diamond for the first time, as soon as I turned the tape recorder on she said, "Now after you record this, are you going to play it for Laura?" (Laura is the program coordinator at Kramer.) At the end of some interviews several residents made a point of subtly reminding me to keep the information confidential. Two residents even used the exact same phrase to convey this information. They said, "Now you can take this and just throw it away somewhere."

During one visit with Yvonne Diamond, I was having a discussion with her about the issues of "getting into trouble" with staff. The conversation grew out of a question I asked her about the usefulness of group meetings at Kramer.

JF: Do you think in general that the group meetings are helpful and worthwhile?

YD: Yes, I do.

JF: Why?

YD: Because you get a chance to voice whatever you're feeling. Whether it's acted upon or not, or whether they [staff] do something about it one way or another, that's another question. But at least if you have something to say and you want to say it, you are free to say it. The only problem I find with that is that there are many people here who will voice particular concerns [outside of meetings] but they come to a group meeting and they say nothing.

JF: So, they'll talk outside of the meeting but . . .

YD: It is different than what is said in here [the meetings]. It is so different, not as much is said here.

JF: That's interesting. Is it that people would fear repercussions for saying things?

YD: Yes. They're afraid of retribution. I don't happen to feel that way but . . .

JF: I've had that sense [that people were afraid] here before. People have not wanted to talk to me.

YD: Everybody's afraid.

JF: I think that some of the fear of repercussions is part of the reason why they won't talk to me.

YD: The majority are afraid.

JF: And I wonder why. Is it a fear of being thrown out of here or . . .

YD: I don't know. Some of these people—maybe they'll talk freely to you, I don't know. And some people have a feeling, well, they don't talk at a meeting because "it is pointless." "Nothing is done anyway"—that has been said to me. (interview by author, tape recording, Chicago, Illinois, 3 November 1992)

Yvonne expressed two major reasons why she believes residents keep many opinions to themselves. She claims that residents either fear retribution or they perceive that nothing will be done about their complaints/suggestions.

Reading further into the fear of retribution that several of the residents at Kramer and Wood Glen are expressing, we again see the issues of dependency and liminality. In the liminal state of a rite of passage, initiates are uncertain of their new statuses and the rules that accompany them. This uncertainty leads to cautious behavior because the liminal phase is considered to be precarious precisely because initiates are uninformed. Residents in assisted living are often uncertain about the rules of staying or leaving the setting so they are constantly suspended in time. As a result, residents often become fearful of saying anything negative to staff since, in their view, staff has the power to send them to an even *more* liminal place: the nursing home. Residents are afraid to exert their own control because of their loss of economy of action. This fear of "getting into trouble," coupled with their lack of control, leads many residents at Kramer and Wood Glen to allow themselves to be treated like children.

Shield (1988) suggests that people undergoing a rite of passage "are often likened to children because of their ignorance about their new role" (Shield 1988:194). Unfortunately, this childlike state cannot be overcome for nursing home residents because they are never taught their new role. Instead they remain helpless and very dependent on staff for direction and functioning. Staff then learn to treat the residents as children. "Treated as if he were a child, without a past, without accumulated experiences, honors, and achievements, the aged individual is reduced to his bodily ailments, which now are the sole focus of the people—work that consumes the staff members who attend to them" (Shield 1988:194–95). This appears to be the case in many assisted living environments as well. Staff may often seek to establish a parent-child relationship rather than an adult-adult relationship with elderly residents. "When patients are treated like children, staff do not have to take their life-long accomplishments into consideration and they can more easily exercise their authority" (pp. 194–95). This statement does not mean that all staff at Kramer and Wood Glen talk down to residents or belittle them constantly, rather that conditions are predisposed to it.

Many residents assume a childlike role themselves through learned dependency. They forget how to do things for themselves and constantly ask authority figures for help. Residents keep their complaints to themselves as a child would, out of fear of punishment. Assisted living residents often passively take on the childlike role because they have no other role to assume.

Many of the activities offered to assisted living and nursing home residents resemble children's activities. Monthly birthday parties, outings for ice cream, and trips to the circus are all activities offered at either Kramer or Wood Glen. When outsiders come into the assisted living environment for a special activity, I often witness the speaker addressing the residents as if they were a kindergarten class. Much like children, assisted living residents are also dependent on "adults" (staff) for their daily needs. This childlike status leads to feelings of invisibility. According to Goffman (1963), adults who are treated as children are accorded a nonperson status. It should be noted that although dependency and liminality exist in assisted living, it is not as extreme as in a nursing home. Residents do have more choices and freedom than nursing home patients, although they still feel as though they have to defer to staff.

My discussion of the relationship of residents to staff should not imply that all assisted living residents hate or resent the staff. On the contrary, at Wood Glen and Kramer several residents had very positive things to say about staff and administrators. There were several residents who expressed a great deal of praise for the staff at their assisted living sites. These residents believe that staff try hard to accommodate them and make them feel at home. When asked if there is anything that the Wood Glen Home could do to enhance the experience or make it more homelike for her, Wendy James said, "No, they are doing a wonderful job. Everyone here is great. They do a hell of a job here" (interview by author, tape recording, Chicago, Illinois, 19 November 1992). I asked Clara Martin if she thinks the staff listen to residents, and she said, "Oh, they are great" (interview by author, tape recording, Chicago, Illinois, 23 November 1992).

Residents at Kramer and Wood Glen have mixed feelings about staff. There are certain situations that occur when residents feel let down or annoyed by staff. The two most prominent are when they voice complaints, and when they avoid saying certain things because they fear retribution. Both of these situa-tions represent occasions when residents perceive they have little control. Un-able to solve a problem on their own, residents feel frustrated because they are dependent upon other people, in this case staff, for help. Since assisted living residents no longer have control over many aspects of their lives, they may tar-get staff to vent their frustrations. Much of residents' disappointment stems from their inability to reciprocate with other residents and staff. Reciprocity is an important aspect of independence and deserves closer attention.

"To give and receive are basic in human life. Reciprocal relations are crucial to power, choice, and control" (Shield 1990:333). People in all cultures and so-cieties are bound together by mutual giving and receiving that help to solidify relationships. Help, time, and services are exchanged in all ongoing relation-ships between individuals. However, reciprocity and the relationships it ce-ments can be violated when one side always gives or receives, especially if the recipients have little or no opportunity to reciprocate. Such is the case with as-sisted living and nursing home residents. As Shield points out,

Because the residents of the nursing home are in the liminal part of the passage from adulthood to death, they are already dependent and vulnerable. Another layer of de-pendency is added because . . . the basic facts of life in the nursing home are that the res-idents receive care and the staff members dispense care. The lack of resources with which the residents can repay staff members reduces their control and increases their dependency. Given this unequal power balance, staff-resident interactions take on par-ticular forms. (Shield 1990:334)

Residents become passive recipients of staff time and care while feeling frus-trated that they cannot pay staff back for their assistance. As examples from Kramer and Wood Glen have shown, residents are also disappointed that they can no longer perform certain tasks and are forced to rely on others for help. Residents cannot reciprocate for services that they need and are simultaneously angry that they need them in the first place. It is difficult for Wood Glen and Kramer residents to try to be more independent when the nature of their rela-tionships with staff create dependencies. The same can be said for residents' re-lationships to each other. Reciprocity is not always possible because of health or mobility constraints. The fear of loss also prevents residents from getting in-volved with each other. This point is especially evident when examining friendships in assisted living.

FRIENDSHIPS AND SOCIAL LIFE

Part of what makes people feel confident in any environment are the people around them: how they get along, what they have in common, and whether or not they choose to live with them. Some of the problems with assisted living, as with any communal living situation, are that one does not always get to choose. While this circumstance does not necessarily mean that residents will be unhappy, it points to the importance of the social environment and sense of control.

At both Kramer and Wood Glen, residents in general expressed only neutral feelings toward planned activities. Though many people participate in activities such as current events, painting, ceramics, book reviews, and Bible study, they do not rely on these to keep themselves busy or entertained all day. There are simply not enough events at either assisted living site to do this. Instead, residents spend much of their time alone in their rooms, "trying to keep busy." In a place where one is surrounded by other people, why is it that these older adults are not more social? The answer is complicated and involves a variety of factors, the first of which is general perceptions about other residents.

I asked respondents if they find the other residents stimulating or interesting to talk with. There were an array of responses, most of them negative. Sara Vernon does not see her fellow residents as interesting. When asked if she finds the others interesting to talk with, Sara simply said, "No, not at all." When I asked her to expand on her statement, she told me the following:

I don't know. They [other residents] are just somehow removed from my kind of thinking and I look at some of them and I just know there is no point in even pursuing this. And then I have gone to many of the groups [activities] because there you can hear what they [other residents] have to say. And, there are very few that even read the newspaper! They [staff] read the paper to some of them on *this floor* [the assisted living floor]. This is supposed to be an independent floor, you should be able to read your own newspaper!

I am just grateful that I have this [one] friend here. If I did not have her I don't know if I'd be too comfortable. Because we [my friend and I] can share some things. . . . See, so many people are not—I don't mean to say "on the ball" but you know what I mean? They are not that observant, and they weren't exposed to a lot of the things that she and I were. (interview by author, tape recording, Chicago, Illinois, 18 November 1992)

Wood Glen resident Gertrude Farmer is suspicious of the actions of other residents. "I think that people talk different to different people. They don't tell you everything and they don't tell me everything. And—when I ask a question I like the truth and that does not always come out either so" (interview by author, tape recording, Chicago, Illinois, 15 December 1992).

Tillie Von Deurst is surprised to be as annoyed with other residents as she is. "I find—like just sitting at a table with five older ladies—it is very catty, very petty, very back biting. Somehow I used to think that the older you got the more spiritual you got—but I don't find it that way, see? I have difficulty loving these people" (interview by author, tape recording, Chicago, Illinois, 17 November 1992). Some residents cite health decline when explaining their dissatisfaction with other assisted living residents. First, there are the complaints. Yvonne Diamond says, "Most of the time they're talking about their illnesses and their medication and their doctors and not things that are interesting." Resident Wendy James is somewhat more sympathetic. I asked her if other residents are stimulating or interesting. "Some of them, yes and some of them— the poor people can't help themselves. But I am nice to them all. I think, *there but for the grace of God go I*. Some of them are in wheelchairs and can't even talk, they just sit there you know?" (interview by author, tape recording, Chicago, Illinois, 19 November 1992).

Generally, the residents had little to say about each other unless it was negative. Most of the respondents at Kramer and Wood Glen simply do not find their co-habitants very interesting. This is not to say that residents are not making any friends. They are, but again it becomes a clash between ideal expectations and the true reality of their situation. Part of the reason older adults enter assisted living is for friendship and companionship, but they do not always get it. Zelda Arnold said, "Well, you know I talk to the people here. I can't say that I have made one particular friend that I can call a real close friend." Yvonne Diamond, like Sara Vernon, feels she has little in common with her fellow residents.

YD: Well, you come in contact with a lot of different people here, and you have very little in common with them. You come from different . . . everything is different about your previous life.

JF: So, is it that assisted living is a group of people, put together in one environment, who are at different places individually?

YD: That's right. And it's not like they're your friends, you know. You come in and everybody [in assisted living] has different ideas and . . . and that is why it's not always easy to make friends. You can have—you can *know* everybody, but you're lucky if you get close with a couple of people. (interview by author, tape recording, Chicago, Illinois, 9 October 1992)

A few residents, such as Tillie Von Deurst, believe that they have made a few friends by accident or by default. "I will say yes, I have [made friends]. I would say so, but I don't know what exactly you would call a friend. Well, there is one woman here who has more or less attached herself to me. She is very lovable in some ways and in other ways she drives me up a wall! Maybe I drive her up a wall! [laughs]" (interview by author, tape recording, Chicago, Illinois, 31 March 1992). Gertrude Farmer found it hard to synchronize her desire to spend time with a resident and the resident's own availability. "Oh, I'd rather kind of stay on my own because people are temperamental. You go to their door and they are either busy or they are going someplace or—it is better to have your own activities" (interview by author, tape recording, Chicago, Illinois, 15 December 1992).

Residents do not generally believe they have made new friends at Kramer or Wood Glen. A few had even stronger words to say. Bertha Edmonds says that many people at Wood Glen dislike her. "You see, I have quite a few enemies here. I don't know what it is but. . . . I hate to say this of myself but somebody once told me that I have a very strong personality and that I can rub people the wrong way without meaning to. And I did rub Sara Vernon the wrong way" (interview by author, tape recording, Chicago, Illinois, 18 December 1992). Kramer resident Fannie Isaacs has a similar assessment of herself. She blames herself for a lack of friends, claiming that she does not socialize well. Fannie believes that she does not fit in well with the other residents at Kramer. "I live in my room—I am a very bad mixer. I can talk to somebody half an hour but then I am gone. Some people can stay with somebody but. . . . People are very nice here but I have no connection. I have one woman, she lives here, she sits at my table [for meals] she 'talks my language.' I know I am different. . . . I try to fit in but I don't" (interview by author, tape recording, Chicago, Illinois, 18 January 1993).

Making friends is sometimes quite difficult in a group living situation. Even if occupants do make new friends, they tend to be reluctant to spend a great deal of time with them. Gail Young explains it this way: "Even when you like someone here, you don't get too close because you know it won't be a long-term thing. It is really too hard to get close now." Residents want companionship but on their own terms. Gail goes on, "Being in group living is hard. You come for the companionship but you only seem to get it when other people want it. You don't seem to have a choice of when you get to be social" (interview by author, Chicago, Illinois, 15 March 1993).

In 1983 Tim Booth conducted a participant-observation study of several homes for the elderly in England. He, too, found that residents did not interact much with each other. "For most of everyday they [residents] sit and do nothing, simply staring into space or dozing. Moreover, the greater part of their time is spent alone in groups, lacking companionship and communication with others around them. They enjoy the same sort of company they would have at a bus stop" (Booth 1983:30). Booth's research also reveals that "in old people's homes, residents spent an average of 88% of their waking day not talking to anyone, while in hospitals the equivalent figure was 85%" (p. 30).

Perhaps the real reason why residents do not get close to each other is that, in the words of Gail Young, "nothing here is permanent." The residents know that their health as well as the health of those around them will decline over time. Residents realize that sooner or later the limbo of assisted living will end and that, most likely, they will be asked to leave. Since these older adults see assisted living as a temporary stop, they are not comfortable enough to take the emotional risk of making new friends. The ideal for these older adults was that assisted living would lead to companionship, but in reality, it does not. Assisted living offers an opportunity to avoid being alone, not an escape from loneliness. A consequence is that residents sometimes isolate themselves from others and spend a great deal of time alone, coming out of their rooms only for meals. Kramer resident Helen Finks says she believes that being in assisted living creates an "every man for himself type of attitude. Residents don't help each other out as much as they could." Many assisted living residents at Wood Glen and Kramer share this opinion. Unfortunately, such feelings lead to further isolation and time spent alone. Everyone is in the same situation, and they are all protecting themselves from being hurt or used. According to Kramer resident Gail Young, "You can't have feelings or be compassionate here or you'll never survive. People will take advantage of you. In this type of environment you have to be looking out for yourself. You need to be selfish" (interview by author, Chicago, Illinois, 15 March 1992). This viewpoint, though totally counterproductive to obtaining companionship and a social life, is the reality for most residents. Finding no solace in their common situation, residents instead retreat even further. Renee Rose Shield found the same situation in her study of the Franklin nursing home. Her comments on friendship avoidance can be directly applied to the residents of Wood Glen and Kramer. "For self-protection, many residents keep to themselves. Wary of involvement many of the residents consider it a virtue 'not to bother anyone' and to 'behave' oneself. A bland, superficial interaction style is characteristic of the relationship that evolve[s]" (Shield 1988:139). The result of this detachment is that no sense of community ever forms among the residents. Instead of feeling like they are part of something bigger that has emotional support and commonality of experience, residents remain in an isolated, liminal state. They are detached from their old community and way of life, yet they have no connection to their new setting. Residents never complete the rite of passage. Perhaps Fannie Isaacs best sums up the sentiments of her fellow assisted living residents: "My children did not want me to live alone in South Carolina. So, now they move me up here [to Chicago and Kramer], and I am still alone" (interview by author, tape recording, Chicago, Illinois, 18 January 1993).

I FEEL USELESS HERE

Although residents are hard on each other, they are even harder on themselves. Closely related to isolation and friendship issues is the experience of personal uselessness. Residents at Kramer and Wood Glen repeatedly told me that they felt useless. Elderly people want to feel as though they can still contribute to society. Most of the residents I spoke with feel as though they no longer serve a purpose in society. These candid thoughts did not arise from direct questioning. Rather, over time residents began making passing comments in front of me, such as, "I feel useless here." Such comments really caught my attention. Then, looking back through my transcriptions and field notes, I realized that this was a serious underlying problem among many residents.

One afternoon at Kramer, I overheard a conversation among five residents. They were discussing aging. One woman began, "I never expected to get this old." As the conversation continued, the residents discussed what it means to be old now compared to a generation ago. One resident interjected, "Sixty used to be old, and then seventy was old, and now." As she trailed off, the rest of the group sat in silence, perhaps contemplating what they thought it means to "be old." Then another resident suggested that perhaps humans today live too long and that maybe ninety, ninety-one, or ninety-two is simply *too old*. As the conversation among these five women continued, one bravely asked, "What purpose do you serve when you're that old?"

This outlook parallels the opinion of many fellow Kramer and Wood Glen residents. My research notes are filled with entries regarding the frequency of comments, such as, "Oh I am old and have served my purpose," or "Oh, I am old and useless now." Residents almost exclusively link the words "old" and "useless." When these people feel old, they feel useless, and when they feel useless, they feel old. It is a vicious cycle. Age is the key that connects all of the emotions involved in loss of independence, control, and freedom. Resident Yvonne Diamond claims, "You or anyone else who is not going through it cannot possibly understand what it is like to feel a loss of control because of your age" (interview by author, tape recording, Chicago, Illinois, 9 October 1992). Fannie Isaacs adds the following: "If you come [to Kramer] from living forty years by yourself [as I have done], you have confidence. You come here and you look for something to hold on to. Sometimes you find it, and sometimes you don't. But we are old. You know it is very hard to be old, *very hard*. It is no Golden Age. Everything is gray" (interview by author, tape recording, Chicago, Illinois, 18 January 1993).

Many processes contribute to an older adult's sense of uselessness. Both Kramer and Wood Glen residents are often at a loss to pinpoint exactly what might give them some purpose in life. One point on which residents agree is that they do not want to entertain themselves with planned activities. Most of these projects do not alleviate their boredom or build their self-esteem. Feeling useful in one's life and in the lives of others is a very individual matter. Residents have differing opinions about how they might feel useful again. Several residents simply do not know what could be done to make them feel like contributing members of society. Wilkin and Hughes (1987) found similar results in their study of six old people's homes in England. "Although most residents would have liked some sort of additional activity with which to fill the time, they were unable to be specific about what they wanted to do" (p. 181).

Most residents I spoke with agree that assisted living serves as a catalyst for their feelings of uselessness and of being "old." Zelda Arnold says, "There was always something to do in your own home, cook or clean—here there's nothing." Kramer resident Yetta Davis agrees, "In your own apartment you kept busy, there were a lot of things to do." Residents believe that the chores they performed in their own homes gave them some purpose. Now, according to one resident, they "sit all day" because they have no responsibilities beyond making their beds and keeping themselves alive. Ultimately, what I learn from these residents is that feeling useless is intricately intertwined with feelings of not only loss and liminality, but also loneliness. And loneliness can also lead to boredom. Goffman says that residents of many total institutions tend to feel this way. "Sometimes so little work is required that inmates . . . suffer extremes of boredom" (Goffman 1961:10). There is no new role for the assisted living residents to embrace so there is nothing to jar them out of their liminal state.

JF: There isn't always enough to do here I guess?

ZA: Well, there is *nothing* to do.

JF: What are weekends like here? Any different than weekdays?

ZA: Every day is the same, there's nothing to do [laughs]. You watch the clock, it tells you the day and the date and the time. (Arnold interview, 11 November 1992)

Wilkin and Hughes received similar responses from residents they interviewed in England. "Not surprisingly, most residents said that they were bored at least some of the time, but many simply accepted boredom as a fact of life in the home" (Wilkin and Hughes 1987:179).

As part of any rite of passage, the liminal phase is marked by a peculiar sense of time. It seems to hang, suspended in the air until a new role is learned and reincorporation into society can take place. As I demonstrated earlier, institutional settings such as nursing homes and assisted living never reincorporate the initiates into a new role. Instead, residents remain uninitiated in their new environment. Adding to this point is the fact that elderly residents of assisted living do not know how long they will be staying in the assisted living community.

On a daily basis, time is paradoxical: scheduled yet loose. For instance, meals and activities may occur at fixed times every day, but the rest of the day is unstructured and sometimes endless. Assisted living residents have no responsibilities; yet, they have all the time in the world to do nothing. Residents may want to rush time along from one day to the next. But, on a long-term basis residents want time to slow down because death or the nursing home await them once they escape the limbo of assisted living.

Shield (1988) points out that in institutional environments there are three types of time. There is the cyclical time of days and weeks, marked by the calendar and the seasons. Second, there is static time "in which everything seems the same" (Shield 1988:192). The days seem to be the same and blend together in a blur of boring repetition. There are no roles and responsibilities to help fill the time and make life active. Finally, and perhaps most important, there is the "time of future peril." Here, each passing day brings with it fears for the elderly residents that new deficits and health limitations will increase to the point that they will require more and more care.

The time of future peril anticipates the increased dependency and helplessness that, due to their adherence to the elderly mystique, many older adults believe will inevitably occur. The risk of increasing health problems and dependency leads residents to be fearful of making friends with other residents. Instead of appreciating the benefits of emotional support in the here and now, residents push others away because the time of future peril looms large. The real loss for residents is that, since they have no idea how long they can stay in assisted living, they sacrifice their present needs for their future fears by keeping others at a distance.

The danger of future health decline also leads assisted living residents to cling to their assisted living settings. Residents are in limbo, not knowing when death or a nursing home will become their fate. Assisted living is not home for the residents and they do not necessarily like who they live with but at least "it's not a nursing home—anything is better than that." Residents in assisted living are paralyzed: they fear the future, they dislike the present, and they cannot return to the past. They are suspended in an ill-defined time span that could bring more losses at any moment. Assisted living residents are trapped in their present sense of uselessness.

The comments throughout this chapter point to the fact that assisted living residents do not believe that activities or other residents are going to give them the sense of purpose and fulfillment they need. The ideal that relatives have for assisted living is that "mom" will move into assisted living, make new friends, and feel better. The reality for many older adults is that coming to assisted living represents a loss of control and independence in their lives.

According to many residents at Kramer and Wood Glen, assisted living accentuates their perceptions of themselves as old and useless. They feel as though their placement in assisted living represents a loss of control and an end to any real life. Residents are simply marking time. As Goffman notes, this is often the case in total institutions. "[T]here is a strong feeling that time spent in the establishment is time wasted or destroyed or taken from one's life; it is time that must be written off" (Goffman 1961:67). Katie Jacobs, a ninety-year-old Kramer resident told me her feelings on the subject.

JF: What are the benefits of group living?

KJ: I don't really know if there are any because [when] you come into a place like this *your life is over.*

JF: Are there activities that you like here?

KJ: Well, they have art but I don't go in. . . . The woman who gives the lessons saw me yesterday and she said, "Katie, why don't you come in?" I said, "I am too old to learn something new." I used to sew, I was a dressmaker for three years in Europe . . . but that wasn't the thing I wanted. What I wanted was to learn things. To find out new things. But you get older and you lose your interest. It's not the same. You know I used to go to everything [the shows] that they take us to. . . . I used to love it. I loved the singing and I used to love everything. Now I don't get a kick out of it. I go and it doesn't interest me anymore. (interview by author, tape recording, Chicago, Illinois, 27 October 1992)

Katie's sentiments speak for many of her fellow assisted living residents: "When you come here your life is over." Some residents feel conflicted because they do not want to be perceived as old and they want to have the power to change this image. Yet, assisted living residents are caught up in the reality of living in a place that emphasizes their frailty to the wider society.

When older adults leave the wider community for life in an assisted living setting they not only lose the roles and statuses they held in the community, but they also have no new role to assume in assisted living. Their liminality in assisted living leads to dependency akin to that of a child. However, there are differences between the dependencies of children and those of older adults. Shield refers to these differences as the "dependency up" of childhood and the "dependency down" of old age. Children are dependent upon others to have their daily needs met. Yet, as children grow they become more independent and more active in society. The opposite may be said for many elderly people. Their status is diminishing because their dependency is increasing. The dependency of older adults is seen as a downward spiral. American society looks down upon dependency and assigns "nonperson" status to anyone other than children who need assistance. Not only have institutionalized elderly persons lost their past roles and responsibilities, but, in the eyes of some, institutionalized elderly persons have also lost their status as useful, contributing members of society.

This chapter has illustrated that residents experience moving into assisted living as an incomplete rite of passage that leads them to feel a sense of dependency and liminality. The lives of elderly people often involve a series of losses: the loss of a spouse, the loss of a home, and the loss of their friends. Moving into an institutional environment adds to these losses.

Once they move into assisted living, residents try to adjust to their lives as best they can. However, their liminality and losses permeate all aspects of their new lives. Residents become dependent on staff and sometimes resentful because they cannot take care of things as they used to. Wood Glen and Kramer residents do not make many friends because they fear the new losses that their liminal state may bring. Assisted living is not home for residents because they do not know how long they can remain there. Residents cannot go backward and they cannot go forward. They feel useless in their present limbo and worry about the time of future peril.

Unfortunately, many assisted living operators inadvertently increase residents' feelings of liminality through the policies and procedures that shape their assisted living communities. As the next chapter will show, marketing, resident contracts, and regulatory confusion can all add to residents' feelings of uncertainty in assisted living.

CHAPTER 6

New Visions, Old Problems

The field of assisted living and the number of assisted living communities have continued to expand over the past fifteen years. Chapters 3, 4, and 5 conveyed the providers' experiences and the residents' realities in assisted living. Additional narratives will now be used to help address unanswered questions surrounding assisted living. The information offered by providers and residents can also guide assisted living proponents through some persistent obstacles faced by the assisted living industry.

I begin this chapter with an in-depth discussion of various models of assisted living. This discussion will serve as a foundation for an analysis of the current regulatory environment surrounding assisted living. The regulatory discussion will then give way to an analysis of marketing materials (including language and information used). This section will also explore the relationship between marketing materials and resident contracts. Next, I turn to community policies and resident rights. How do policies outlined by providers and assisted living communities affect resident rights and autonomy? What do these policies look like at Kramer and Wood Glen? Quantitative data collected at Wood Glen and Kramer will be used to analyze the contrasting perspectives between residents and staff. This data also illustrate residents' perceptions of policies and rules in their assisted living environments. Finally, aging in place will be examined in relation to all of the other issues discussed in this chapter. How do models of assisted living, marketing materials, contracts, and residents' experiences inform us about aging in place in assisted living?

EVOLUTION OF ASSISTED LIVING MODELS

As stated in chapter 3, assisted living refers to a housing/health care alternative for elderly persons who are no longer able to live independently in their own homes but do not require twenty-four-hour nursing care (Regnier 1991). A unique dimension of assisted living is the fact that there is no one standard definition for this residential option. The Assisted Living Federation of America (ALFA), the American Association of Homes and Services for the Aging (AAHSA), and the U.S. Health Care Financing Administration (HCFA), as well as various scholars such as Regnier (1996), Mollica and Snow (1996), and Wilson (1996), have all proposed definitions of assisted living. Although the definitions may differ, there is a component present in virtually all definitions. This commonality includes considering assisted living as a combination of some kind of housing *and* services. This is where the similarities often end. Individual states then decide what is meant by "housing" and "services" as they relate to definitions, policies, and procedures surrounding assisted living.

In order to clarify some of the confusion, ALFA (1999) offered two general models of assisted living that I discussed in chapter 3. In a separate work, Hawes, Rose, and Phillips (1999) proposed a more detailed division of assisted living than that offered by ALFA. Their study, based on a survey of 1,251 sites in the United States, found that four basic types of assisted living are represented across the country. Although not related to the models proposed by ALFA, Hawes's four categories fit nicely into the classifications proposed by ALFA.

The first type described by Hawes is termed Low Service/Low Privacy. Based on their nationwide survey, Hawes, Rose, and Phillips found that this form represents 59 percent of the places that call themselves assisted living. In the Low Service/Low Privacy model, the majority of rooms are shared and the only activities of daily living (ADL) assistance offered is with bathing and dressing. Most of the services provided for this type would be instrumental activities of daily living (IADL) assistance such as help with laundry and transportation.

The second type of assisted living community Hawes refers to is called Low Service/High Privacy. Approximately 18 percent of the 1,251 assisted living sites in their survey exemplify this model. Here, residents are more likely to have a private room (or apartment) and a private bathroom but not much in the way of ADL assistance. Hawes also referred to this model as the "cruise ship" model because of its emphasis on luxury, privacy, and hospitality services. Of my two research sites, Kramer's assisted living community would fit into this category.

The third type of assisted living described by Hawes is High Service/Low Privacy. In these assisted living settings, two-thirds of residents live in rooms rather than apartments, and slightly over 20 percent of the rooms are shared.

All of the High Service/Low Privacy sites in Hawes's study had a registered nurse on staff and the respondents for these sites all claimed they would retain a resident who needed nursing care. Nationally, only 12 percent of assisted living communities fall into this category. Assisted living at Wood Glen conforms to the High Service/Low Privacy category.

The final model Hawes presents is called High Service/High Privacy. This group offers both private dwellings for residents as well as a high level of services to meet both ADL and IADL needs. Approximately 11 percent of assisted living sites nationwide qualify for this category.

The Low Service/Low Privacy model and the Low Service/High Privacy model both conform to the first ALFA category discussed in chapter 3, Senior Housing with Non-Health Care Services. Hawes's two models could be seen as a subcategory of the ALFA classification because both of these models have a lower emphasis on services, and virtually no emphasis on health-related care. The High Service/Low Privacy model and the High Service/High Privacy models qualify under the second ALFA model, Senior Housing with Health Care Services. Both models are geared toward meeting the health needs of residents and both offer a better possibility of aging in place because they can supply the needed health care assistance and advanced ADL assistance that a resident may require to remain in assisted living. However, even the high service models do not guarantee that residents will be permitted to fully age in place.

The distinctions between these four models are critical because several of the models Hawes discusses do not adhere to the basic philosophy of care that is so central to assisted living. "Assisted living's philosophy is to provide physically and cognitively impaired older persons the personal and health-related services that they require to age in place in a homelike environment that maximizes their dignity, privacy, independence, and autonomy" (Wilson 1996:10). Three of the four assisted living models outlined by Hawes would not qualify as complying with the philosophy of care stated here by Wilson and others, and, therefore, would lack the essence of what assisted living strives to be. The numerous models of assisted living and their varying characteristics create a plethora of possibilities for regulating this housing option. They may also lead to great incongruity between legislators, providers, residents, and their families.

REGULATORY CONFUSION

Further complicating the abundance of assisted living models presented above is the reality of state regulations. Assisted living not only changes its name from state to state but it also varies by licensure category and definition. According to Hawes, Rose, and Phillips (1999), "The best estimate is that there are more than thirty names for licensed residential care facilities and they are regulated by more than 60 state agencies" (p. 1).

For example, in the state of Massachusetts, assisted living is defined as "any entity that provides room and board and provides and arranges for personal care services and activities of daily living for three or more adults" (NCAL 2001:35). In Massachusetts, assisted living has a separate licensure category and is administered under the Office of Elder Affairs. By comparison, in Minnesota, assisted living is not licensed but rather is certified by the Minnesota Department of Health under the category of Elderly Housing with Services Establishments. It is defined as "an establishment providing sleeping accommodations to one or more adult residents, at least eighty percent of which are 55 years of age or older, and offering, for a fee, one or more regularly scheduled health-related services or two or more regularly scheduled supportive services" (NCAL 2001:39).

In Illinois, where my study took place, assisted living is administered under the Department of Public Health. As of 1 January 2001, Illinois' new Assisted Living and Shared Housing Establishment Act went into effect, creating a new licensure category for assisted living in Illinois. The new act defines assisted living as follows:

a home, building, residence or any other place where sleeping accommodations are provided for at least three unrelated adults, at least 80% of whom are 55 years of age or older and where the following are provided: (1) services consistent with a social model that is based on the premise that the resident's unit in assisted living and shared housing is his or her own home; (2) a physical environment that is a homelike setting; (3) community-based residential care for persons who need assistance with activities of daily living. (Illinois Assisted Living and Shared Housing Act, 210 ILCS Section 10)

It is noteworthy that "home" and "homelike" both appear in the new state regulations, although neither term is defined in the act.

Regulation is gaining momentum across the country. By the beginning of 2000, twenty-nine states had regulations in place that used the specific term "assisted living" and two more states had pending legislation using this term (Melia 2000:54). Further, as of June 2001, the National Conference of State Legislatures claims that "more than 450 assisted living bills are currently under consideration in states" (Blankenheim 2001:13).

Manard et al. (1992) propose to regulate assisted living by acknowledging three possible fields of regulation and letting states act according to the domain they most emphasize. Using Donabedian's trilogy (1972), Manard et al. (1992) state that the structural domain, the process domain, and the outcome domain are all possible fields for regulating assisted living. Depending on what the individual state most closely links to quality of life, the state may regulate accordingly. For instance, some states have put forth strict parameters regarding the physical setting (structural domain). States such as Oregon define assisted living based on architectural attributes of the site (e.g., each person must have a separate apartment with a kitchen in order for it to qualify as assisted living). Therefore, in Oregon, it makes sense to emphasize regulation in the structural domain in order to best complement the state's definition of assisted living.

Other states, such as California and Washington, have chosen to regulate under the process domain; thus regulating is based on what services may be provided in the assisted living community. A third possibility is to regulate based on outcomes. For example, "a regulatory approach might be crafted where those aspects of quality a state decides are most directly linked to the philosophy of assisted living (including tenant autonomy) and tenant well-being are regulated, but the myriad of other aspects of care and facility operations are not" (Manard et al. 1992:vi–9).

Rather than arguing which of these domains should be prioritized, it is useful to point out that *all three* areas should be integrated into assisted living regulations. Manard et al. (1992) point out that "it is the *connections* between structure, process, and outcome that lead to quality care" (pp. vi–9). I firmly believe that the linkages between these three domains are critical to regulating assisted living. It is only by integrating the structural, process, and outcome domains that the industry can guarantee a holistic approach to assisted living. And a holistic approach is the only way to adhere entirely to the philosophy of assisted living and offer any possibility of full aging in place. This integrated approach would allow providers to remove assisted living from the continuum of care and offer residents the highest measure of autonomy.

There are still unanswered questions associated with regulating assisted living, such as, Should the federal government regulate assisted living? How can we actually regulate "risk"? Should marketing and advertising be regulated? Finally, should aging in place be regulated? I will return to these questions in the next chapter. Presently, I turn to an analysis of assisted living marketing materials and advertisements.

MARKETING MATERIALS AND RESIDENT CONTRACTS: WHO IS "THE CUSTOMER"?

The population in assisted living continues to grow as record numbers of assisted living settings are being built and marketed all over the country. With this boom in the assisted living industry several critical questions arise: Who are the marketers selling to? Who initiates the decision to move? What is included in the advertisements? Where are resident rights within the tenancy documents?

After completing a variety of types of research including participant-observation fieldwork, interviews, and an extensive literature review, I have concluded that the potential resident is *not* the person the marketers are aiming to impress. The senior may end up living in assisted living but he or she is *not* necessarily the person the industry or residence tries to please. This point becomes evident when examining the decision-making process surrounding a move. Having conducted a number of interviews with administrators at various assisted living sites, I found that most of them talk about the family making the choice regarding a potential resident's move. It is only natural that family members would be consulted during the decision-making process, as this is a major choice for the senior to make. Oftentimes, however, family consultation with the senior does not even take place. Family members tour the site, gather the marketing materials, and make the decisions. In chapter 5, Kramer residents Fannie Isaacs, Zelda Arnold, and Wilma Rose all expressed their lack of involvement in the decision-making process and their frustration at their insufficient participation in the determination to move into Kramer. It is somewhat disquieting that many assisted living sites do not require or at least strongly encourage the potential resident to even tour the building before moving in.

More interesting is the fact that national studies on assisted living support the idea that the resident is not the customer. "Most industry participants would agree that the family and/or advisor is the true 'customer' for assisted living since few residents move without anyone else involved in the decision" (NIC 1998:xiii). This statement is extremely problematic. How can the industry *not* believe that the older adult is the true customer when he or she will ultimately be living in the assisted living residence? Who is the industry looking to satisfy? Should it not be the person living in the building? This same study also states that "advertisements should focus more on the family/advisor since only 6% of residents said they first learned about the community from an advertisement" (NIC 1998:xiv). Assisted living tenants may not be the first to read the marketing materials, but it is still the potential resident that the site *should* appeal to. After all, he or she is the one who will live there. Potentially, one might argue that family members should be marketed more strongly because they will pay for assisted living, therefore making them the "real" customer. Nevertheless, this is not the case. Of the approximately 1,000 residents included in the NIC study, approximately 65 percent of residents "were reported as totally self-pay, receiving no forms of financial assistance from their family or government agency" (NIC 1998:xxxii). Further data from this study show that only 15.8 percent of assisted living residents receive any payment assistance from family members. So, why does the industry market to family members? How are they true "customers"? This action contradicts the entire philosophy of assisted living.

A second critical question connected to marketing and "customer" choices asks who initiates the decision to move into assisted living. The NIC national survey calculated the answer to this question based on a series of age ranges for the potential resident. The age categories ranged from less than seventy-five years to ninety years. Averaging all age-ranges together shows that in approximately 47 percent of cases it was the resident's idea to move into assisted living and 53 percent of the time it was "mostly someone else's" idea to move (NIC 1998:128). The person likely to be the most influential in the decision to move is either the resident's daughter or son (accounting for 55% of cases).

Tying together data on decisions to move with earlier survey statements about who the "true customer" is could present a scenario of little empowerment in the decision-making process for the resident. Members of the industry believe that they should be marketing to family members, perhaps because the decision to move, in over half of cases, is made by someone other than the resident. However, it is the resident who pays for assisted living in the majority of cases. Why isn't the senior seen by the industry as the key player to be satisfied? The son or daughter may initiate the move with brochures and advertisements but the elderly person has to live in assisted living. Another trend illustrating the lack of self-determination in the decision-making process can be seen in the number of residences considered.

The National Investment Conference reports that a mean of 1.4 communities are considered when looking into assisted living sites. The question posed to the assisted living residents in the survey was, "[H]ow many assisted living communities . . . did you consider before moving into this residence?" (NIC 1998:132). An astounding 45 percent of residents answered, "They had not considered any residence" (p. 132). If residents were not considering any assisted living communities before their move, who was? And why wasn't the resident consulted?

Visiting a residence prior to moving in is an important step for a resident in order to know if he or she will feel "at home" there and to help make the transition easier when it is time to move. According to the national survey conducted by NIC, 72 percent of assisted living residents claimed they had visited the building in which they now live prior to moving in. Reversing the numbers shows that 28 percent of residents had never set foot inside the assisted living residence until the day they moved in. How can residents know how homelike an assisted living community will be if over one-fourth of them never see the place before they move? How would they even know what to take with them if they have never seen the living space? How many people in the general population move into a new dwelling before seeing it? Why would administrators and marketers *allow* this to happen? By contrast, what if it is residents in the majority of cases who choose not to see the place before they move? What does this say about their involvement in their lives or their perceptions about their future? A critical piece of missing data from the NIC study is the reason *why* residents did not visit the assisted living community ahead of time. This information could offer critical clues regarding resident choice, autonomy, the philosophy of assisted living, and adherence to the elderly mystique.

Analyzing reasons for moving to assisted living reveal some enlightening information for marketers and the assisted living industry. As part of the 1998 National Investment Conference survey of assisted living communities, over 1,000 residents from 178 assisted living communities were asked about their choice of a particular assisted living residence and the life circumstances surrounding their move. The most important reasons residents cited for choosing their present assisted living residence are as follows: services offered at the site (31.9%); convenient for family and friends (21.7%); appearance of residence (12.9%); and staff (6.6%). It seems noteworthy that only 12.9% of respondents cited appearance of the residence as the most important reason for selecting a particular community. Marketers in the assisted living industry are putting significant resources into emphasizing the appearance and design of assisted living, but this is not residents' primary concern or motivation for choosing a residence. Reasonably, it could not be a primary concern if 28 percent of residents never see the community before moving in.

Life circumstances underlying a senior's choice to move to assisted living were varied but seemed to cluster into two broad categories: (1) health-related reasons; or (2) needed assistance with activities of daily living. According to the National Investment Conference, health reasons account for 28.5 percent of circumstances underlying seniors' decisions to move to assisted living. The need for assistance or inability to live alone accounted for 27.7 percent of respondents' answers. Other reasons cited include death of a spouse or caregiver, recent hospitalization, inability to maintain his or her home, not wanting to "live with or be a burden to family," and not feeling safe in his or her present home. The vast majority of responses were *need driven*. The older adult chose to move because of a need (health problems, ADL deficiencies, and loneliness). The 1,000 resident responses show that seniors are choosing assisted living communities out of necessity rather than a desire to move to assisted living. According to the NIC national survey, "only 5.8% of the respondents volunteered a reason [for moving to assisted living] that suggested the assisted living community had a positive pull, as opposed to a negative push from their former living environment" (NIC 1998:141). Marketers need to pay careful attention to this statistic because it indicates that many older adults are moving away *from* their own homes, not *to* assisted living. There are a few industry experts who do acknowledge this situation. According to David Schless, executive director of the American Seniors Housing Association, "There is no question that seniors' housing is a need-driven product. That is to say, the vast majority of older adults will attempt to remain wherever it is they call home for as long as possible; the vast majority of people who do move into seniors' housing do so because of some event, whether it is the death of a spouse or some other type of situation, particularly health related, that compels them to move" (Zaner 1997:52). However, most industry participants are not as perceptive as Schless. As will be discussed later, this fact can have enormous implications for resident autonomy and ability to age in place.

Another aspect of the marketing process is the actual content of the advertisements and company literature. How do communities advertise their sites and how does this connect to or contradict assisted living's basic philosophy?

Marketing information and advertisements will obviously focus on the positive aspects of assisted living. But positive in whose eyes? As discussed in chapter 3, the physical design and architecture are a very important component of assisted living. Nonetheless, as the numbers in this chapter illustrate, residents are placing their emphasis on things other than the physical environment.

A critical point I noted in many marketing and trade journals is the manner in which assisted living is labeled and discussed. Semantics can be very powerful as well as convey subtle messages about what the author or assisted living community wishes to sell. A 1996 article in the trade publication, *Continuing Care,* referred to assisted living as a "long-term care facility" (Retzlaff 1996:30). One of the major missions of assisted living creators is to develop a homelike environment for older adults—a long-term care facility sounds like a nursing home. Assisted living, as many operators are quick to point out, is not a nursing home. Further, a number of authors (in both scholarly and trade journals) continue to refer to assisted living communities as "facilities" (Namazi and Chafetz 2001; Barton 1997; Scott, Kender, and Townsley 1999; Fisher 1995; Innes 1998; Gold 1996; Fairchild and Lindh 1998; Redmond and Chafetz 2001; Tarlach 1998; Allen 1999a; Moos and Lemke 1996; Hodlewsky 2001; Lewin-VHI 1996).[1] In a recent *Chicago Tribune* article, assisted living is decribed as a "facility" and "senior housing" in the same sentence (Adler 2001:sec. 16, p. 3). Some scholars in the field of assisted living have repeatedly stated the need to avoid using such terminology regarding assisted living if we really want providers and residents to see it as something other than an institutional environment. How can someone see a place as "home" if everyone around him or her calls it a "facility"? Kane and Wilson (1993) claim it is very necessary to avoid terminology such as facility if we want residents to make their home there but also admit that "no ideal noun is available" to describe assisted living (p. 12).

Trade publications and academic literature both need to be careful about the words used to describe assisted living communities. If a place is labeled as a "facility" by developers, administrators, and staff then maybe they view seniors living there as "patients" rather than residents or tenants. Facility is a word that offers no ownership or sense of community for those living there. How can we "maximize residents' dignity" (Wilson 1996; Regnier 1996; ALFA 2000; Allen 1999a) if we tell them and everyone else that they are living in a facility?

It is interesting that terminology is most problematic when it comes to the residential nature of the assisted living community, because it is the residential and homelike nature of assisted living that is supposed to be the big selling point and what distinguishes assisted living from other senior housing and health care options. Yet, the word "facility" is used constantly by trade journals and academic journals. Other terms appear that also contradict the residential nature of assisted living. A 1998 study compiled by the National Center for Assisted Living (NCAL) refers to residents' living quarters as "beds" (NCAL 1998:40). Interestingly, this is a nursing home or hospital term. How does an assisted living "facility" with thirty "beds" sound any more residential or homelike than a nursing home? If the National Center for Assisted Living is collecting data about "beds" and "facilities," then how are developers, providers, and architects going to integrate the assisted living philosophy into their buildings? The philosophy strives to treat frail older adults *not* as patients but as residents who can exercise autonomy and retain control and choice.

A national survey, conducted by the Assisted Living Federation of America (1998) does call assisted living "communities" rather than facilities. Also of note is the fact that in 1996 ALFA changed its name from the Assisted Living Facilities Association of America to the Assisted Living Federation of America, thus dropping the word "facilities" from its organizational title. However, other organizations and marketing materials have not made such a transformation. "Facility" is still the most common word used to describe assisted living and this term contradicts the goal of a "homelike" environment. Another perplexing issue in the marketing literature is the depiction of residents in assisted living settings.

Portrayal of Elders in Trade Publications: "Super Seniors"

An examination of articles and advertisements in trade journals yields an interesting picture of assisted living residents. As discussed in chapter 3, the profile of the typical assisted living resident is an eighty-four-year-old female who requires assistance with approximately two activities of daily living. However, in trade publications, the depiction of residents is frequently anything but typical. The following description illustrates one such example.

In a particular advertisement for an assisted living company, an elderly woman is pictured in sky-diving gear with the following caption above her picture: "Assisted living. It's not the same old business." The advertisement then continues on to describe several of this company's residences, pointing out that they are "a far cry from stereotypical residences for seniors." Evidently, their residents are also a far cry from typical resident. Based on this advertisement, a reader might believe that assisted living is occupied by active, vigorous seniors rather than frail eighty-four year olds who need assistance with shopping, cooking, dressing, and bathing. While there may be a few seniors in assisted living who do sky-dive or go kayaking, this is *not* the typical resident profile. Of more concern is the fact that a contradiction seems to exist within the trade publications when discussing residents. Ads such as the one described here imply that seniors in advertiser's residences are energetic, healthy individuals. However, the same trade journal publication in which this ad appears calls assisted living residences "facilities" and tells providers how many "beds" may best suit their design. Again, "facilities" and "beds" are terms that imply nursing care, and frail residents—not sky divers. Why the paradox? Such contradictions make it difficult to know how these providers actually view their residents.

A second example of "super seniors" appearing in trade journal publications comes from an article in a 1998 issue of *Assisted Living Today* (the monthly magazine of the Assisted Living Federation of America). This particular issue features a cover story of a woman named Maggie and her life in assisted living. The woman, recovering from a stroke, has been living in assisted living because she needed "a little help" with her daily routine. Maggie is described as being in her sixties (a full twenty years younger than the average assisted living resident), and very active (helping with Meals on Wheels, exercising, painting, and playing bingo). The article is inspirational, uplifting, and perhaps misleading. If this is the number one publication in the assisted living industry is it not possible that providers and new operators might read this cover story and have skewed expectations about the functional ability of their residents? Maggie is *not* the typical assisted living resident. The fact that she is featured on the cover of *Assisted Living Today* illustrates contradictions regarding what population assisted living is supposed to serve. Are assisted living settings for vital seniors like Maggie who just need a helping hand or are assisted living communities created for frail elders in their eighties who require increasing amounts of assistance? Perhaps it depends on which model of assisted living the operator is adhering to.

Another important issue is the link between the philosophy of assisted living and the marketing literature. Paula Carder (2002) conducted content analysis on brochures from sixty-three assisted living communities in the state of Oregon. Carder sought to measure the frequency of the six assisted living principles including privacy, dignity, independence, choice, individuality, and homelike environment in order to see which concepts were used most often in the marketing literature. Of the six assisted living principles, their frequencies were as follows. Independence was mentioned most frequently in the marketing brochures (28.8%). This figure is followed by individuality (19.9%), choice (18.4%), and home (18.1%). Privacy and dignity were least mentioned of the six principles, with frequencies of 10.8 percent and 7.0 percent, respectively (Carder 2002:116). Implications for these frequencies will be addressed later on in the chapter. In order to more thoroughly understand the links between the philosophy of assisted living and the marketing of assisted living, it is important to examine other documents pertaining to this residential option.

Resident contracts are instruments used to convey the policies that a particular residence sets for its occupants. Ideally, these contracts clarify questions that a potential resident and his or her family may have regarding rules for occupancy. These contracts can frequently be as puzzling as the marketing literature.

Resident Contracts: Room for Confusion

"Who are suitable candidates for assisted living?" "When is it time for a resident to leave?" These are questions that every assisted living operator must grapple with and both are central to aging in place. The reality of the ten assisted living sites I visited in the Chicago area was that none had a standard discharge policy written into residents' contracts or marketing materials. This fact reflects the findings of a study conducted by Kathryn Allen (1999b). She found that of the over 700 assisted living communities she studied, only 48 percent have resident contracts that specify discharge criteria. Further, in a closer examination of marketing materials and contracts from sixty assisted living sites, Allen found that twenty of these sites "contained language that was unclear or potentially misleading, usually concerning the circumstances under which a resident could be required to leave a facility" (Allen 1999b:9). Since it is by way of these policies that the concept of aging in place becomes evident, it is valuable to examine several providers' verbal policies in order to highlight the complexity of assisted living as a combination of housing and services.

All ten assisted living settings I visited have some sort of criteria for admission into their assisted living program; yet all of these were vague and sometimes contradictory. This, too, is not uncommon among assisted living communities. "Many assisted living providers have poor admission agreements, which resemble real estate property leases more than they do care agreements" (Gordon 1997b:39). While this may promote a more residential atmosphere, it also creates ethical and legal problems for assisted living residents and their families. Such confusion can begin at the state level and trickle down to individual assisted living communities. "States without clear standards [for assisted living] leave facilities a great deal of room in which to maneuver, creating a burden on consumers who must decipher the contract to determine which services to expect" (Edelstein 1998:337).

Admission agreements and resident contracts have been an area of much discussion in the assisted living literature over the past few years (Epstein 1998; Allen 1999b; Wilson 1996; Manard et al. 1992; NIC 1998; Hawes, Rose, and Phillips 1999; Edelstein 1998; Gordon 1997a; Eckert, Zimmerman, and Morgan 2001). Several national studies show little consistency among residency requirements from one assisted living community to the next.

A 1999 report to the Senate Special Committee on Aging showed that a number of assisted living sites across the United States possessed "numerous examples of vague, misleading, or even contradictory information contained in written materials that facilities provide to consumers" (Allen 1999a:2). It may be that some of the marketing materials were vague because of the variety of definitions for assisted living and the variability of regulations from one state to the next. But, how can this be explained to a potential resident who is trying to decide where to move? During a 1999 Senate hearing on assisted living, several family members of assisted living residents testified before the Special Committee on Aging in an attempt to describe their experiences with resident contracts. One woman on the panel has a parent in assisted living and is also president of an organization that serves the elderly in a variety of living arrangements including assisted living. Her testimony reveals much about the nebulous nature of assisted living contracts. "Do I feel it [the resident's contract] is adequate? No, I do not feel that it is adequate. I think that it does not answer questions. There are great big voids in that contract that can be—you could almost fall in them. But the contracts are industry-oriented. They are slanted toward the side of the facility, not toward the side of the consumer" (testimony of Collette Appolito before the Special Committee on Aging, U.S. Senate, 26 April 1999).

Reading the residential contract before applying to the residence would be helpful for a potential resident so the person would know what to expect regarding procedures and rules. Of 753 sites surveyed, Allen (1999b) found that only 25 percent "routinely provide a copy of the contract to consumers before they make a decision to apply for admission" (p. 8). A total of 65 percent of the sites surveyed will provide a sample contract upon request. Why wouldn't all sites do this? Is there something they do not want potential residents to know? Knowing contradictions abound in the marketing material and resident contracts, one cannot help but wonder.

As noted in chapter 4, it is in the area of discharge criteria where assisted living policies can be especially vague or contradictory. Each of the ten assisted living providers I interviewed in Illinois struggle to deal with this issue. Nationally, Allen found that less than 50 percent of 753 sites surveyed provide written information to prospective residents regarding discharge criteria. While it may be difficult for a provider to explicitly outline every scenario resulting in discharge, it is very unfair to the potential resident. How "homelike" can an environment be if one has no idea how long he or she can live there? "The marketing material one Florida facility uses is potentially misleading in specifying that residents can be assured that if their health changes, the facility can meet their needs and they will not have to move again. However, the facility's contract specifies a range of health-related criteria for immediate discharge including changes in a resident's condition" (Allen 1999b:9). Interestingly enough, the law regarding eviction from assisted living sides with operators of assisted living communities. "In many states the ALF may have the sole discretion to evict a resident without providing the resident any notice or appeal rights" (Siemon, Edelstein, and Dresner 1996:581–82). Further, attorney Paul Gordon (1997b) explains, "[A]ssisted living facilities are not generally subject to the limited grounds for termination that apply to nursing facilities, and a contract theoretically can be terminated for no specific reason" (p. 40). Attorney Stephanie Edelstein, associate director of the American Bar Association's Commission on Legal Problems of the Elderly, agrees: "Ironically, assisted living residents may have fewer legal rights to contest arbitrary facility decisions that affect their residency than they would have if they lived in either rental housing or a nursing home" (Edelstein 1998:378). Such was the case with a resident in Oregon in 1998. "A resident was told on admission that she could stay until she dies. However, the facility issued an eviction notice when she began to wander within the facility and it raised her monthly charges from approximately $1,600 to more that $6,400" (Allen 1999b:15).

Resident contracts and marketing materials can cause a great deal of confusion and stress for assisted living residents and their families. Much of the printed information on assisted living does not clarify the target population for assisted living or state how long a resident may expect to stay. Much of the assisted living industry does not even consider residents the "true customers" of this residential option. New companies are building assisted living sites without understanding the great need to balance the housing and health care portions of this residential option. "A lot of people getting into this business do not recognize the intensity of the need or the difference from what they did before. The key thing to understand is this is not a hotel. And it is not a nursing facility" (Wilson, quoted in Fisher 1997:64).

COMMUNITY POLICIES AND RESIDENT RIGHTS

An integral part of the assisted living philosophy is "to maximize residents' dignity, autonomy, privacy, and safety" (Assisted Living Quality Coalition 1998:65). These goals are most apparent in policies assisted living administrators create for their residents. Whether residents are allowed to do things such as come and go as they please, have visitors when they choose, smoke, and drink reveals much about the particular assisted living community and its adherence to the philosophy of assisted living.

First, it is important to note that even though several major assisted living surveys and assessments have been undertaken in the past five years (Hawes, Rose, and Phillips 1999; NIC 1998; Lewin-VHI 1996; Allen 1999a), only one of these reports consulted residents on *their* experiences in assisted living or their opinions about living in this setting. The National Investment Conference survey asks seniors many demographic questions on topics such as former occupation, educational level, vision and hearing capacity, and financial status. However, only a handful of questions address their opinions and expectations. I believe it is critical to note the overall lack of resident perspective when beginning a discussion of assisted living policies and resident rights. Could it be that the assisted living industry is convinced that the resident is *not* the consumer, and, therefore, feels there is no need to consult residents in national studies of assisted living? All of the data that will be discussed in this section are based on providers' answers to questions *about* their assisted living community and resident rights issues.

Visitation is one area where residents seem to be offered a great deal of flexibility. According to the NIC survey, 90 percent of assisted living sites allow visitors to come anytime. Only 10 percent impose restrictions on visitation by assigning set visiting hours. There are no restrictions on visitors in one's own home (unless the person living there sets them). If assisted living is supposed to be seen by residents as their *home*, then unrestricted visitation should exist at all sites.

Freedom of movement is key to resident autonomy. Knowing one can come and go as he or she pleases can make a person feel a stronger sense of control over his or her life. According to the NIC national survey, 72 percent of assisted living communities surveyed allow residents to leave the site without obtaining any type of permission. Residents' movements are totally unencumbered at these sites. Conversely, a full 28 percent of residences required tenants to "obtain permission before leaving the community" (NIC 1998:72). This means more than one in four assisted living communities are violating residents' privacy and autonomy by requiring formal authorization from administration before exiting the building. This policy suggests an institutional atmosphere rather than one that is homelike.

Kramer and Wood Glen have been faced with the challenge of creating programs and policies that are advantageous to residents and flexible for staff. Since assisted living is still evolving, there are no set rules or procedures to follow when fashioning a program that will suit the needs of each individual setting. It is worthwhile here to examine different methods and approaches to administering an assisted living site. As in chapter four, results from the Multiphasic Environment Assessment Procedure (MEAP) will be used to aid in the comparison of Kramer and Wood Glen.

The Policy and Program Information Form (POLIF)

The POLIF portion of the Multiphasic Environment Assessment Procedure assesses characteristics related to a setting's programs and policies. In this way it serves as a vehicle for examining differences between Kramer and Wood Glen's approaches to assisted living. There are nine dimensions on the POLIF scale, each of which measures some aspect of a setting's practices. Table 6.1 outlines the nine dimensions and their characteristics.

Table 6.1
Policy and Program Information Form (POLIF): Subscale Descriptions and Item Examples

---

1. Expectations for Functioning—Measures the minimum capacity to perform daily living functions that is acceptable in the facility. (Is inability to clean one's own room tolerated?)

2. Tolerance for Deviance—Measures the extent to which aggressive, defiant, destructive, or eccentric behavior is tolerated. (Is refusing to bathe tolerated? Is pilfering or stealing tolerated?)

3. Policy Choice—Reflects the extent to which the facility provides options from which residents can select individual patterns of daily living. (Is there a curfew? Are residents allowed to drink a glass of beer or wine at mealtimes?)

4. Resident Control—Assesses the extent of formal institutional structures that provide residents with a voice in running the facility and the influence that residents have over policy. (Is there a residents' council? Are residents involved in deciding what kinds of new activities or programs will occur?)

5. Policy Clarity—Measures the extent of formal institutional mechanisms that contribute to clear definitions of expected behavior and open communication of ideas. (Is there a handbook for residents? Is there a newsletter?)

6. Provision for Privacy—Measures the amount of privacy given to residents. (How many residents have private rooms? Are residents allowed to lock the doors to their rooms?)

7. Availability of Health Services—Measures the availability of health services in the facility. (Is there an on-site medical clinic? Is there physical therapy?)

8. Availability of Daily Living Assistance—Measures the availability of services provided by the facility that assist residents in tasks of daily living. (Is there assistance with personal grooming? Is dinner served each day?)

9. Availability of Social/Recreational Activities—Assesses the availability of organized activities within the facility. (How often is there outside entertainment? How often are there classes or lectures? How often are there parties?)

Source: Rudolf H. Moos and Sonne Lemke. *Evaluating Residential Facilities: The Multiphasic Environment Assessment Procedures*, p. 83, copyright © 1996 Sage Publications, Inc. Reprinted by permission of Sage Publications, Inc. and Sonne Lemke.

The nine dimensions have been placed into larger groups by Moos and Lemke based on subject categorization. The first two dimensions "reflect the extent to which behavioral requirements are imposed on the residents" (Moos and Lemke 1996:82). The next four dimensions appraise "the balance between individual freedom and institutional order and stability" (p. 82). The last three POLIF dimensions gauge the availability of activities and services.

The scores for Kramer and Wood Glen are illustrated in Figure 6.1. The graph shows how these two sites compare for each of the aforementioned dimensions. In general, a number of differences are evident.

First, the tolerance for deviant behavior at Kramer is much higher than at the Wood Glen Home. This finding can be linked to characteristics of many free-standing assisted living environments versus assisted living sites connected to a larger health care facility. Studies have shown that free-standing assisted living sites generally tend to house a more frail population (Kane and Wilson 1993). When these findings are coupled with the fact that no higher level of care exists at Kramer, they suggest that staff is more likely to tolerate atypical behavior rather than ask a resident to leave.

Wood Glen shows a substantially lower tolerance for deviant behavior, possibly reflecting the presence of higher levels of care on site. Since Wood Glen residents can easily be transferred to a floor with more advanced levels of care, the staff is not pressured to maintain the residents in assisted living as long as possible. There is little risk that "problem" residents will be evicted from the Wood Glen Home. Rather, they will be moved to a level of care better suited to deal with such behaviors. At Kramer, however, there is nowhere to go but "out."

Another dimension of the POLIF scale, which ties into these findings, is that of resident control. As Figure 6.1 shows, Wood Glen appears to offer residents much more control in the decision-making process than Kramer does, at least in the view of administrators. These scores, coupled with the low tolerance for deviant behavior, suggest that residents at Wood Glen have more control because they are held much more accountable for their behavior. Conversely, Kramer offers residents little control in policy-making or procedural domains, but staff and administrators tolerate a much higher level of "defiant" or "eccentric" behavior.

Figure 6.1
Policy and Program Resources Dimensions

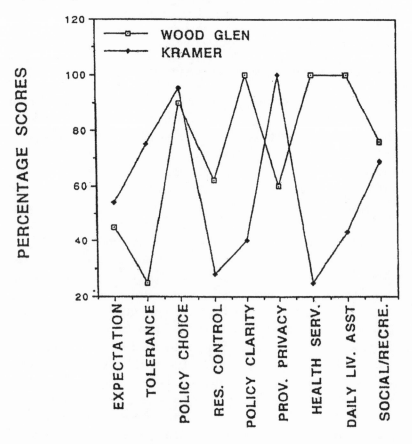

Provision for privacy, thought to be a key feature in assisted living, is a dimension where Kramer scored exceptionally high compared to Wood Glen. This is due to the differences in the architectural design of the two sites. Kramer's suite-style design, shared kitchenettes, and private full bathrooms help to ensure that residents will have more than adequate privacy. Residents at Wood Glen have one small room and sometimes a private half-bath. Also contributing to the dissimilar scores is the difference in size between Kramer and Wood Glen. Kramer houses a maximum of twenty-nine residents and has a staff of under ten people. Therefore, residents never feel crowded. The entire Wood Glen Home houses a total of 115 residents (only seventeen of whom are assisted living residents) and has a staff of over sixty people. It is much more difficult for both staff and residents to find adequate privacy in the Wood Glen Home. To understand exactly where Kramer and Wood Glen differ in their policies and programs, I narrow the focus to an examination of one particular subscale of the POLIF.

Expectations for Functioning

If we closely examine expectations for functioning at Wood Glen and Kramer, clear differences emerge. This particular POLIF dimension is revealing because policies regarding residents' functional abilities highlight a fundamental question relevant to all assisted living providers: "What population is assisted living supposed to serve?" As alluded to in chapter 4, there are separate but equally popular answers to this question. One group of providers seems to believe that assisted living should house healthier, basically independent older adults who require virtually no assistance with their activities of daily living (ADLs). The second group of providers believes that assisted living should house more impaired older adults who require at least moderate ADL assistance. Kramer is an example of the former group, and the Wood Glen Home is an example of the latter group.

The POLIF asks providers, "[W]hat is the policy [here] with respect to the following [nine] behaviors and activities?" The respondent is then supposed to answer the questions in relation to a resident's *inability* to perform the designated behavior. For example, "[W]hat is the policy with respect to a resident's . . . inability to make his or her bed?" Providers at Wood Glen and Kramer answer the question by checking one of the following answers: "allowed," "tolerated," "discouraged," or "intolerable." Five of the nine questions are related to ADLs: eating, bathing, dressing, toileting, and ambulating. Ambulating is actually separated from the rest of the questions and asked in regard to in-coming residents only. Providers are simply supposed to circle "yes" or "no" to the following question: "[M]ust an in-coming resident be ambulatory at time of entry?" The expectations for resident functioning at Kramer and Wood Glen indicate decidedly different policies and outlooks.

First, Kramer's policy is that prospective residents must be ambulatory at their time of entry. This is not the case for assisted living residents at Wood Glen. In regard to the other four ADLs, there are also significant deviations between the two sites. Kramer's policy is either to discourage or not tolerate any inability among residents to feed, bathe, toilet, or dress themselves. Basically, any ADL dysfunction was severely looked down upon, if not totally prohibited. By contrast, Wood Glen expects residents to require moderate ADL assistance. Although Wood Glen providers do not tolerate residents who cannot feed themselves or who are incontinent, they do allow residents to have assistance with bathing and dressing. Summing up findings for this subscale can illuminate broader policy contradictions in the field of assisted living. It is evident that Kramer's policies are much more in line with the "cruise ship" model of assisted living discussed earlier (Hawes, Rose, and Phillips 1999). Kramer views its "assistance" portion of assisted living as pertaining only to *instrumental activities of daily living* (IADLs) such as help with shopping, meal preparation, and housekeeping. As Hawes et al. state, the cruise ship model of assisted living (also known as the Low Service/High Privacy model) emphasizes luxury and privacy while downplaying any medical or health-related services. Kramer offers much privacy and an elegant living environment with few medical services in place. Kramer and other "cruise ship" model settings view assisted living as fundamentally a helping hand for those older adults who are basically independent but may require IADL assistance with grocery shopping or housework. Providers who adhere to the Low Service/High Privacy model create policies based on this perspective and then target clientele whose time spent in assisted living is likely to be brief because the setting cannot (or will not) accommodate any health-related needs.

Wood Glen's structure is more in line with the "High Service/Low Privacy" model. As noted in the POLIF, administrators at Wood Glen believe residents have little privacy in their environment due to architectural details and sheer number of residents in the building. However, providers at Wood Glen expect that their new residents are going to move in with some ADL needs and Wood Glen is ready to meet these needs. Since the differences between Wood Glen and Kramer center on the expected resident population of both sites, I turn now to a closer focus on questions involving assisted living residents.

The Sheltered Care Environment Scale (SCES)

The Sheltered Care Environment Scale (SCES) assesses the social environments of sheltered care settings. This tool can also be used to evaluate the social conditions in assisted living communities. For the SCES, staff and residents are asked individually about "the usual patterns of behavior in their setting" (Moos and Lemke 1988:47). The POLIF and Resident and Staff Information Form (RESIF) focus on objective information about the assisted living community while the SCES draws upon resident and staff perceptions. The SCES can shed light on how individuals living and working in assisted living perceive each other, themselves, and the site.

The SCES is a sixty-three-question survey that covers seven social dimensions (see Appendix II for a copy of the survey). As Table 6.2 shows, these seven subscales are grouped into three broader domains: relationship dimensions, personal growth dimensions, and system maintenance and change dimensions. Moos and Lemke have since made slight revisions to the SCES (1996), but, because I administered the 1984 version to residents at Kramer and Wood Glen, it is logical to reprint this earlier version. Within each of the subscales, a sample question is presented from the actual survey. Each of the seven subscales for the SCES has nine corresponding questions. These questions are arranged in a pattern throughout the survey so that the respondent is unaware of the seven dimensions. For example, questions one, eight, fifteen, twenty-two, twenty-nine, and so forth correspond to the cohesion subscale.

Table 6.2
Sheltered Care Environment Scale (SCES): Subscale Descriptions and Item Examples

---

Relationship Dimensions

1. Cohesion—Measures how helpful and supportive staff members are toward residents and how involved and supportive residents are with each other. (Do residents get a lot of individual attention?)

2. Conflict—Measures the extent to which residents express anger and are critical of each other and of the facility. (Do residents ever start arguments?)

Personal Growth Dimensions

3. Independence—Assesses how self-sufficient residents are encouraged to be in their personal affairs and how much responsibility and self-direction they are encouraged to exercise. (Do residents sometimes take charge of activities?)

4. Self-Exploration—Measures the extent to which the residents are encouraged to openly express their feelings and concerns. (Are personal problems openly talked about?)

System Maintenance and Change Dimensions

5. Organization—Assesses how important order and organization are in the facility, the extent to which residents know what to expect in their day-to-day routine, and the clarity of rules and procedures. (Are activities for residents carefully planned?)

6. Resident Influence—Measures the extent to which the residents can influence the rules and policies of the facility and the degree to which the staff directs the residents through regulations. (Are suggestions made by the residents acted upon?)

7. Physical Comfort—Taps the extent to which comfort, privacy, pleasant décor, and sensory satisfaction are provided by the physical environment. (Can residents have privacy whenever they want?)

Source: Rudolf H. Moos and Sonne Lemke. *Evaluating Residential Facilities: The Multiphasic Environment Assessment Procedures,* p. 111, copyright © 1996 Sage Publications, Inc. Reprinted by permission of Sage Publications, Inc. and Sonne Lemke.

It is important to note that the number of residents at Kramer and Wood Glen fluctuated during the period of my research. At the time I administered the SCES to residents, there were thirteen residents living on the assisted living floor at Wood Glen (of a possible 17), and at Kramer there were twenty-two residents (of a possible 29 total). Therefore, I should make a few qualifications at this point. Because my sample at both sites was small, it is impossible to draw any grandiose, statistically significant conclusions for the field of assisted living as a whole. However, this was not my purpose in using this tool. My objective was to shed more light on information gathered in my interviews and participant observation research. Another goal was to elicit feedback on issues that were uncomfortable for residents to address in formal interviews. I believe that I succeeded in attaining both of the aims with the SCES.

Another critical fact should be made before beginning the analysis of the SCES. Almost all of the questions in this survey focus on residents rather than staff. This means that residents are the sole objects of most of the dimension questions. Re-examining Table 6.2, one can see that only two of the subscales, cohesion and resident influence, mention staff. Subscales such as conflict, independence, and self-exploration focus only on residents. All nine questions in the SCES related to the conflict dimension allude to conflict among *residents*, not conflict at the assisted living site in general (see Appendix II).

In general, the survey places primary responsibility for the quality of the social environment on the residents. Thirty-five of a total of sixty-three questions exclusively mention residents—for example, "Do residents ever start arguments?" and "Are residents careful about what they say to each other?" Only one of the sixty-three questions mentions staff only: "Are staff strict about rules and regulations?" A total of seven questions on the SCES mentions both staff and residents—for instance, "Do staff members sometimes talk down to residents?" The twenty remaining questions mention neither staff nor residents—for example, "Are there a lot of social activities?" and "Is the furniture here comfortable and homey?" The general findings from the SCES are especially illuminating.

For the SCES it is useful to first examine the two assisted living communities separately and then compare their overall results. Figure 6.2 illustrates the staff and resident impressions for those at Wood Glen. The graph shows how staff and residents rate the seven dimensions for their assisted living setting. Staff and residents perceive comparable levels of independence and self-exploration among residents yet divergent levels of cohesion, conflict, and resident influence. The largest difference can be seen in the resident influence dimension. Staff clearly believes that residents have much more influence on policymaking than the residents themselves believe. Staff scored 82 percent for resident influence while residents scored only 55 percent for the same scale.

Figure 6.2
Social Climate Resources for Wood Glen

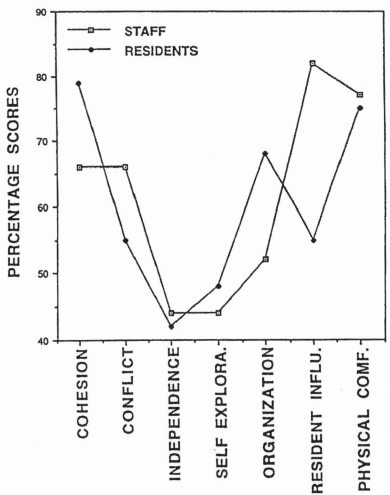

At Kramer, the outcomes between residents and staff were much more extreme. As Figure 6.3 shows, staff and residents had agreement on only one of the seven SCES dimensions. Scores for cohesion, conflict, and resident influence all show significant differences between staff and residents. Residents' average score for the resident influence dimension was 31 percent while the score for staff was 66 percent. Staff perceived that residents had twice as much ability to influence rules and policies as residents did.

Figure 6.3
Social Climate Resources for Kramer

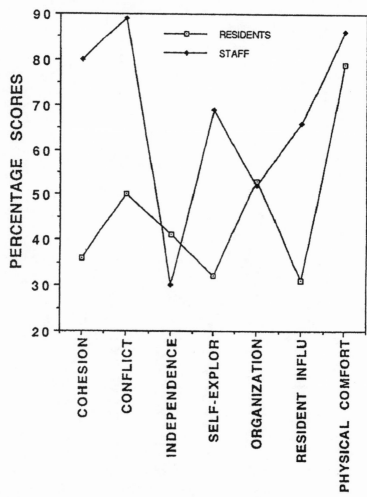

Residents reported that their overall level of conflict was 50 percent. How-ever, staff rated resident conflict at 89 percent. Cohesion is the subscale dimen-sion showing the most divergence at Kramer. Residents scored 36 percent for their sense of resident cohesion at Kramer while staff scored residents at 80 per-cent. This represents a 44 percent difference between staff and residents' im-pressions of the level of social cohesion at Kramer. At first glance, it appears contradictory for staff to score residents so high for both cohesion and conflict. I believe the explanation for some of this contradiction lies within the ques-tions themselves. As discussed above, the vast majority of the SCES questions place the responsibility for the quality of the social environment on residents.

Since the scales measure perceptions of staff and residents, we can look to the questions within the scales to explain some of the discrepancies.

Cohesion and conflict measure two very different, nearly antithetical types of behavior. Therefore, it is improbable that someone who believes there is a high level of cohesion would think the same for conflict. But, if we examine the nine questions related to the cohesion subscale, three of the questions mention staff directly and a total of seven questions relate to staff behavior and responsibility (e.g., "Do staff members spend a lot of time with residents?").

Cohesion Questions from SCES

1. Do residents get a lot of individual attention?
2. Do staff members spend a lot of time with residents?
3. Do staff members sometimes talk down to residents?
4. Are there a lot of social activities?
5. Do a lot of the residents just seem to be passing time here?
6. Are requests made by residents usually taken care of right away?
7. Do staff members sometimes criticize residents over minor things?
8. Do residents tend to keep to themselves here?
9. Are the discussions very interesting?

Taking into account the nature of the cohesion subscale questions, we may now analyze the scores more accurately. Kramer residents scored 36 percent for cohesion, a subscale that is largely staff centered (as evidenced by these nine questions). The staff scored 80 percent for the cohesion subscale. The differences in scores between the two groups point to strong differences in perception. Kramer residents discern that staff is not doing an adequate job of fulfilling their responsibilities. Conversely, the staff perceives that they are performing quite well.

The reverse scenario occurred for the conflict dimension. First, of the nine conflict questions, eight mention residents specifically and none of the questions mention staff.

Conflict Subscale Questions

1. Do residents ever start arguments?
2. Is it unusual for residents to openly express their anger?
3. Do residents sometimes criticize or make fun of this place?
4. Do residents usually keep their disagreements to themselves?
5. Is it unusual for residents to complain about each other?

6. Is it always peaceful and quiet here?

7. Do residents often get impatient with each other?

8. Do residents complain a lot?

9. Do residents criticize each other a lot?

These subjective questions target resident behavior only. Comparing scores for residents and staff, we can see the opposite trend from the cohesion subscale discussed previously. Residents' perceived level of conflict among themselves was 50 percent at Kramer. Staff, however, perceived an 89 percent level of conflict among residents, a much higher number than residents expressed.

The scores for cohesion and conflict demonstrate that staff and residents have more positive perceptions of their *own* responsibility and role in the social environment. Staff had high scores for cohesion, a dimension with many questions related to them, while they also noted a high level of conflict, a dimension based solely on resident behaviors and interactions. Both groups viewed the other as more responsible for the *negative aspects* of the social environment. The questions themselves are partly responsible for this outcome because they suggest two troublesome assumptions: (1) if there is a high level of cohesion in an assisted living setting, it is due to staff; and (2) if there is a high level of conflict in an assisted living community, it is due to residents.

Now, I would like to compare residents from Wood Glen and Kramer on the SCES dimensions. Insights gained from residents' perspectives reinforce many of the policy concerns raised throughout this chapter. Figure 6.4 indicates a significant difference between Kramer and Wood Glen residents for many of the seven dimensions. Kramer residents scored lower on all dimensions except independence and physical comfort. Kramer and Wood Glen residents exhibited exactly the same independence level scores (41%), indicating that residents at both sites perceive their fellow co-habitants as moderately independent. Wood Glen and Kramer exhibited very similar scores for physical comfort, 75 percent and 79 percent respectively. The disparity between the five remaining dimensions is more striking when we examine them separately. By narrowing the focus to specific SCES questions within the dimensions, I call attention to the policy-related issues most meaningful to residents in both assisted living communities.

Scholars of assisted living and providers in the assisted living industry are both quite concerned with whether a homelike environment can be created in assisted living communities. Therefore, it is pertinent to isolate two of the questions addressing the issue of physical comfort in order to understand if assisted living proponents are reaching their goal. The two questions are as follows: "Is the furniture here comfortable and homey?" and "Do the colors and decorations make this a warm and cheerful place?" Combining resident re-

Figure 6.4
Social Climate Resources for Wood Glen and Kramer Residents

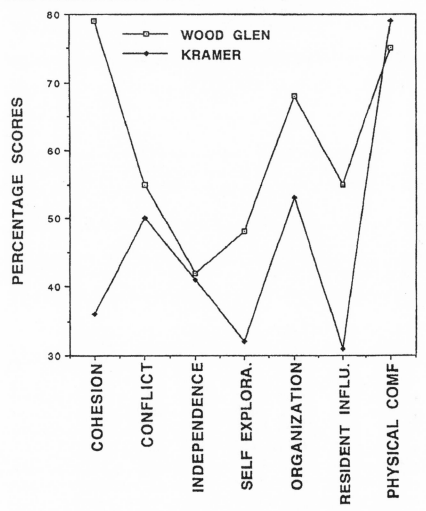

sponses from both sites, 95 percent of inhabitants said "yes" to the first question and 90 percent said "yes" to the second question. Evidently, residents at Kramer and Wood Glen are quite satisfied with their physical environment. These results reinforce residents' comments from chapters 2 and 5 that the physical design is among the least of their concerns in assisted living.

In the domain of conflict, there are some interesting contradictions between responses to questions. I have isolated two questions below in order to analyze the relationship between them: "Do residents ever start arguments?" and "Do residents usually keep their disagreements to themselves?" When measuring the presence of conflict among residents, Moos and Lemke report that the responses should be "yes" for the first question and "no" for question two as evidence of a high level of conflict. Seemingly, these two questions would force a response of either yes/no or no/yes. Yet, this was not the case among residents at Kramer and Wood Glen. First, a profile cannot even be drawn for residents at Wood Glen because 50 percent of residents surveyed chose not to answer either one or both of these questions. This fact is interesting in itself.

As for Kramer, the results were divergent. A total of 38 percent of Kramer residents answered "yes" to both questions—meaning that residents tend to start arguments while at the same time they usually keep to themselves. Who is starting all these arguments if residents are keeping their disagreements to themselves? A total of 31 percent of Kramer residents said "yes," residents do start arguments, and "no," residents do not tend to keep their disagreements to themselves. In addition, 23 percent of Kramer residents answered "no" to the first question and "yes" to the second question, meaning that residents do not tend to start arguments and they do keep disagreements to themselves. The divergent numbers indicate an interesting pattern of resident responses at Kramer. For many of the questions, Kramer residents were fairly evenly split with opposing viewpoints. For instance, one SCES question was, "Are residents careful about what they say to each other?" Fifty-seven percent of Kramer residents said "yes" to this question, while 43 percent said "no." On such subjective questions it is interesting to note the lack of consensus.

Yet another question in the conflict domain yielded a similar result. The question asked, "Is it unusual for residents to openly express their anger?" Forty-six percent of residents said "yes" and 54 percent said "no." Finally, a separate question on the SCES related to conflict asked, "Is it hard to tell how the residents are feeling?" There was little accord in the responses here. Forty percent of Kramer residents said "yes" and 60 percent said "no." What do these different answers indicate?

One possible explanation for the division in resident responses at Kramer is that these numbers represent two distinct groups: those who are actively involved at Kramer and those who isolate themselves from the rest of the group. Even if this were the case, it still does not fully explain these divided responses. After all, how can residents be so isolated at a small place like Kramer that they could not perceive whether or not residents start arguments? How can half of the residents perceive that their fellow residents do not express their anger and half say they do? Maybe all of these responses support the very low level of cohesion at Kramer. They also suggest ambiguity among some of the questions.

There were several questions on the SCES that exhibited almost unanimous agreement between residents at Kramer and Wood Glen. Question number twenty-nine on the SCES is, "Do a lot of residents just seem to be passing time here?" The responses were very revealing. Of those who answered this question, 83 percent said "yes." The vast majority of residents at Kramer and Wood Glen discern that many co-habitants are merely "sitting idle" in assisted living. Importantly, this question had one of the highest agreement factors of all sixty-three questions. Residents may have disagreed on many points but most of them answered "yes" to this particular question, thus illustrating a strong sense of their own liminality. As was mentioned in chapter 5, Booth (1983) and Wilkin and Hughes (1987) reported similar findings from their research on homes for the aged in England.

Another question on the SCES showing great consensus among the answers was, "Do residents often get impatient with each other?" Seventy percent of those answering the question said "yes." Finally, question twenty-five from the SCES asked, "Do residents talk much about their fears?" The answer to this question showed the most consensus of the sixty-three-question SCES with ninety percent of residents saying "no."

These scores do not suggest a positive atmosphere. Residents generally seem to see each other in a negative light and believe that others stay alone and do not share problems and feelings with each other. These quantitative responses support qualitative data revealed throughout the book.

The Sheltered Care Environment Scale also asks residents about their perceptions of policies in their assisted living sites. A particular question asks residents, "Are things sometimes unclear around here" (in reference to policies and procedures)? The results show that 65 percent of residents at Kramer and Wood Glen believe that policies are sometimes unclear in their communities. In addition, residents are pessimistic about their own capacity to change vague policies in their residences. Residents were asked, "Can residents change things here if they really try?" Of those who answered, 44 percent said "no." Nearly half of Wood Glen and Kramer residents do not believe they have the power to change rules and policies in their domicile.

It is important to point out that residents at Kramer and Wood Glen experienced a real quandary when completing the surveys. Residents repeatedly told me that they thought the questionnaire was problematic. First, residents informed me that they perceived many of the questions to be very ambiguous. For instance, question number thirty-two asks, "Is it hard to tell how the residents are feeling?" Residents were not sure if the question was referring to their health or their emotions. Another example of a problematic question is, "Do some residents look messy? Wood Glen resident Susanna Frost told me, "yes, I think so, but maybe some people think I look messy" (interview by author, tape recording, Chicago, Illinois, 21 December 1992). In other words, she believes that type of question is too subjective.

The other major problem residents had with the survey was that they thought several of the questions merited both a "yes" and a "no" response. For instance, question number thirty-four asks, "Are suggestions made by the residents acted upon?" Residents told me "sometimes." Several respondents circled both yes and no for several questions. Residents summed up their opinion of the SCES with the statement that "some questions were difficult to answer." Had I not been conducting qualitative interviews with residents, I might have felt much more concern about ambiguous responses on this survey. Residents' comments about the SCES simply reinforced to me the need for in-depth interviews and participant observation, along with the survey.

Overall, residents' answers to the SCES survey illustrate their confusion and mixed feelings about each other and about the policies at Wood Glen and Kramer. Policies are created to clarify issues for residents but, as illustrated through residents' answers and data regarding marketing materials and resident contracts, residents at Kramer and Wood Glen appear to be perplexed. Perhaps the most confounding issue for residents as well as providers continues to be aging in place.

AGING IN PLACE: POLICIES AND PERSPECTIVES

The last part of this chapter focuses on aging in place and its connection to marketing material, residency contracts, regulations, policies, and the philosophy of assisted living. Because such friction exists surrounding aging in place it is important to analyze it from these various viewpoints.

Marketing materials such as brochures and advertisements can mislead family and residents about the ability to age in place in assisted living. Much of this deception is unintentional and is often due to vague wording in ads and brochures. Currently "aging in place" appears to be a popular buzz phrase in both trade journals and academic publications (ALFA 1999; NCAL 2001; Mollica and Snow 1996; Regnier 1991; Wagner 1995; Fisher 1995; Yee et al. 1999; Zaner 1997; Consumer Consortium for Assisted Living 1996; Kane and Wilson 1993). The problem is that many marketers use this phrase in their publications and either (1) do not define it; or (2) do not know what it means; or (3) both. The lack of understanding about what it means to age in place can cause a great strain on potential residents and their families. Marketers use this phrase to retail their community but may not follow through with it. "A major selling point for assisted living is offering consumers the ability to age in place, but aging in place can be a misnomer. Advertisements frequently lead prospective residents to assume that they can remain in the assisted living facility as long as they want, no matter how frail they become" (Siemon, Edelstein, and Dresner 1996:581). The thought of aging in place is often what gives potential residents and family members peace of mind, knowing (or thinking) that "no matter how sick 'mom' gets, she can stay here until she dies." This is not the reality for the majority of consumers of assisted living. The promise to "age in place" in assisted living does not materialize because marketers and industry representatives really mean *prolonged residence* when they talk of aging in place. Part of the reason is that the vast majority of providers see assisted living as simply one slot on the continuum of care. So, when one assisted living community advertising in *Assisted Living Today* claims, "Our unique vision of assisted living allows our residents to age in place by meeting their changing personal and health care needs," it does not mean *full* aging in place. The ad actually goes on to say, "Our assisted living facilities serve as a foundation to provide a continuum of care for our residents." This is not aging in place in assisted living. However, ads such as this one are not seen by the assisted living industry as problematic because "aging in place" in most operators' view is a temporary thing; staving off nursing home placement for as long as possible rather than fully aging in place in assisted living.

A 2001 study by Chapin and Dobbs-Kepper support my findings. In their research of assisted living settings in Kansas, they state, "the findings on admission and retention policies regarding physical and cognitive suggest that assisted living is serving as part of a continuum of care rather than a setting where residents can age in place and remain until death" (Chapin and Dobbs-Kepper 2001:48).

In a wider scope, what does the marketing material tell consumers and their families about aging in place? When looking closely at trade journal publications one sees mixed messages. *Provider* magazine interviewed John Knutson, vice president of operations for Leisure Care in Washington State. When asked about aging in place Knutson said,

Providers across the country all have a different attitude and approach to aging in place. . . . Many see assisted living and aging in place as a replacement for all other methods of housing and care for seniors. Other providers, whose focus is on retirement housing, have a tendency to think of assisted living as just a part of the continuum of care and believe that when residents become too mentally or physically frail, they should go to a nursing facility or some other arrangement that provides a more skilled level of care. (Wagner 1995:55)

Knutson points out that some interpret aging in place one way and some interpret it another way. However, based on an extensive literature review, the majority of providers in the assisted living industry are interpreting aging in place as prolonged residence. One representative from the Arizona Association of Homes for the Aging claims, "[W]e need to promote aging in place, but only to a point" (Rajecki 1992:48). What point might this be? Who determines this point? How does an assisted living residence communicate this "point" to potential residents?

Aging in place is often portrayed in a contrary manner, based on the setting in which the older person resides. When speaking of an elderly woman in her own home, the interpretation of aging in place is literal: residing there until she dies. When describing aging in place in assisted living (or any other housing for seniors) the definition for most operators of assisted living becomes prolonged residence. A resident can only stay until an undetermined point in time when the assisted living administrators and staff decide they can no longer sustain the resident. The resident must then go somewhere else to die.

Some organizations have attempted to contain the confusion surrounding aging in place by avoiding use of the term all together. According to the National Center for Assisted Living (NCAL), "Once used to describe a commitment to minimize the need to move, the phrase 'aging in place' has evolved to mean different things to different people. To prevent any consumer confusion or misunderstanding, NCAL discourages the use of the phrase 'aging in place' unless accompanied by an explanation that includes any health-related occupancy restrictions mandated by the residence and/or state regulation" (NCAL 2000:2). NCAL believes that providers should not use aging in place without a careful explanation of what this term means in that particular assisted living setting. Trying to prevent confusion among consumers is an admirable idea. However, trade journals and scholarly articles still use the phrase "aging in place" throughout their publications, and at this point, family members and consumers are familiar with the phrase from advertisements and marketing brochures. Further, if this phrase is going to bring in new residents to an assisted living community, operators are not going to stop using it. NCAL states that if providers in the industry wish to continue using the phrase "aging in place," then they need to define it based on the caveat in the above quotation. This statement is a paradox because when such restrictions exist, then aging in place is actually prolonged residence. "Part of the dilemma surrounding aging in place stems from the industry's attempt to manage it" (Wagner 1995:55). How can full aging in place be managed? Only prolonged residence can be managed. Perhaps the real reason assisted living providers try to "manage" aging in place is because they wish to manage *dying in place*. I return to this issue in the next chapter.

A recent study by Hawes, Phillips, and Rose (2000) shows disturbing repercussions that have emerged from the confusing marketing literature and vague resident contracts. Hawes et al. conducted research on 300 assisted living settings that qualified as either High Service or High Privacy assisted living sites (these are considered the highest quality assisted living sites).[2] Using a representative sample of residents from High Privacy and High Service assisted living sites, the researchers sought to gather information on residents' under-standing of discharge policies and aging in place. Their findings are alarming. "Less than one-third of the residents in the study (30%) reported being in-formed of their facility's discharge policies. Thus, almost 70% were unin-formed about conditions under which they might be discharged from the facility" (p. 32).

Residents' families were also tapped for their knowledge of discharge poli-cies. A total of 32 percent of families "reported that they either did not know whether the facility had policies about discharge (17%), or that the facility had no such policies (15%)" (Hawes, Phillips, and Rose 2000:33). Of the family members who claimed they did know of the existence of discharge policies, many felt the policies were somewhat to very unclear.

According to assisted living expert Robert Mollica, "consumer expectations are shaped by marketing materials and resident agreements, and clear and un-derstandable agreements promote satisfaction with and understanding of as-sisted living" (Mollica 2001:18). Here, Mollica directly links resident happiness with their receipt of clear information provided by the assisted living community. Perhaps many residents are not as satisfied with assisted living as they could be because they are not provided with clear and understandable agreements, especiallly in the domain of discharge criteria.

More disquieting than the data on discharge policies were Hawes et al.'s data on beliefs about aging in place. In spite of the fact that both residents and family members voiced confusion and concern regarding discharge policies, most were confident about residents' ability to remain in assisted living (to age in place). An astounding 98.2 percent of residents surveyed believed that "they would be able to reside in their present ALF [assisted living facility] for as long as they wished" (p. 33). Almost every assisted living resident asked thought he or she could fully age in place. Further, family members concurred. Eighty-nine per-cent of family members surveyed expected that "their relative would be able to stay at the ALF as long as they wanted the relative to stay" (p. 33).

Carder's 2002 study of marketing literature failing to address againg in place by way of discharge criteria on asssisted living shows an even more startling ex-ample. When examining the marketing materials for sixty-three assisted living settings in Oregon (considered by many to be the most progressive state for as-sisted living) "only one out of 63 facilities addressed the issue of potential moves" (Carder 2002:117). Only one out of 63! By failing to address the po-tential criteria for eviction, these sites are misleading residents and family members about the ability to fully age in place in their settings.

In the midst of confusing marketing literature and vague policies, assisted living residents and their families are thoroughly convinced that residents can stay there until they die. Are marketers, operators, and regulators aware of this fact? Evidently not.

Thus it appears that the topic of aging in place continues to be confounded by marketing literature, community policies, and state regulations. If full aging in place is going to occur, providers and the assisted living industry as a whole must support it. According to Bill Lasky, president of Alternative Living Services and member of the ALFA Leadership Council, "[A]ssisted living operators have to address their responsibility to allow residents to age in place. I don't know why when someone needs more services they need a change of address" (Fisher 1995:63). Lin Noyes, director of Family Respite Care Center in Virginia, agrees: "Though aging in place is what we all want, assisted living facilities must provide services to allow a person to do that in order for that ideal to be a reality" (Wagner 1995:67). The question remains, Is aging in place what all providers truly want? If so, why is it not occurring? These questions set the stage for the final chapter of this book and a critical look at the true meaning of aging in place.

NOTES

1. It should be noted that I, too, used this term in my writing until recently. However, the more I thought about the purpose of assisted living and its philosophy, it became apparent that "facility" is an inappropriate term to use for this residential option.

2. Hawes, Phillips, and Rose (2000) used criteria for inclusion in either the High Privacy or High Service categories. Minimal qualifications for High Privacy were that "80%–100% of the units were private" (p. 17). In order to qualify as High Service, the assisted living site had to provide at least the following:

- 24-hour staff oversight
- housekeeping
- at least two meals a day
- personal assistance, defined as help with at least two of the following: medications, bathing, or dressing
- at least one full-time registered nurse (RN) on staff
- nursing care (monitoring or services) with its own staff. (p. 17)

CHAPTER 7

Sitting Here in Limbo:
Aging in Place in Assisted Living

Assisted living is a complex residential option for seniors that evokes conflicting perspectives from the different players associated with it. Aging in place in assisted living could be perceived as an intricate puzzle whose pieces somehow fit together to create a complete whole, meeting needs for residents, their families, and providers. This book has been an attempt to put the pieces together. The overarching question for the last chapter of this book is, "How do the pieces fit together (both conceptually and in practice)?" Before answering this question, several pieces of the puzzle must be reexamined to reveal their interlocking nature and to link them to the issue of aging in place in assisted living.

This chapter critically examines the holistic picture of aging in place in assisted living. Beginning with the concept of home and the philosophy of assisted living as building blocks, I then turn to the notion of autonomy and its critical role in the lives of seniors in group-living arrangements. From here, residents' experiences at Wood Glen and Kramer are utilized to see if the concept of autonomy is actualized in assisted living or if it is hindered by internalization of the elderly mystique by both residents and staff. Further, how do residents' feelings of liminality prevent them from seeing assisted living as their home? These pieces will then be placed next to assisted living policies and the issues of regulation: Do these two segments match or create a schism in the puzzle of aging in place? What picture is created? Is it merely prolonged residence? If so, what does this mean for the future of this residential option and especially for those who must live with the reality of this puzzle, even if the pieces do not conform to the idealized notion of assisted living.

THE MEANING OF HOME AND THE PHILOSOPHY OF ASSISTED LIVING

As discussed in chapter 2, there are two levels to the concept of home. First, there is home as a physical structure, a dwelling where we live and feel comfortable to express ourselves. Second, there is the deeper level of a *sense of home*. Here, home is disconnected from a specific place and conveys emotions, relationships, and identity. The first level of home could be referred to as the *product* (a place, a thing), while the second level is *process* oriented (a positive evaluation or mental state) (Rapoport 1995).

The assisted living industry is trying hard to sell assisted living as *home* to older adults and their families. Marketers attempt to retail *both* the product *and* the process of home to a population of older adults who might otherwise end up in more institutional environments. While the idea is somewhat commendable, is it reasonable to believe that assisted living providers should sell the processual aspects of home, even if they cannot deliver these things to residents once they move in? The mental states involved in the process domain of home involve "feelings of security, control, being at ease and relaxed and are related to . . . family, kinship, comfort, friendship . . . and other positive attributes" (Rapoport 1995:29). Much of the marketing and trade journal literature purports to supply these processual aspects of assisted living to its inhabitants. How can this be? Much like "aging in place," the words "home" and "homelike" are used as buzz phrases. Does the industry have an idea of the vastness of what they are promising residents when they promise them "home?" I do not believe so, mainly because many providers do not fully understand or embrace the philosophy of assisted living discussed throughout this book.

What is fascinating about the depth of home as a concept among researchers is that many of the core components found in the concept of home are the *same exact* core components embodied in the philosophy of assisted living. In order to illustrate the impact of this finding, I present a comparison of these two concepts below. I begin by fleshing out the various dimensions of "home."

According to researchers (Hayward 1977; Dovey 1978; Sebba and Churchman 1986; Despres 1991; Brummett 1998), there are many dimensions that compose the notion of "home." Brummett (1998) asserts that there exist six separate dimensions of home, some of which refer to functions of the physical dwelling, while others are concerned with emotional or relational connections. These dimensions include: (1) self-projection/identity/self-symbol (called individuality and self-identity by other researchers); (2) connectedness/belonging (also referred to as relationship with others and community building); (3) a vessel of memory and soul (also known as continuity); (4) privacy/territoriality (also referred to as refuge); (5) control/autonomy; and (6) choice/opportunity.

Based on a thorough investigation of the assisted living literature, I found a significant parallel between the above definitions of home and the philosophy of assisted living. *Almost every dimension mentioned above is also considered an important dimension in the philosophy of assisted living.* To more clearly illustrate this point, I have developed the following diagram. In Table 7.1, I have listed the domains of home mentioned above. Then, next to this I have created a heading titled *Philosophy of Assisted Living.* Under this heading I have written the names of authors who have articulated their philosophy of assisted living and in the process have used the *exact* term shown in column one. Of the six dimensions of home, only "vessel of memory and soul" had no equivalent listed in the philosophy of assisted living descriptions. Among the other five dimensions of home, privacy is cited most often under the philosophy of assisted living followed by choice and autonomy. Clearly, these three concepts are regarded as critical to the philosophy of assisted living. It is interesting to note that privacy is the term cited most often as strategic to the philosophy of assisted living (as well as the concept of home) because privacy is sorely lacking in many assisted living sites. As seen in several national assisted living surveys, assisted living dwelling units are frequently shared spaces (with as many as *four* people sharing a room in some states). According to Hawes, Rose, and Phillips (1999), only 27 percent of assisted living communities have all private rooms on site and 45 percent of the sites surveyed said they had some shared rooms on site.[1] Additionally, less than two-thirds (or 62%) of the 1,251 providers surveyed had private *full* bathrooms (i.e., sink, toilet, and shower or tub) in their assisted living communities. Further, more than one-third (38%) of assisted living sites require residents to share a bathroom. Therefore, there seems to be little privacy in assisted living sites although the idea of privacy is so central to the philosophy of assisted living. And, if privacy is also a key dimension of home, then we can certainly begin to understand why so many residents do not consider assisted living their home: they have no privacy.

Autonomy is a second dimension of home that plays a pivotal role in the philosophy of assisted living. Because autonomy is so highly emphasized as a value in both the academic and trade literature on assisted living, I would like to turn the focus below to an in-depth analysis of autonomy. What is it? How do elders assert it? Why do so many residents in assisted living believe they possess such a minimal amount of it?

Autonomy for Elders in Institutional Environments

Those who determine their own ends (at least to some degree) are recognized as having the dignity that moral agency bestows. Moreover, from the agents' own point of view autonomy promotes self-esteem. (Young 1986:2)

Table 7.1

A Comparison of Home and the Philosophy of Assisted Living

Home	*Philosophy of Assisted Living*
1. Self-projection/identity/self-symbol/ (Individuality/self identity)	ALFA 2000—"individuality" Manard et al. 1992—individuality Carder 2002—individuality
2. Connectedness/belonging (Relationship w/others, community)	Manard et al. 1992—"community" ALFA 2000—community
3. Privacy/territoriality (Refuge)	Wilson 1996—"privacy" ALQC 1998—privacy Manard et al. 1992—privacy Regnier 1991—privacy Mollica et al. 1992—privacy Clemmer 1995—privacy ALFA 2000—privacy GAO 1997—privacy Carder 2002—privacy
4. Vessel of memory and soul	———
5. Control/autonomy	ALQC 1998—"autonomy" Chapin and Dobbs-Kepper 2001— "control" CCAL 1996—autonomy Wilson 1996—autonomy Manard et al. 1992—autonomy Regnier 1991—autonomy Clemmer 1995—autonomy
6. Choice/opportunity	NCAL 2001—"choice" Regnier 1991—choice Mollica et al. 1992—choice GAO 1997—choice Clemmer 1995—choice ALFA 2000—choice

My discussion of assisted living residents would not be complete without an analysis of *autonomy*. This term is complex because it is accompanied by many value-laden ideas. It is also seen by some in black and white terms—either an "all or nothing" scenario. It is important to realize that this extreme should not be used as the archetype of autonomy, especially when speaking of frail older adults. According to Collopy (1988), autonomy needs to be seen as "a notional field, a loose system of inter-orbiting concepts that trace out the varied paths of self-determination. Accordingly, autonomy is understood as a cluster of notions including self-determination, freedom, independence, liberty of choice and action" (p. 10).

The paradoxical nature of autonomy for frail older adults warrants closer scrutiny. Frail older adults, especially those living in long-term care settings, frequently require care from others. This reality tends to contradict our basic definition of autonomy as "self-rule." Although needing care should not mean surrendering autonomy, it often does for seniors. This is partially due to the fact that caregivers looking after older adults often unintentionally override residents' autonomy in the guise of looking out for the seniors' best interests. Part of the reason why this occurs is due to the tensions that are inherent within the cluster of notions that make up the concept of *autonomy.*

There are a number of dichotomies that exist when looking at older adults in long-term care environments. First is the polarity between decisional versus executional autonomy. According to Collopy (1988), decisional autonomy refers to having preferences and making decisions, while executional autonomy refers to the ability to implement decisions or carry out preferences. Historically, long-term care environments have focused on executional autonomy: "Can the patient complete a task himself or herself?" This focus on executional autonomy for older adults has tended to negate decisional autonomy all together. However, "decisional autonomy can exist without the ability or freedom to execute decisions" (Collopy 1988:11). Individuals may still possess the capacity to be intellectually autonomous while being unable to act (perhaps because of mobility limitations or compromised health). The resident or "patient" of a long-term care environment should not face the abrogation of decisional autonomy simply because he or she is unable to execute it. This dichotomy is perhaps the most basic to understand when considering frail elderly people, such as those residing in assisted living. "For the elderly in long term care, this is, then a pivotal distinction with advancing frailty, autonomy of execution frequently shrinks or disappears completely. Consequently, if autonomy is defined principally in terms of execution, the frail elderly will be relegated to a non-autonomous status" (p. 11). The need for assistance should not mean diminished autonomy. Philosophically, assisted living is based on this principle (promoting autonomy by involving the resident as much as possible in the decision-making process). In reality, however, sometimes residents themselves internalize the idea that executional autonomy is exclusively linked with decisional autonomy. Kramer resident Helen Finks frequently relinquishes her decisional autonomy because of her executional limitations. Helen uses a walker for ambulatory assistance. When I asked her about her participation in the group outings that Kramer offers, she said, "No. I feel a bit more helpless because of my walker . . . I don't want to bother anybody, so I don't sign up for the trips" (interview by author, Chicago, Illinois, 16 March 1993). Helen could still participate in group trips with a bit of assistance. But, since Helen cannot "execute" her plans without assistance, she makes her choices based on feeling a bit "more helpless," thus limiting her decisional autonomy.

The second polarity in autonomy for the frail elderly is direct versus delegated autonomy. When exercising direct autonomy, people are acting on their own behalf when making decisions regarding their care. By contrast, delegated autonomy involves the involvement of other persons by "authorizing others to make decisions and carry out activities in their place" (Collopy 1988:12). Residential settings for seniors tend to focus on direct autonomy as a sign of residents' independence and capabilities. Administrators may perceive the delegation of autonomy as "acquiescence," which, therefore, translates into dependency in the eyes of many care providers. What often goes unrecognized is the fact that the frail senior exercised autonomy when he or she made the decision to ask others for assistance or input.

As illustrated throughout this book, many providers (including those at Wood Glen and Kramer) do not validate delegated autonomy. Instead, they see delegation as a signal of growing dependency. By contrast, however, there are many situations at Kramer and Wood Glen where staff and administrators have taken away opportunities for both direct and delegated autonomy. By taking care of laundry and cleaning responsibilities, providers believe they are helping residents in their daily lives. Nonetheless, residents may experience this as a removal of their direct autonomy and believe they have too much time on their hands to do nothing. Another example can be seen in the realm of meals and food preparation. Meals in group settings occur every day at a designated time. This may seem necessary for feeding a group of people; however, there are no cooking apparatuses present at Kramer or Wood Glen. Therefore, residents do not even have the choice to exercise *either* direct autonomy (by cooking for themselves or eating when they want) or delegated autonomy (by telling others what or when they want to eat).

Another disparity is between what are referred to as competent autonomy and incapacitated autonomy.

This is the most highly sanctioned and widely discussed distinction in the area of autonomy. Competent autonomy is choice or behavior that is informed, rationally defensible, and judgmentally effective in choosing appropriate means to desired ends. Incapacitated autonomy consists in choice or activity that is substantially uninformed, unreasonable, or judgmentally unsound. The distinction is crucial because incapacity, when it leads to harmful choice, provides defensible grounds for intervening in the choice and behavior of the elderly. (Collopy 1988:13)

Obviously, competent and incapacitated autonomy can be used to refer to those seniors with diminished cognitive capacity. However, before focusing on seniors with cognitive problems, we should first focus on another part of competent or incapacitated autonomy.

In order to understand whether one has decisional capacity, it is necessary to examine *authentic* versus *inauthentic* autonomy. When a person makes decisions that reflect his or her true history, personality, and norms, then the decision is said to represent *authentic autonomy.* For example, Wood Glen resident Tillie Von Deurst explained to me that she likes to participate in solitary activities: piano playing, reading, and walking in the neighborhood. So, her decision not to participate in scheduled activities would be representative of Tillie's true nature: independent and solitary.

By contrast, *inauthentic autonomy* represents a course of action or behaviors that show serious discontinuity from the person's illustrative values, history, and previous patterns. If an assisted living resident makes a decision that seems "irrational" to staff, one must examine the situation closely in order to deduce authenticity versus inauthenticity. Authenticity challenges staff and administrators to focus on the *person* as an individual, not what is "reasonable" based on societal standards or the desires of staff. In order for one to determine whether a decision is authentic for the person making the decision, it is necessary for the persons involved to *know* the resident: know his or her personality, likes and dislikes, attitudes about certain issues. It is impossible to assess whether or not the decision the resident makes is authentic without an interactive relationship with the older adult. In the previous example, one would have to spend time with Tillie Von Deurst, and have gotten to know her personality and preferences, in order to realize that her decision to avoid group activities is authentic for *her*. Contrast this scenario with that of Katie Jacobs. When she first moved to Kramer, Katie said she would participate in almost all of the planned activities. But now, she does not. "You know, I used to go to everything that they [Kramer] took us to [shows, concerts, shopping]. I used to love it. I used to love the singing. I used to love everything that we did [at Kramer]. Now I don't get a kick out of it. Once in a great while I go, and it doesn't interest me anymore" (interview by author, tape recording, Chicago, Illinois, 27 October 1992). Katie's recent decision to stop participating in group activities is very likely an exercise of *inauthentic* autonomy. Katie may be depressed or becoming ill. But again, staff would need to have a relationship with Katie in order to know her history, personality, and norms. This knowledge would be critical to decipher the fact that Katie's decision not to participate in activities may represent inauthentic autonomy.

Notions of authentic and inauthentic autonomy are naturally made more complicated by the presence of cognitive incapacity. I now return to the issue of competent versus incapacitated autonomy. It is currently estimated that between 30 and 40 percent of assisted living residents suffer from some form of cognitive impairment (Hyde 2001; Hawes, Rose, and Phillips 1999). How to approach autonomy for those with Alzheimer's disease and related dementias is a critical issue that will require increasing attention in the immediate future. Special care and training will certainly be needed in order to prevent staff and caregivers from over-reacting to residents' perceived irrational decisions. However, the topic of training staff to distinguish between competent and incapacitated autonomy in cases of cognitive impairment is beyond the scope of the present book. Therefore, I would like to turn to a comparison of immediate and long-range autonomy.

A frequent area of conflict between long-term care residents and administrators is immediate versus long-range autonomy. Immediate autonomy is very present oriented. An older adult may choose immediate freedom, instead of making choices based on future options and long-range considerations. As noted earlier in the book, many residents at Kramer and Wood Glen opt solely for immediate autonomy, sacrificing the possibility of integrating these two polarities (Collopy 1988). Throughout this volume residents from Kramer and Wood Glen have illustrated the inherent stresses between choosing for "today" or a "tomorrow" that may never come. Unfortunately, assisted living residents frequently see immediate versus long-range autonomy as mutually exclusive as do many developers of assisted living. They are anxious to plan assisted living settings and to have seniors move in. However, they do not plan for long-range health complications, resident wants, and individual choices. By its very nature, assisted living muddies immediate versus long-range autonomy because residents and administrators do not know exactly what kind of "long range" plans they should be making. Residents do not know how long they can remain in assisted living, so they may be much more willing to grab for immediate autonomy (as evidenced through their harsh comments about the frailty of their fellow residents) rather than plan for an indefinite future. "Present choice can delimit or thwart future choice; autonomous action in one area of life can foreclose on such action in another area" (Collopy 1988:15).

By contrast, many providers of care discourage immediate autonomy. "Long-term care professionals are primarily committed to long-range autonomy for the elderly, immediate choice or behavior which threatens this autonomy will seem ripe for well-intentioned intervention" (p. 15). For residents at Wood Glen and Kramer, perhaps the most striking contrast between immediate versus long-range autonomy is their desire to have ailing residents removed from assisted living *now* (immediate autonomy), even if this decision means that they are sacrificing their *own* long-range autonomy (the ability to stay in assisted living themselves) by supporting a policy that removes those who require increasing assistance.

Immediate versus long-range autonomy is even more conflicted in an assisted living environment because of the confusion surrounding aging in place. Because residents will most likely experience *prolonged residence* rather than full aging in place, they may feel forced to opt for immediate autonomy because they know their long-range autonomy is precarious at best. Why choose long-range autonomy when they do not know how long they will be allowed to remain in assisted living? Conversely, staff and administrators tend to push for long-range autonomy by encouraging residents to make plans and set goals for the future. The goals may be physical in nature, such as improving a resident's mobility to the point where he or she can ambulate with a cane instead of a walker.

Autonomy in institutions is sometimes viewed as a paradox. How can an older adult be autonomous when so many rules and regulations surround him or her? If one examines the daily routines of seniors in long-term care settings, one can see many features of Goffman's *total institution* (1961). As discussed in Chapter 2, assisted living environments, like nursing homes, possess many features of total institutions. For example, people residing in total institutions carry on almost all of their activities while surrounded by others. And, "unlike persons outside of the nursing home, patients did not choose the people with whom to spend their days" (Lidz and Arnold 1990:66). Several residents at Kramer and Wood Glen pointed out this fact as a reason why they do not see assisted living as "home." Recall Sara Vernon who said about her fellow Wood Glen residents, "These are all strangers to me and they will forever be strangers to me" (interview by author, tape recording, Chicago, Illinois, 18 November 1992). Other scholars have found similar situations in the elderly housing settings they research. "Boredom and inactivity generate frustration, which leads to irritability and places a strain on personal relationships in the residential setting. This problem is aggravated by the fact that residents have no voice in choosing with whom they live" (Booth 1983:31).

Another inhibitor of autonomy is the strict scheduling found in total institutions. Although assisted living attempts to distance itself from institutional life, much of what goes on there is similar to what goes on in nursing homes. In assisted living meals are served at certain times, activities occur at certain times, and transportation is available at certain times. It is understandable that scheduling can make things easier for staff and even for some residents. However, often this is not what occurs in one's own *home*. For many residents of assisted living, the last time they experienced this much regimentation in their lives was when they were children.

Autonomy in assisted living can be greatly affected by a lack of privacy, another prominent feature of total institutions. As stated at the beginning of the chapter, privacy is emphasized as a key component of both home and the philosophy of assisted living. There seems to be a breach between the philosophy of assisted living and the reality of life for many residents when we speak of privacy. This brings us back to autonomy. As people at Kramer and Wood Glen have expressed, they do not perceive they possess much autonomy, and objectively they do not seem to exercise much of it. The question is, why? Some critical answers can be found by returning to "the elderly mystique" and linking it to assisted living residents.

Relinquishing Autonomy: The Elderly Mystique

The elderly mystique "holds that the potentials for growth, development, and continuing engagement virtually disappear when disabled" (Cohen 1988:24). Of greatest concern is the fact that older people buy into this negative view of growing older and focus only on the losses associated with old age. This mystique, formerly applied to the general population of aged individuals, is now focused specifically on those elders who are considered "frail" (either physically or mentally). Buying into the elderly mystique may emotionally paralyze older adults and narrow their life focus to a struggle to remain in their home. "The elderly themselves have concluded that when disability arrives, hope of continued growth, self-realization, and full participation in family and society must be abandoned so that all energy can be directed to avoiding the ultimate defeat, which is not death but institutionalization, which is regarded as a living death" (Cohen 1988:25).

For those who subscribe to the elderly mystique, what happens after institutionalization? Since "the nursing home is regarded as the ultimate assault on autonomy" (p. 25), many older adults simply give up and sink further into the belief that they are biologically inferior and totally dependent. This raises a fascinating question: what about those older adults in assisted living? Assisted living is supposed to be a noninstitutional environment that promotes choice, independence, and autonomy. Assisted living was founded on the belief that frail older adults could maintain a sense of dignity and self-worth by living in a homelike setting that fully integrates their housing and health care needs. My research repeatedly shows that residents in assisted living settings embrace the elderly mystique just as surely as nursing home residents are purported to do. I have cited numerous examples of residents at Kramer and Wood Glen relinquishing their autonomy and giving up any sense of empowerment (Frank 1994, 1999, 2001). Kramer resident Gail Young illustrated her adherence to the elderly mystique when she told me, "The useful, productive part of our lives is over" (interview by author, Chicago, Illinois, 15 March 1993). In reference to herself and her co-habitants, fellow resident Helen Finks told me, "We are not independent people anymore." Such comments illustrate how residents in assisted living may surrender all aspects of their autonomy, based on this perception of themselves as dependent.

The philosophy of assisted living drives hard against the elderly mystique; yet, residents are still investing into this false mystique. Why? The explanation I propose is that many family members, assisted living providers, and marketers are also buying into the elderly mystique. Family members often believe that their aged relatives are too frail to take care of themselves. And while this may sometimes be the case, it does not mean the older adult cannot or should not take part in the decision-making process. Marketers advertise assisted living "facilities," thereby reinforcing all of the ideas of powerlessness that accompany this term. If the assisted living industry considers assisted living residences "facilities," than how can they expect residents to consider the place their home?

Further, many in the assisted living industry, like others in the long-term care industry, utilize jargon that has come to carry negative connotations for our society. Terms and phrases used to describe older adults with disabilities can reinforce the elderly mystique because they are juxtaposed with notions of "well" and "functional" elderly. For instance, terms such as "impaired elderly," "wheelchair-bound elderly," "institutionalized elderly," "vulnerable elderly," "elderly-at-risk," and "patient" (rather than resident) are all used in contrast with "healthy" and "independent" elderly people. Society views the latter terms as positive reflections of older adults, while they view the former terms as negative.

Each of these [pessimistic] terms carries a negative connotation emphasizing weakness, captivity, and diminished capacity for effecting control, expressing preferences, and exercising dominion. This is the language of long term care programs. . . . It is the language of nursing homes, personal care homes, and retirement homes that set schedules for rising and retiring, eating, recreating, coming and going, dressing and undressing. It is the language that conveys to the elderly person with disabilities what he or she is and is not. (Cohen 1990:14–15)

Bearing this statement in mind, it is neither surprising nor unexpected that older adults and those in the assisted living industry subscribe to the elderly mystique. Residents relinquish autonomy and opportunities for control while providers support this action. The elderly mystique, thirty-five years after its introduction, continues to be subconsciously accepted by our ageist society, even among many of those who advocate on behalf of the older population.

As long as the elderly mystique continues to be embraced by frail elderly persons, their family members, and advocates in the long-term care system, autonomy will continue to be stifled in assisted living settings. A reflection of the perpetuation of the elderly mystique is the inability of the philosophy of assisted living (as well as the components of home) to penetrate the policies of assisted living communities and the psyche of assisted living residents.

Continuum of Care versus Aging in Place: Residents' Views

The inner conflict that residents face as those around them encounter sickness and decline speaks to a larger issue of whether or not residents should be allowed to fully age in place. This debate underlies all of the issues discussed in this book. Therefore, it is critical to return to the issue and evaluate what residents think about aging in place.

The continuum of care model of assisted living is medically oriented and emphasizes both the health care environment and nursing services. Under this model, assisted living is seen as a bridge between residing independently in the community and living in a nursing home. The proponents of this model believe that assisted living serves a very useful role as part of a progression of increasingly medicalized environments. Supporters of the "continuum of care" believe it is inappropriate to allow older adults to remain in assisted living if their health declines significantly. The alternative to the continuum is aging in place in assisted living. Defenders of this model believe that elderly persons should be allowed to remain in assisted living until they die. Supporters not only believe that residents' quality of life will be enhanced by staying in a more residential environment, but they also believe that residents will not have to worry constantly about when they will have to leave. The friction between these two models of care influences all losses, liminality, and loneliness. It is useful to address these two models, as they are experienced in the everyday lives of Wood Glen and Kramer residents. The dilemmas these two models present for residents combine to make assisted living less than an ideal home for them. The discord between the models becomes most evident when residents ask the question, "How long can I stay?"

Residents at both Kramer and Wood Glen have strong but mixed feelings on the subject of aging in place. Although the presence of very frail and dependent residents upsets them, they themselves want to be able to remain in assisted living, and to know they will not be cast out when they become more impaired. Residents voice compassion and concern for their co-habitants who are in failing health. "It could be me" and "there but for the grace of God go I" are common sentiments. Yet, long-time assisted living residents also express distress at the increasing numbers of frail and cognitively impaired elderly who are living at Kramer and Wood Glen. If regulations remove assisted living from the continuum of care, allowing residents to remain until they die, then healthier residents might become even more depressed than they already are. Wood Glen and Kramer residents definitely do not want to see their fellow residents ailing. In many ways, residents would rather cling to their liminality than face the issues of impairment and death. And yet, some residents are annoyed that Kramer and Wood Glen accept "unsuitable candidates." Retaining the continuum of care model might mean that more assisted living communities could maintain a more noninstitutional ambiance. Many residents I interviewed drew a direct link between increasing frailty among fellow residents and their inability to call their assisted living community home. Perhaps tenants such as those whose voices are presented throughout this book might feel more comfortable in assisted living if impaired residents continue to move into advanced-care facilities. Paradoxically, residents may never think of assisted living as home unless they themselves can remain there indefinitely.

Full aging in place supports residents' capacity to feel at home in their environment. Proponents of this philosophy could target a much broader range of potential residents because providers would not have to worry about "inappropriate placement." Another asset would be the general move away from nursing home placement and all of the institutional trappings that accompany it. As Kane and Wilson (1993) say, "Assisted living can be seen as a promising way to change the paradigm for delivering care to persons with substantial disabilities" (p. xviii). Providers could spare themselves the agonizing decision about when a resident should be asked to leave.

As noted in chapter 4, assisted living providers in the Chicago area find that discharge criteria are one of their most difficult policy-making areas. Many experience the dilemma between allowing and preventing aging in place. Providers indicate they may want to allow residents to remain in the homelike setting that assisted living offers, but because of policies, resident pressure, and state regulations, they cannot or will not always do so. For the short term, most of these providers are willing to reshape the rules so that a resident may remain in assisted living longer than might have been previously considered appropriate. However, providers do not interpret aging in place to mean that occupants can remain in assisted living until they die; most interpret aging in place as prolonged residence, which means that residents can stay in assisted living until some undetermined point in time when they need a higher level of assistance. Then their prolonged residence is terminated, and they are moved to a higher level of care. Is this what proponents of assisted living are striving for? Prolonged residence does not do justice to the aging in place model because it denies older adults the opportunity to remain in a homelike environment. It also brings into question the necessity of design innovations and environmental alterations. Why make the environment more accessible and more homelike if residents cannot remain there to use it and if they are not seen as the "real" consumer?

Residents at Kramer and Wood Glen told me that before moving into these residences they were led to believe that no "sick" elderly persons would be present at their assisted living site. Then, after moving in, they compared themselves to those around them and wondered why deteriorating residents were being allowed to stay. Healthy residents seem to prefer that sick residents be removed. An explanation for this behavior is that healthy residents really do not want to admit the obvious: that populations at Kramer and Wood Glen are not static, people who are eighty-five and ninety years old will decline over time. Residents do not want to face this reality for three major reasons. First, it is very painful to befriend someone and then watch him or her slip away. Second, the scenario of the infirm residents in assisted living is contrary to what they thought they were promised when they moved in. Third, and most significant, residents are fearful. They are not being cruel when they say, "There are people who do not belong here." Rather, they are scared about facing death: their own as well as the deaths of those around them. This avoidance of death is typical in our society and gets to the root of the issue of aging in place.

Aging in Place Equals Dying in Place

In the previous chapters, aging in place has been a common thread that has woven its way through all of the issues covered in the book. I have shown that for the majority of providers in the assisted living industry, aging in place is interpreted as prolonged residence. Despite my lengthy discussion and analysis, the issue of aging in place in assisted living is still unresolved. Why are providers opting for prolonged residence? Why are they not allowing residents to remain in assisted living until they die? Some would say that regulations hinder the ability of assisted living residents to fully age in place. However, according to Victor Regnier, architect and expert in the field of assisted living, regulations are not necessarily the culprit. In a recent presentation at the 10th National Alzheimer's Disease Education Conference, Regnier spoke about the barriers facing further design innovation in assisted living. He said, "It is not the regulations, it is our mindset that is the problem." I believe this statement applies to aging in place in assisted living as well. Many assisted living operators claim regulations prohibit them from allowing residents to stay in assisted living until they die. However, my extensive research leads me to a different conclusion: that the American mindset about death and dying is the root of the problem. After all, what does it mean to fully age in place? It means *dying in place*.

Popular culture in America seeks to avoid the subject of death entirely and masks the process of dying as much as possible. "American society goes out of its way to hide death and to dissociate it from the flow of everyday life. Dying people are often hidden away in hospitals or nursing homes, and upon death they are swept away from 'the corridors of the living' to the basement morgue as quickly and discreetly as possible" (Moller 1996:175). It is my contention that this attitude infiltrates the assisted living industry (and long-term care industry) and prevents aging in place.

The medical field in the United States holds the predominant view that dying is considered a "failure" of science (Moller 1990; Pierson 2000; Braun, Pietsch, and Blanchette 2000). Such a perspective has become standard for almost all physicians practicing medicine and has crept into the psyche of the general population. "This ethic of curing and lifesaving is so routine that to do otherwise requires a special order, that is the 'do-not-resuscitate' (DNR) order" (Pierson 2000:234). In other words, we require special *permission* to die in health care settings. Our society is so disturbed by death that we do not *allow* people to die in nursing homes or hospitals without legal authorization.

Another part of this view is that people should only die in hospitals, not residential settings (and only after everything possible has been done to "save" the person). This "institutionalization of death" (Pierson 2000) dilutes the process of dying by removing it from the public eye. Death is a taboo subject; therefore, by institutionalizing death, the medical community has managed to assist the general public in avoiding it.[2] Interwoven in this institutionalization of death is an attitude of "you cannot die here," held by most assisted living communities, continuing care retirement communities (CCRCs), and nursing homes.

One might grow old in his or her own home, an assisted living setting, or a nursing home, but a person should only die in a medicalized environment (where death may be prevented by the use of medical devices). A colleague of mine, "Brenda," relayed a personal anecdote to me about the dying process for her elderly mother. Brenda told me that although medical staff in the assisted living community (and then the nursing home) cared for her mother, they also held an attitude of "don't die on my shift." Brenda expressed her frustration at the fact that her mother was passed around like a hot potato the closer she came to dying. Brenda's mother moved from assisted living to a hospital following a fall, then to a "rehabilitation and convalescent hospital," then to a nursing home that allowed hospice care. Brenda said that several times during her mother's decline, the nursing home would send her mother to the hospital at the first sign of any further medical complication. Brenda asserts that these trips to the hospital did not help her mother at all, rather they seemed to make her mother worse both mentally and physically, and her mother concurred. Brenda's experience with her mother's frequent delivery to a hospital is not uncommon. Scholar Charon Pierson, a medical sociologist and nurse, explains that shifting a patient to a hospital is common in long-term care facilities. Medical emergencies in long-term care facilities are "time-consuming, emotionally draining, and create havoc with the normal routines of the facility"

(Pierson 2000:235). Therefore, what happens is that nurses will try to "anticipate the patient's downward trajectory and transfer the patient to the hospital
before the actual need for a code [CPR] occurs" (p. 235). Moving a resident to a
hospital makes it easier on staff in long-term care facilities and creates a situation where patients will not die in the nursing home.

Narrowing in on the issue of dying in place in assisted living actually connects many of the points raised thus far. Most assisted living residents are de-
nied the ultimate demonstration of autonomy: choosing where they are going
to die. Currently, approximately 22 percent of assisted living residents die
while residing in their assisted living setting (NCAL 1998). Residents are not
afforded the opportunity to stay in a homelike environment until the end of
their lives. Although some scholars believe that "the place where we grow old
and the place where we die should be without separation" (Brent 1999:76),
the assisted living industry (and indeed the long-term care industry) does not
support this argument. The same sort of anticipatory removal from the pre-
mises that Pierson describes above occurs in assisted living. If a resident is perceived as failing, then he or she is moved to a more medicalized, less residential
environment.

The liminality residents face in assisted living can ultimately be traced to the
issue of dying. How close or far from death will residents be when they are
asked to move? Many people fear death because it is the greatest unknown that
we will face in our lives. According to Powers,

In general, the fear of death has been broken down into the specific fears of pain, loneliness, abandonment, mutilation, and, somewhat more difficult to define, fear of the
loss of self. This is not just another way of saying fear of death, but a kind of disassocia-
tion of the self as a conscious entity (the sense of *me*-ness one feels) from the self as a
particular individual, with his particular history in the everyday world. That individual is one's closest associate and one fears his loss. (Powers 1982:251)

The fears that Powers describes are interesting in that (on a broader level)
they reflect the same feelings residents told me they experience every day in assisted living. Throughout this text, residents have expressed feeling lonely while
in the company of other residents, feeling abandoned by family even though
they have visitors, and feeling a loss of identity (self) because of role loss and diminished autonomy. Residents at Kramer and Wood Glen have especially con-
verged on this area of losing one's self. Although residents do not speak of this
feeling specifically in relation to death, I believe the loss of self permeates much
of their daily existence, as illustrated by statements made to me, such as "my life
is basically over" and "at my age I am not sure where I fit in" (see chapters 1 and
5). Residents already feel that they have lost much of their "self." Therefore, not
allowing them to die in place just reinforces their status in limbo.

A very interesting point to note is, according to one study of 366 assisted living communities, 65 percent offered hospice services as of 1998 (NCAL). If this sample is representative of the total number of assisted living sites in the United States, it would seem that more than 22 percent of the assisted living residents should be dying in place. Perhaps the gap between these numbers reflects the fact that simply because hospice care is offered does not mean the resident (or their family members) will want to utilize the option.

The concept and practice of a "continuum of care" conditions health care professionals to view assisted living residents as situated along a linear path whereby a person is supposed to move from one setting to the next before he or she dies. The analogy might be envisioned as a moving walkway where the track transports the person from one level of care to the next and the machinery controls when the person disembarks. The continuum of care seems to pressure assisted living settings to discharge residents to a higher (and more institutionalized) level of care. Being able to fully age in place (and therefore die in place) will only happen if the health care industry moves away from the mindset of fitting elderly residents into a slot along a designated path. Many Americans accept the idea that as an elderly person becomes more frail, the medical model takes over.

The continuum of care does not offer assisted living residents the autonomy, dignity, control, privacy, and choice that full aging in place does. The continuum of care pushes residents from assisted living to higher levels of care because operators do not know exactly when a resident will begin dying. The decision to move a resident plays into the medical culture in the United States as well as into society's fears about dying.

Full aging in place in assisted living is a radical concept that goes against the entire medical approach to dying. This is because in assisted living settings there is much less medical care available for residents. Therefore, little can be done medically to "save" a person if he or she becomes acutely ill. Full aging in place opposes the medical model because it re-empowers the elderly person to die as he or she chooses, without interference of extensive and invasive medical procedures. The medical model is not in control in assisted living. Perhaps assisted living really is a radical idea because residents are more actively confronting death (because no life-saving machinery is present at assisted living sites), and they are actively exercising autonomy by living in a setting where they lack an opportunity for instant rescue. The point is that full aging in place in assisted living would give residents the *choice* to exercise their *autonomy* by dying where *they* want to. This ideal embraces the true spirit of the philosophy of care so important to the uniqueness of assisted living.

Liminality, Prolonged Residence, and Aging in Place in Assisted Living

Providers and residents both confront the challenge posed by the idea of aging in place. Providers ask: "Who qualifies for entrance?" "When should residents be asked to leave?" "What does aging in place actually mean?" Trying to answer these questions while pursuing the practice of prolonged residence is difficult because providers must decide just when the individual resident's condition warrants movement out of the assisted living community. Concurrently, residents ask their own set of questions: "Why is such a sickly resident here?" "When will they ask him or her to leave?" "How long can I stay?" "If I cannot stay until I die, why should he or she?" The limbo of the incomplete rite of passage does not help residents to answer their questions either. Prolonged residence places assisted living at one stop along a trajectory of increasing medical care, or as Heumann and Boldy (1993b) term it, "the conveyor belt approach to housing for seniors." However, questions that arise along this continuum remain unanswered for assisted living, due to the diversity of this environment and its multilayered definitions in the industry.

Providers' interpretation of aging in place as prolonged residence merely adds to seniors' sense of liminality and insecurity in assisted living. Since residents do not know what the rules are regarding exit criteria and procedures in the assisted living community, they are likely to be more apprehensive about their own failing health. Residents sense this limbo in all aspects of their lives, even in the personal domain, and it increases their isolation. Assisted living resident Gail Young asserts, "Nothing here is permanent, so, when you like someone at Kramer, even then you don't get close because you know that it won't be a long-term thing" (interview by author, Chicago, Illinois, 15 March 1993). This reality does not help residents to feel at home in assisted living. Yet residents still want to stay in assisted living until they die. This residential option, while not "home," is still preferable to a nursing home.

Providers are struggling just as much with aging in place. According to one assisted living provider in Chicago, "Most definitely, everybody who is doing elderly housing is dealing with that aging in place issue. And now that we are getting older, more frail clients, we have to be in a position to deal with that" (interview by author, tape recording, Chicago, Illinois, 24 March 1993). The question now is, *how?*

Presently, prolonged residence is occurring by default in many assisted living environments. This is because either the provider allows older adults to remain in assisted living by stretching the model of assisted living the home follows or there are no specific regulations or policies at that site to force someone to leave at a designated point in time. On the national level, concern regarding aging in place can be seen in recent research study. In a 1999 National Survey of Assisted Living, Hawes, Rose, and Phillips pose the question: "Can ALF (assisted living facility) residents age in place?"

The answer depends on one's concept of aging in place. For example, in most ALFs,

> a resident could move from relative independence (e.g., needing or wanting only meal preparation, housekeeping, and staff that can respond to emergencies) to a more complex stage at which the resident needed help with bathing, dressing, and managing medications and used a wheelchair to get around. If this "span" or change in needs were the definition of "aging in place," then the admission and retention policies of ALFs suggested that they were willing to allow residents to age in place.
>
> On the other hand, if aging in place meant that the average consumer could select an assisted living facility and reasonably expect to live there to the end of his or her life, regardless of changes in health or physical and cognitive functioning, then the answer must be "no." In most ALFs, a resident whose functional limitations necessitated help with transfers or whose cognitive impairment progressed from mild to moderate or severe or who exhibited behavioral symptoms would be discharged from the facility. (Hawes, Rose, and Phillips 1999:E–11)

The above statements represent the two opposing interpretations of aging in place. First, Hawes et al. explain that it *is* possible to age in place—at least temporarily. This of course is prolonged residence. The second statement addresses full aging in place and their conclusion that it is virtually impossible in assisted living.

A major hindrance to the possibility of fully aging in place in assisted living is the outlook of some providers and participants in the assisted living industry. As shown in comments by several Chicago assisted living providers and industry representatives, many still view assisted living as a temporary stop along a set continuum of care. Karen Abrams, an administrator at Wood Glen claims, "The people we have attracted to assisted living pretty much conform to what I expected, which would be relatively frail, compromised elderly who might have a good year or two in assisted living but would likely need more supervised care shortly." Abrams and other people in the assisted living industry with this mindset will never get beyond prolonged residence in their assisted living communities. Unfortunately, it would certainly be possible for residents to pick up this unspoken attitude from administrators, thereby increasing their sense of liminality and decreasing their ability to call assisted living "home." Assisted living resident Fannie Isaacs draws a clear connection between the limbo of her life at Kramer and her incapacity to feel at home there: "How can it [Kramer] be home? It is a station before you go there [she points upward].

And, in between you are here" (interview by author, tape recording, Chicago, Illinois, 18 January 1993).[3]

A strong component of residents' discontinuity is a feeling of uselessness and role loss connected to the elderly mystique. Residents feel suspended: they have no clearly defined role in their assisted living community and do not know how long they can remain there. In their own homes, residents knew better what roles to assume and how they fit in. At Kramer and Wood Glen, residents frequently seem lost. Kramer resident Zelda Arnold makes this point very clear in one of our interviews.

JF: Do you feel like you belong here [at Kramer]?

ZA: Well, I don't know where I belong [laughs]. I've got to live somewhere.

JF: Do you feel more like you belong here than at the last senior housing complex you lived?

ZA: [laughs] I don't really know where I belong. When you get to be my age, you don't know where you belong. (interview by author, tapr recording, Chicago, Illinois, 11 November 1992)

Liminality breeds feelings of isolation for a number of residents, and the majority of assisted living models that exist in the United States only enhance these feelings. Assisted living residents in Chicago do not feel at home in assisted living. The incomplete rite of passage residents undergo when entering assisted living leaves them feeling roleless, frustrated, and bored. Resident Katie Jacobs says, "I am bored a lot here [at Kramer]. When I am bored I go into my room and watch TV. Sometimes I go into my room when I am bored and I cry, I don't know why, but I cry" (interview by author, tape recording, Chicago, Illinois, 27 October 1992).

Kramer and Wood Glen residents are very conflicted. They definitely *do not* want to see their fellow residents ailing because they are empathetic and they realize that they, too, will become more frail and then could be asked to leave. Nevertheless, they cling to their liminality by saying, "There are people who should not be here." This is especially true because they realize they will likely die in a nursing home, the most dreaded place of all (Gubrium 1975; Cohen 1988; Goffman 1961; Savishinsky 1991). Presently, the only thing prolonged residence offers an older adult is prolonged anxiety. Residents do not want this. Seniors in assisted living want to know how long they can stay. They want to know that they *can* stay. Right now, in most assisted living communities, they cannot stay. Therefore, residents struggle to determine what combination of instrumental activities of daily living (IADLs) and activities of daily living (ADLs) deficiencies will create the formula for their eviction. The formula differs from one setting to the next, since different settings follow different models of assisted living. Residents are left to constantly compare their abilities to those of their fellow residents on a daily basis. Identifying those who are "worse off" than they gives healthier residents a temporary sense of security. They think, "After all, if 'Betty' is more dependent than me, then Betty will be asked to leave before me." The way to diminish resident liminality and halt the comparisons would be to allow seniors to fully age in place: to stay until they die. However, it must be acknowledged that if residents can remain until they die, they will not be spared the reality of witnessing their co-habitants' decline and death. What they *will* avoid is a sense of insecurity about their own status and having to face yet another move.

According to Victor Regnier, expert in the field of assisted living, " 'assisted living' is a phrase which means a care philosophy to some people, a building type to others, and to others it defines a regulatory category" (Regnier 1996:1). In order for an assisted living resident to have the opportunity to fully age in place, I argue that all three ingredients mentioned by Regnier need to be present in assisted living. Providers must integrate the philosophy of assisted living into their sites if they want to provide the highest quality of life for residents and honor their dignity. As a building type, assisted living must be residential in character if we want a resident to truly feel "at home" rather than institutionalized. Assisted living must also be understood in relation to regulations and standards. Services that can be provided are framed by the regulatory category in which assisted living exists for each state. Residents need to know which health services can and will be provided once they move into assisted living. Developers and industry participants must understand and incorporate all three of these components if there is any possibility of residents completely aging in place. In addition, those in the assisted living industry need to understand what it means to age in place, not just use the phrase in their marketing literature.

It is important to point out that an evolution has been occurring over the past decade regarding the level of frailty among assisted living residents. Overall, Kramer and Wood Glen have not remained completely static or rigid in their policies. They are allowing residents to stay longer and utilize more support services. Nancy Simpson has noted the change at Kramer, a community that provides no health care services.

I think what is wonderful is when I first started working at Kramer, things were pretty set in that a person had to be independent physically and intact cognitively—alert and oriented. And Kramer only provided the program—which is meals and housekeeping—and that's it. And what I have seen over the years is much more flexibility. Allowing a person to age in place, allowing bathing assistance, allowing a companion to come for maybe three or four hours to help a person. (interview by author, tape recording, Chicago, Illinois, 26 October 1992)

Kramer still does not supply any health care services, but now it allows residents to hire personal care workers to come in and help them. The changes that have been made, while positive, are leading to prolonged residence rather than aging in place. Unfortunately, the situation is problematic for residents because it forces them to deal with ailing residents around them while they are simultaneously unaware of the actual standards for remaining in assisted living.

Perhaps the most positive point to be made about prolonged residence is the fact that it is happening at all. Prolonged residence represents a progression for many assisted living sites across the country. Providers are letting residents stay longer than they did seven or eight years ago. This movement represents an encouraging shift, but it still leaves residents in limbo. Maybe prolonged residence can be seen as a necessary step in the transformation of assisted living from a majority of Low Service/Low Privacy sites to a majority of High Service/High Privacy sites.

Finally, although providers and residents are both conflicted about the aging in place model, there is one important point to bear in mind about the nature of our current elderly housing industry. In the United States the continuum of care penalizes our elderly population for aging and it neglects the very population it is supposed to serve.

Though useful to place assisted living on a continuum for definitional purposes, doing so may be inconsistent with assisted living's philosophy of promoting "aging in place." It is important to emphasize that one important intent of assisted living is to design environments to accommodate individual needs that change over time. A continuum of care orientation, therefore, may emphasize facility types more than individual needs. (Manard et al. 1992:ii–15)

Historically, the more frail and sick an older person becomes, the *less* homelike his or her living environment becomes. "Industrial society devalues non-productive people, thus when human beings are no longer productive, they become expendable" (Heumann and Boldy 1993a:27). We seem to be sending elderly people in this country a message: *When your health declines you will be moved through a continuum of care into more and more institutional environments, until you end up in a nursing home.* Presently, while a senior may *reside* in the homelike environment of assisted living, he or she is not unconditionally allowed *to stay* in this homelike environment of assisted living until death. Our home is a place that symbolizes security and comfort for us (Rybczynski 1986; Saile 1985; Korosec-Serfaty 1985). How can assisted living be seen as home if providers are evicting residents? Seldom are people expelled from their own homes; yet, they can be removed easily from assisted living. Perhaps many providers are interpreting "homelike" merely to mean *the design and décor*, not the philosophy of care.

Thus far, prolonged residence appears to be a shaky compromise for aging in place in assisted living. And, as illustrated throughout this book, it has not worked. Instead, this temporary solution to the growing tension between these two models is having negative repercussions for providers and residents. Operators, researchers, and assisted living advocates must remember that the process of leaving one's home and moving to assisted living is difficult for older adults. "Most older adults are not planning a move, when they do move, they are being pushed out of their previous homes rather than pulled to the retirement housing" (Merrill and Hunt 1990:73). In addition, once pushed out of their old housing into assisted living, residents become suspended in limbo where they give up their old roles without the feeling of acquiring new ones. And, most critically, they give up the certainty of their old environment in exchange for a sense of alienation, few social bonds, and uncertain tenure in their new environment.

NOTES

1. Hawes, Rose, and Phillips (1999) point out that 28 percent of assisted living administrators in their survey admitted that their residences had at least one room at their site that was shared by *three or more residents*.

2. According to Thomas Powers, "In 1967 a number of doctors in New York created the Foundation of Thanatology to encourage the study of death and dying from a broad perspective. They chose the word thanatology to make it easier to raise funds, figuring that philanthropists, like others, would find the word death so disturbing they would prefer to have nothing to do with it" (Powers 1982:251).

3. As Fannie's statements reveal, facing death itself may produce liminality, isolation, uncertainty, and even fear. How much of each an individual feels will vary.

APPENDIX I

The MEAP: Procedures and Challenges

The Multiphasic Environment Assessment Procedure (MEAP) is a tool developed by Rudolf H. Moos and Sonne Lemke (1996; 1984; 1980) in order to evaluate the social and physical environments of elderly housing settings. There are five parts to the MEAP. According to Moos and Lemke (1996), the sections may be used individually or as a whole, depending on what the site wishes to evaluate. Briefly, the parts are as follows:

1. *The Physical and Architectural Features Checklist* (PAF) assesses eight dimensions and covers questions about the facility's location, its external and internal physical features, and its space allowances.
2. *The Policy and Program Information Form* (POLIF) assesses nine dimensions, including questions about the types of rooms or apartments available, the way in which the facility is organized, and the services provided for residents.
3. *The Resident and Staff Information Form* (RESIF) measures nine dimensions describing the residents' social backgrounds and functional abilities, their participation in activities, their utilization of services, and the characteristics of staff and volunteers.
4. *The Sheltered Care Environment Scale* (SCES) assesses residents' and staff members' perceptions of seven characteristics of a facility's social environment. The items cover the quality of interpersonal relationships, the opportunities for personal growth, and the mechanisms for system maintenance and change.
5. *The Rating Scale* (RS) taps observers' impressions of the physical environment and of resident and staff functioning. (Moos and Lemke 1984:2)

This book presents results from parts 2, 3, and 4 of the MEAP.

Before Moos and Lemke tested their tool on actual housing sites, they wanted to develop eligibility criteria. What they came up with was a set of three requirements for inclusion: "Each facility had to have a minimum of ten residents, a majority of the residents had to be elderly (60 years or older), and the facility had to offer at least a meal plan for residents" (Moos and Lemke 1984:3). If a site filled these three criteria then it was labeled a "sheltered care setting" and was considered for their study. Based on the services and care provided, Lemke and Moos divided their sample sheltered care settings into three categories: skilled nursing facilities (SNFs), residential care facilities (RCFs), and apartment facilities (APTs). An initial version of the MEAP was tested in ninety-three separate sites in California. The sites included forty-one SNFs, twenty-eight RCFs, and twenty-four APTs. Building on the California sample, the MEAP was revised and tested on a national reference group consisting of 151 sites in twenty states. The same three criteria were used for qualification as a sheltered care setting. The breakdown for the sites was as follows: eighty-six SNFs, twenty-seven RCFs, and thirty-eight APTs. Because of the similarity in facility characteristics, Moos and Lemke later combined the national and California samples.

BASIC PROCEDURES

In their original 1988 manual and handbook for users, Moos and Lemke offer advice and suggestions regarding how to administer the parts of the MEAP. Because the MEAP is a flexible tool, a number of options exist for executing it. Some of these choices are shaped by the subsection itself. For example, the PAF consists of over a hundred questions, many of which are technical numbers and measurements. Therefore, it is most useful to simply give the administrator a copy of the PAF and allow him or her to complete it when there is ample time to concentrate. Also, sections one through three of the MEAP only need to be completed by one knowledgeable person in the setting. Moos and Lemke (1996), therefore, advise that researchers choose a staff member who is very experienced with the setting and the residents. It should be noted that the administrator or staff person who completes the PAF does not necessarily have to be the person who completes the POLIF and RESIF sections. If the provider thinks that a specific staff member has more knowledge and experience in these areas, then that person may complete these sections.

For the Sheltered Care Environment Scale (SCES), a different set of issues comes into play due to the fact that the SCES is the only portion of the MEAP administered to residents as well as staff. The SCES is a sixty-three-question yes/no survey measuring perceptions of the social environment (see Appendix

II for a copy of the SCES survey). Moos and Lemke (1996) suggest that the researcher proceed in one of three ways dependent on what he or she deems best.

1. Administer the SCES orally during a resident function. This way, many residents can complete the survey at once and any confusion regarding the questions can be easily clarified.
2. Administer the SCES individually to each resident. The benefit to this method is that the researcher can sit down one on one with residents, possibly alleviating pressure that residents might feel in a group setting.
3. Administer the SCES survey anonymously. The benefit here is that residents receive the survey without any contact with the researcher, complete it, and return it to a specified location where the researcher will pick it up.

I chose the third method. I will discuss how and why I chose this particular method in the next section of the appendix.

The SCES

The Sheltered Care Environment Scale was by far the most valuable part of the MEAP for my research. This was in large part due to the fact that residents themselves participated in the SCES. This tool allowed me to directly compare resident and staff perceptions of their social environment. Both staff and residents complete the SCES, but different guidelines apply to residents versus staff.

Lemke and Moos outline some basic parameters to follow when administering the questionnaire. As mentioned above, I chose to anonymously give the survey to residents and staff and have them return surveys to a covered box that I used for collection purposes. I opted to use this method for several reasons. First, I believed that staff and especially residents would be more honest if I was not present while they answered the questions. Second, I did not want to expose respondents to possible pressures that the presence of other residents may cause. Last, I had experienced reluctance from residents when I tried to convince them to consent to personal, tape-recorded interviews. I did not want the same situation to occur with the surveys. Therefore, I adopted what I refer to as the "hands-off" policy: leave the surveys under the residents' doors with a cover letter and then let them choose when, where, and if they wished to complete it. This method turned out to be more successful that I had expected, based on my earlier experience with trying to solicit tape-recorded interviews.

The Sheltered Care Environment Scale turned out to be powerful tool for my research. The results I received from the SCES fleshed out many of the issues raised in the formal interviews about which many residents were reluctant to speak. The SCES was particularly important because the basis of much of my research was to try to understand the ideals versus the realities of assisted living. The importance of perceptions elicited by the SCES cannot be underestimated in this domain. "Resident and staff perceptions represent an important perspective on the reality of sheltered care facilities. Information about such facilities can be obtained by outside observers who may be more 'objective,' but it is difficult for such people to know what the setting is like without actually experiencing it as participants" (Moos, Gauvain, Lemke, Wax, and Mehren 1979:75).

In terms of response rates for the survey, Moos and Lemke offer guidelines here as well.

Practically achievable response rates from residents vary considerably among facilities. Although the upper limit on the achievable return rate in community care home, domiciliaries, and apartment buildings is usually over 70%, it can be as low as 20–40% in facilities in which residents' functional abilities are low or literacy is a problem. A 20% response rate can be achieved in the majority of nursing homes, whereas response rates of around 30% are obtainable in those nursing homes that have some intermediate care beds. (Moos and Lemke 1988:53)

My response rates from residents were quite good at both sites. At Wood Glen I achieved a 46 percent response rate and at Kramer I received a 73 percent response rate. Moos and Lemke advise that a researcher "should try to obtain a minimum of ten completed questionnaires from residents and five completed questionnaires from staff" (p. 53). My percent return rate falls within the expected norms that Lemke and Moos gave for returned surveys, but Wood Glen does not qualify if strictly numbers are used. At the time I administered the survey, there were only thirteen of a possible seventeen residents living on the assisted living floor at Wood Glen. I received six completed surveys from residents, therefore falling short of the desired ten. At Kramer, sixteen of the twenty-two residents there completed the surveys. I realize the actual numbers of residents completing the survey is small and not statistically significant. However, my main purpose in using the SCES was to elicit comparative perspectives from residents and staff. Additionally, the SCES allowed residents to remain anonymous while stating their opinions, which I believe was a valuable asset.

In terms of staff, there were restrictions at both sites. The staff population working at the Wood Glen Home is large. Most of these staff members rarely have any contact with the assisted living residents and would therefore be of little help in the SCES. There are approximately eight to ten staff members who come into contact with assisted living residents on a very regular basis. I received four completed surveys from this group. Although this figure falls short of the five suggested by Lemke and Moos, I believe some valuable information can still be gleaned from these four surveys. The staff outcomes from Kramer were also somewhat problematic. At Kramer there are *only* five staff members present (other than kitchen workers and housekeepers). I received surveys back from all five staff/administrative personnel at Kramer. As chapters 3 and 6 show, their responses were also revealing.

While the SCES was undoubtedly the most worthwhile part of the MEAP for my study, at the same time it posed a number of research challenges and obstacles. As mentioned earlier, there were several procedural problems in distributing the survey and securing response from residents. Originally, I had considered administering the survey during a group activity but found this would not be feasible at either site. Timing was also never ideal because resident numbers fluctuated during the course of my research. Therefore, it was difficult to calculate the ideal time to distribute the survey. Ultimately, my solution was to pick a date to distribute the surveys at both sites, regardless of the numbers of residents living at either site at the time or who was away at the hospital.

The RESIF

The dimensions for utilization of health services and utilization of daily living assistance have been omitted from this book and my analysis. Wood Glen activities director Bess Coleman told me that it would be virtually impossible for her to complete these two portions of the RESIF accurately. Coleman said this was due to several factors. First, residents of the assisted living unit employ the on-site community health clinic for their health services. The clinic has dental, podiatric, mental health, and internal medicine components. Residents are treated on an "outpatient" basis when they need care. Coleman said she could not begin to guess how often and what exact services are utilized by assisted living residents. In reference to the daily living assistance, Coleman said that she was not sure that she would be able to accurately discern the residents' assistance from that of the 100 nursing home residents. Since the number for these two sections did not affect the outcomes of the other seven dimensions, the RESIF was still a valid tool for comparison.

I also shortened the RESIF for Kramer. The program coordinator at the residence left a significant number of the questions for the resident social resources section blank. Therefore, it was impossible to score this section and it was eliminated. The utilization of daily living assistance and the utilization of health services are present for Kramer.

The POLIF

The Policy and Program Information Form focuses on the site's policies, organizational set up, and services provided. There are nine POLIF subscales (as explained in chapter 6). The administration of this part of the MEAP was straightforward and there was no need to eliminate any subscales or dimensions.

APPENDIX II

The SCES Resident Questionnaire

SHELTERED CARE ENVIRONMENT SCALE

Name (optional) _____   Age _____

Name of Facility _____

❑ Male   ❑ Female

How long have you lived or worked here?   _____   _____   _____
                                                         Years   Months   Days

If you are a staff member, check the following box ❑

    and indicate your staff position _____

Today's Date _____

    There are 63 questions here. They are statements about the place in which you live or work. Based on your experience here, please answer these questions YES or NO. Ask yourself which answer is *generally* true.

    Circle YES if you think the statement is true or mostly true of this place.

    Circle NO if you think the statement is false or mostly false of this place. Please be sure to answer every question. Thank you for your cooperation.

1. Do residents get a lot of individual attention?   YES   NO
2. Do residents ever start arguments?   YES   NO
3. Do residents usually depend on the staff to set up activities for them?   YES   NO
4. Are residents careful about what they say to each other?   YES   NO
5. Do residents always know when the staff will be around?   YES   NO
6. Is the staff strict about rules and regulations?   YES   NO
7. Is the furniture here comfortable and homey?   YES   NO
8. Do staff members spend a lot of time with residents?   YES   NO
9. Is it unusual for residents to openly express their anger?   YES   NO
10. Do residents usually wait for staff to suggest an idea or activity?   YES   NO
11. Are personal problems openly talked about?   YES   NO
12. Are activities for residents carefully planned?   YES   NO
13. Are new and different ideas often tried out?   YES   NO
14. Is it ever cold and drafty in here?   YES   NO
15. Do staff members sometimes talk down to residents?   YES   NO
16. Do residents sometimes criticize or make fun of this place?   YES   NO
17. Are residents taught how to deal with practical problems?   YES   NO
18. Do residents tend to hide their feelings from one another?   YES   NO
19. Do some residents look messy?   YES   NO
20. If two residents fight with each other, will they get in trouble?   YES   NO
21. Can residents have privacy whenever they want?   YES   NO
22. Are there a lot of social activities?   YES   NO
23. Do residents usually keep their disagreements to themselves?   YES   NO
24. Are many new skills taught here?   YES   NO
25. Do residents talk a lot about their fears?   YES   NO
26. Do things always seem to be changing around here?   YES   NO
27. Do staff allow the residents to break minor rules?   YES   NO
28. Does this place seem crowded?   YES   NO
29. Do a lot of the residents just seem to be passing time here?   YES   NO
30. Is it unusual for residents to complain about each other?   YES   NO
31. Are residents learning to do more things on their own?   YES   NO
32. Is it hard to tell how the residents are feeling?   YES   NO
33. Do residents know what will happen to them if they break a rule?   YES   NO
34. Are suggestions made by the residents acted upon?   YES   NO

35.	Is it sometimes very noisy here?	YES	NO
36.	Are requests made by residents usually taken care of right away?	YES	NO
37.	Is it always peaceful and quiet here?	YES	NO
38.	Are the residents strongly encouraged to make their own decisions?	YES	NO
39.	Do residents talk a lot about their past dreams and ambitions?	YES	NO
40.	Is there a lot of confusion here at times?	YES	NO
41.	Do residents have any say in making the rules?	YES	NO
42.	Does it ever smell bad here?	YES	NO
43.	Do staff members sometimes criticize residents over minor things?	YES	NO
44.	Do residents often get impatient with each other?	YES	NO
45.	Do residents sometimes take charge of activities?	YES	NO
46.	Do residents ever talk about illness and death?	YES	NO
47.	Is this place very well organized?	YES	NO
48.	Are the rules and regulations rather strictly enforced?	YES	NO
49.	Is it ever hot and stuffy in here?	YES	NO
50.	Do residents tend to keep to themselves here?	YES	NO
51.	Do residents complain a lot?	YES	NO
52.	Do residents care more about the past than the future?	YES	NO
53.	Do residents talk about their money problems?	YES	NO
54.	Are things sometimes unclear around here?	YES	NO
55.	Would a resident ever be asked to leave if he/she broke a rule?	YES	NO
56.	Is the lighting very good here?	YES	NO
57.	Are the discussions very interesting?	YES	NO
58.	Do residents criticize each other a lot?	YES	NO
59.	Are some of the residents' activities really challenging?	YES	NO
60.	Do residents keep their personal problems to themselves?	YES	NO
61.	Are people always changing their minds around here?	YES	NO
62.	Can residents change things here if they really try?	YES	NO
63.	Do the colors and decorations make this a warm and cheerful place?	YES	NO

References

Abeles, Ronald. 1991. Sense of control, quality of life, and frail older people. In *The concept and measurement of quality of life in later years*, James E. Birren, James E. Lubben, Janice Cichowlas Rowe, and Donna E. Deutchman, eds. San Diego, CA: Academic Press, Inc.

Adler, Jane. 2001. Study surveys residents of assisted living facilities. *Chicago Tribune* 14 October, section 16, p. 3.

Agich, George J. 1990. Reassessing autonomy in long-term care. *Hastings Center Report* 20: 12–17.

Ahrentzen, Sherry, Douglas W. Levine, and William Michelson. 1989. Space, time, and activity in the home: A gender analysis. *Journal of Environmental Psychology* 9:89–101.

Alexander, Ernest R. 1997. Regulation and evaluation criteria for housing for the elderly: An international comparison. *Journal of Housing for the Elderly* 12:147–68.

Allen, Kathryn G. 1999a. Assisted living: Information, quality concerns. *Consumer's Research* 20–23.

———. 1999b. *Assisted living quality of care and consumer protection issues.* Testimony before the Special Committee on Aging, U.S. Senate, GAO/ T-HEHS 99–111, 26 April.

Altman, Irwin, M. Powell Lawton, and Joachim Wohlwill, eds. 1984. *Elderly people and the environment.* New York: Plenum Press.

Art, Karen Majcher. 1979. The Navajo hogan: Microcosm of the universe. Unpublished paper presented at the Central States Anthropology Society Meetings, Milwaukee, WI, 29 March.

Assisted Living Facilities Association of America (ALFAA). 1992. *1992 ALFAA fact sheet.* Fairfax, VA: Assisted Living Facilities Association of America.

Assisted Living Federation of America (ALFA). 1994. *1994 fact sheet.* Fairfax, VA: Assisted Living Federation of America.

———. 1999. *Assisted living regulations: A state by state profile.* Fairfax, VA: Assisted Living Federation of America.

———. 2000. *Assisted living regulations: A state by state profile.* Fairfax, VA: Assisted Living Federation of America.

Assisted living meets "aging in place." 1997. *Nursing Homes* 46(7):43–45.

Assisted Living Quality Coalition (ALQC). 1998. *Assisted living quality initiative: Building a structure that promotes quality.* Washington, DC: Assisted Living Quality Coalition.

———. 1999. *Assisted living quality coalition outcome measurement summit June 1999.* Washington, DC: Assisted Living Quality Coalition.

Baltes, Margaret, and Paul Baltes, eds. 1986. *The psychology of control and aging.* London: Lawrence Erlbaum Associates.

Barry, Charlotte D. 1999. The experience of moving into an assisted living facility: A Heideggerian hermeneutical phenomenological inquiry. Ph.D. dissertation, University of Miami.

Barton, Linda J. 1997. A shoulder to lean on: Assisted living in the U.S. *American Demographics* (July): 45–51.

Beck, Cornelia K., and Theresa S. Vogelpohl. 1995. Cognitive impairment and autonomy. In *Enhancing autonomy in long-term care: Concepts and strategies,* Lucia M. Gamroth, Joyce Semradek, and Elizabeth M. Tornquist, eds. New York: Springer Publishing Company.

Benjamin, David N. 1995. Afterward, or further research issues in confronting the home concept. In *Home: Words, interpretations, meanings, and environments,* David N. Benjamin and David Stea, eds. Aldershot, UK: Avebury.

Benjamin, David N. and David Stea, eds. 1995. *The Home: Words, interpretations, meanings, and environments.* Aldershot, UK: Avebury.

Blankenheim, Tracy A. 2001. Legislators re-examine the state of assisted living. *McNight's Long-Term Care News,* 18 June, 3, 13.

Blier, Suzanne Preston. 1987. *The anatomy of architecture: Ontology and metaphor in Batammaliba architectural expression.* Cambridge: Cambridge University Press.

Booth, Tim. 1983. Residents' views, rights, and institutional care. In *Speaking of clients,* Mike Fisher, ed. Sheffield, UK: Joint Unit for Social Services Research, University of Sheffield.

Boschetti, Margaret. 1990. Reflections on home: Implications for housing design for elderly persons. *Housing and Society* 17:57–65.

Braun, Kathryn L., James H. Pietsch, and Patricia L. Blanchette, eds. 2000. *Cultural issues in end-of-life decision making.* Thousand Oaks, CA: Sage Publications, Inc.

Brent, Ruth. 1999. Gerontopia: A place to grow old and die. In *Aging, autonomy, and architecture: Advances in assisted living,* Benyamin Schwarz and Ruth Brent, eds. Baltimore: Johns Hopkins University Press.

Brower, Sidney. 1989. Residents' and outsiders' perceptions of the environment. In *Housing, culture, and design: A comparative perspective*, Setha Low and Erve Chambers, eds. Philadelphia: University of Pennsylvania Press.

Brown, Patricia Leigh. 1993. The architecture of those called homeless. *New York Times*, 15 January, part 1, p. 18.

Bruck, Laura. 1996. Assisted living: A snapshot 1995. *Nursing Homes* 45(4):13–15.

Brummett, William. 1997. *The essence of home: Design solutions for assisted living housing*. New York: Van Nostran Reinhold.

———. 1998. Building the character of home. *Assisted Living Today* (January/February): 29–31.

Bulos, Marjorie, and Waheed Chaker. 1995. Sustaining a sense of home and personal identity. In *Home: Words, interpretations, meanings, and environments*, David N. Benjamin and David Stea, eds. Aldershot, UK: Avebury.

Butler, Robert N. 1975. *Why survive? Being old in America*. New York: Harper and Row.

Buttimer, Anne. 1980. Home, reach, and sense of place. In *The human experience of space and place*. Anne Buttimer and David Seamon, eds. London: Croom Helm.

Byetheway, William R. 1982. Living under an umbrella: Problems of identity in sheltered housing. In *Geographical perspectives on the elderly*, A.M. Warnes, ed. Chichester, UK: John Wiley and Sons Ltd.

Calabria, John A. 1997. Assisted living and alternative family care options. *New Jersey Medicine* 94(1):39–41.

Calkins, Margaret. 1995. From aging in place to aging in institutions: Exploring advances in environments for aging. *The Gerontologist* 35:568–70.

Callahan, James J. 1992. Aging in place. *Generations* 16(2):5–6.

———. 1993. Introduction: Aging in place. In *Aging in place*, James Callahan, ed. Generations in Aging Series. Amityville, NY: Baywood Publishing Company, Inc.

Can your loved ones avoid a nursing home? 1995. *Consumer Reports* (October): 656–62.

Caplan, Arthur L. 1990. The morality of the mundane: Ethical issues arising in the daily lives of nursing home residents. In *Everyday ethics: Resolving dilemmas in nursing home life*, Rosalie Kane and Arthur L. Caplan, eds. New York: Springer Publishing Co.

Carder, Paula C. 2002. Promoting independence: As analysis of assisted living facility marketing materials. *Research on Aging* 24(1):106–23.

Cavanaugh, Gene. 1993. Foreword. In *Home sweet home*, C.W. Moore, K. Smith, and P. Becker, eds. New York: Rizzoli International Publications, Inc.

Chapin, Rosemary, and Debra Dobbs-Kepper. 2001. Aging in place in assisted living: Philosophy versus policy. *The Gerontologist* 41(1):43–50.

Clark, Margaret. 1972. Cultural values and dependency in later life. In *Aging and modernization*, Donald Cowgill and Lowell Holmes, eds. New York: Appleton-Century-Crofts.

———. 1973. Contributions of cultural anthropology to the study of the aged. In *Cultural illness and health: Essays in human adaptation,* Laura Nader and Thomas Maretzki, eds. Anthropological Studies Series, David Maybury-Lewis, series ed. Washington, DC: American Anthropological Association. Number 9.

Clark, Margaret M., and Barbara G. Anderson. 1967. *Culture and aging: An anthropological study of older Americans.* Springfield, IL: Charles C. Thomas.

Clements, Mark. 1993. What we say about aging. *St. Petersburg Times, Parade Magazine,* 12 December.

Clemmer, Elizabeth. 1995. *Assisted living and its implications for long-term care.* Washington, DC: American Association of Retired Persons.

Cohen, Elias. 1988. The elderly mystique: Constraints on the autonomy of the elderly with disabilities. *The Gerontologist* 28:24–31.

———. 1990. The elderly mystique: Impediment to advocacy and empowerment. *Generations* (supplement):13–16.

Collopy, Bart J. 1988. Autonomy in long-term care: Some crucial distinctions. *The Gerontologist* 28(supplement):10–17.

———. 1990. Ethical dimensions of autonomy in long-term care. *Generations* (supplement):9–12.

———. 1995. Power, paternalism, and the ambiguities of autonomy. In *Enhancing autonomy in long-term care: Concepts or strategies,* Lucia Gamroth, Joyce Semradek, and Elizabeth Tornquist, eds. New York: Springer Publishing Company.

Consumer Consortium on Assisted Living 1999. *Checklist of questions to ask when choosing an assisted living facility.* www.ccal.org.

Csikszentmihalyi, Mihaly, and Eugene Rochberg-Halton. 1989. *The meaning of things: Domestic symbols and the self.* Cambridge: Cambridge University Press.

Day, Patricia, Rudolf Klein, and Sharon Redmayne. 1996. *Why regulate? Regulating residential care for elderly people.* Bristol, UK: The Policy Press.

Despres, Carole. 1991. The meaning of home: Literature review and directions for future research and theoretical development. *The Journal of Architectural and Planning Research* 8:96–114.

Dill, Ann. 1987. The case of George Sellers: A safe plan. *Generations.* Special issue on coercive placement of elders: Protection or choice? (September):48–53.

Dobkin, Leah. 1992. If you build it they may not come. *Generations: Journal of the American Society on Aging* 14(2):31–33.

Donabedian, Avedis. 1972. Models for organizing the delivery of health services and criteria for evaluating them. *Milbank Quarterly* 50:103–54.

Dostal, James F. 1998. Effectiveness of Assisted living under Minnesota's Housing with Services Act: Residents' comprehension and satisfaction. Masters thesis, St. Cloud State University.

Dovey, Kimberly. 1978. Home: An ordering principle in space. *Landscape* 22(2):27–30.

————. 1985. Home and homelessness. In *Home environments*, Irwin Altman and Carol Werner, eds. New York: Plenum Press.

Dubler, Nancy. 1987. Introduction. *Generations*. Special issue on coercive placement of elders: Protection or choice? (September):6–8.

Duffy, Michael, et al. 1986. Preferences in nursing home design: A comparison of residents, administrators, and designers. *Environment and Behavior* 18:246–47.

Duncan, James. 1985. The house as symbol of social structure: Notes on the language of objectives among collectivist groups. In *Home environments*, Irwin Altman and Carol Werner, eds. New York: Plenum Press.

Dworkin, Gerald. 1988. *The theory and practice of autonomy*. New York: Cambridge University Press.

Eckert, J. Kevin, Sheryl Zimmerman, and Leslie A. Morgan. 2001.Connectedness in residential care: A qualitative perspective. In *Assisted living: Needs, practices, and policies in residential care for the elderly*, Sheryl Zimmerman, Philip D. Sloane, and J. Kevin Eckert, eds. Baltimore: Johns Hopkins University Press.

Edelstein, Stephanie. 1998. Assisted living: Recent developments and issues for older consumers. *Stanford Law & Policy Review* 9(2):373–85.

Epstein, Barry A. 1998. Avoiding wrongful discharge. *Provider* (September):71–73.

Fairchild, Thomas J., and Katrina Lindh. 1998. Seamless care. *Urban Land* (November):66–69.

Farquhar, Morag. 1995. Elderly people's definitions of quality of life. *Social Science and Medicine* 41:1439–46.

Fisher, Christy. 1995. Coming home to assisted living. *Provider* (October):57–64.

————. 1997. Congress eyes care, oversight in assisted living. *Provider* (September):10.

Fisher, Mike. 1983. The meaning of client satisfaction. In *Speaking of clients*, Mike Fisher, ed. Sheffield, UK: Joint Unit for Social Services Research, University of Sheffield.

Fogel, Barry S. 1992. Psychological aspects of staying at home. *Generations: Journal of American Society on Aging* 16(2):15–20.

Frank, Jacquelyn. 1989. Navajo house forms: Transitions and explanations. Unpublished paper, Northwestern University, June.

————. 1994. Nobody's home: The paradox of aging in place in assisted living. Ph.D. dissertation, Northwestern University.

————. 1999. I live here but it is not my home: Residents' experiences in assisted living. In *Aging, autonomy, and architecture: Advances in assisted living*, Benyamin Schwarz and Ruth Brent, eds. Baltimore: Johns Hopkins University Press.

————. 2001. How long can I stay?: The dilemma of aging in place in assisted living. *Journal of Housing for the Elderly* 15(1, 2):5–30.

Fried, Marc. 1963. Grieving for a lost home. In *The urban condition*, L.J. Duhl, ed. New York: Simon and Schuster.

Fry, Christine L. 1980. Toward an anthropology of aging. In *Aging in culture and society: Comparative viewpoints and strategies*, Christine L. Fry, ed. Brooklyn, NY: J. F. Bergin.

————. 1981. Introduction: Anthropology and dimensions of aging. In *Dimensions: Aging, culture, and health*, Christine L. Fry, ed. Brooklyn, NY: J. F. Bergin.

Gamroth, Lucia, Joyce Semradek, and Elizabeth M. Tornquist, eds. 1995. *Enhancing autonomy in long-term care: Concepts and strategies*. New York: Springer Publishing Company.

Gamzon, Mel. 1996. Seniors housing in focus: Assisted living is the segment to watch. *National Real Estate Investor* (March):63, 64, 117–23.

George, Linda K., and Lucille B. Bearon. 1980. *Quality of life in older persons: Meaning and measurement*. New York: Human Services Press.

Glascock, Anthony P. 1990. By any other name, it is still killing: A comparison of the elderly in America and other societies. In *The cultural context of aging: Worldwide perspectives*, Jay Sokolovsky, ed. New York: Bergin and Garvey.

Goffman, Erving. 1961. *Asylums: Essays on the social situation of mental patients and other inmates*. New York: Doubleday.

————. 1963. *Stigma: Notes on the management of spoiled identity*. Englewood Cliffs, NJ: Prentice-Hall, Inc.

Golant, Stephen M. 1984. *A place to grow old: The meaning of environment in old age*. New York: Columbia University Press.

————. 1990. Changing an older person's shelter and care setting: A model to explain personal and environmental outcomes. In *Environment and aging theory: A focus on housing*, Rich Scheidt and Paul Windley, eds. Westport, CT: Greenwood Press.

————. 1992. *Housing america's elderly: Many possibilities, few choices*. Newbury Park, CA: Sage Publications.

————. 1999. The promise of assisted living as a shelter and care alternative for frail American elders: A cautionary essay. In *Aging, autonomy, and architecture: Advances in assisted living*. Benyamin Schwarz and Ruth Brent, eds. Baltimore: Johns Hopkins University Press.

Gold, Daniel. 1996. Managed care is coming—is assisted living ready? *Assisted Living Today* (Spring):20–30.

Goldstein, Andrew. 2001. Better than a nursing home? *Time*, 13 August, 48–53.

Gordon, Paul. 1997a. Licensure and discrimination issues: Traps for the unwary developer. *Urban Land* (June):59, 68, 69.

————. 1997b. When a handshake just won't do. *Provider* (April):39–41.

Greene, Angela, Catherine Hawes, Merry Wood, and Cynthia Woodsong. 1998. How do family members define quality in assisted living facilities? *Generations* (Winter):34–36.

Gubrium, Jaber F., ed. 1974. *Late life: Communities and environmental policy*. Springfield, IL: Charles C Thomas.

————. 1975. *Living and dying at Murray Manor*. New York: St. Martin's Press.

————, ed. 1976. *Time, roles, and self in old age*. New York: Human Sciences Press, Behavioral Sciences, Inc.

Gubrium, Jaber F., and Andrea Sankar, eds. 1994. *Qualitative methods in aging research*. Thousand Oaks, CA: Sage Publications.

Gutheil, Irene. 1991. The physical environment and quality of life in residential facilities for the frail elderly. *Adult Residential Care Journal* 5:131–45.

Harris, Diana K. 1988. *Dictionary of gerontology*. Westport, CT: Greenwood Press.

Hawes, Catherine. 1999a. A key piece of the integration puzzle: Managing the chronic care needs of the frail elderly in residential care settings. *Generations* (Summer):51–55.

———. 1999b. *Shopping for assisted living: What consumers need to make the best buy*. Testimony before the Special Committee on Aging, U.S. Senate, GAO/ T-HEHS 99–111, 26 April.

———. 2001. Introduction. In *Assisted living: Needs, practices, and policies in residential care for the elderly*, Sheryl Zimmerman, Philip D. Sloane, and J. Kevin Eckert, eds. Baltimore: Johns Hopkins University Press.

Hawes, Catherine, Vincent Mor, Judith Wildfire, Vince Iannacchione, and Linda Lux. 1995. *Executive summary: Analysis of the effects of regulation on the quality of board and care homes*. Research Triangle Park, NC: Research Triangle Institute.

Hawes, Catherine, Charles D. Phillips, and Miriam Rose. 2000. High service and high privacy in assisted living facilities, their residents and staff: Results from a national survey. U.S. Department of Health and Human Services, Office of the Assistant Secretary for Planning and Evaluation. Prepared under contract numbers HHS-100-94-0024 and HHS-100-98-0013. Washington, DC.

Hawes, Catherine, Miriam Rose, and Charles D. Phillips. 1999. *A national study of assisted living for the frail elderly: Results of a national survey of facilities*. Report prepared for the Office of Disability, Aging, and Long-Term Care Policy, Assistant Secretary for Planning and Evaluation, U.S. Department of Health and Human Services. Beachwood, OH: Menorah Park, Center for Senior Living. Contract numbers HHS-100-94-0024 and HHS-100-98-0013.

Hawryluk, Markian. 1995. Regulations in the assisted living community: States seem willing to adapt rules. *Provider* 21:71–74.

Hayward, D. Geoffrey. 1977. Psychological concepts of "home." *HUD Challenge* (February):10–13.

Hazan, Haim. 1980. *The limbo people: A study of the constitution of the time universe among the aged*. London: Routlege and Kegan Paul.

———. 1994. *Old age: Constructions and deconstructions*. Cambridge: Cambridge University Press.

Hendersen, Neil. 1990. Anthropology, health and aging. In *Anthropology and aging: Comprehensive reviews*, Robert L. Rubinstein, ed. Boston: Kluwer Academic Publishers.

Hendrickson, Michael C. 1988. Assisted living: An emerging focus in an expanding market. *Contemporary Long-Term Care* 11:20–23.

Heumann, Leonard, and Duncan Boldy. 1993a. Aging in place: The growing need for new solutions. In *Aging in place with dignity: International solutions re-*

lating to the low-income and frail elderly, Leonard Heumann and Duncan Boldy, eds. Westport, CT: Praeger Publishers.

———. 1993b. The basic benefits and limitations of an aging in place policy. In *Aging in place with dignity: International solutions relating to the low-income and frail elderly*, Leonard Heumann and Duncan Boldy, eds. Westport, CT: Praeger Publishers.

Hodlewsky, R. Tamara. 2001. Staffing problems and strategies in assisted living. In *Assisted living: Needs, practices, and policies in residential care for the elderly*, Sheryl Zimmerman, Philip D. Sloane, and J. Kevin Eckert, eds. Batimore: Johns Hopkins University Press.

Hofland, Brian F. 1988. Autonomy in long term care: Background issues and a programmatic response. *The Gerontologist* 28 (supplement): 3–9.

———. 1990a. Introduction. *Generations* (supplement):5–8.

———. 1990b. Value and ethical issues in residential environments for the elderly. In *Aging in place: Supporting the frail elderly in residential environments*, David Tilson, ed. Glenview, IL: Professional Books on Aging, Scott, Foresman, and Company.

———. 1995. Resident autonomy in long-term care: Paradoxes and challenges. In *Enhancing autonomy in long-term care: Concepts or strategies*. Lucia Gamroth, Joyce Semradek, and Elizabeth Tornquist, eds. New York: Springer Publishing Company.

Holmes, Lowell D. 1980. Anthropology and age: An assessment. In *Aging in culture and society: Comparative viewpoints and strategies*. Christine L. Fry, ed. New York: Praeger Publishers.

Howell, Sandra C. 1985. Home: A source of meaning in elder's lives. *Generations* 9:58–60.

Huntington, Richard, and Peter Metcalf. 1979. *Celebrations of death: The anthropology of mortuary ritual.* Cambridge: Cambridge University Press.

Hyde, Joan. 2001. Understanding the context of assisted living. In *Assisted living: Current issues in management and resident care,* Kevan H. Namazi and Paul K. Chafetz, eds. Westport, CT: Auburn House.

Illinois, Compiled Statutes. 2001. *Assisted Living and Shared Housing Act.* (210 ILCS/9). P.A. 91–656.

Innes, J. Bruce. 1998. Listen to your elders! (Assisted living facilities management). *Nursing Homes* 47(3):43–45.

Jacobs, Jerry. 1974. *Fun city: An ethnographic study of a retirement community.* New York: Holt, Rinehardt, and Winston, Inc.

Jett, Stephen C., and Virginia E. Spencer. 1981. *Navajo architecture: Forms, history, distribution.* Tucson: University of Arizona Press.

Johnson, Colleen, and Barbara Barer. 1993. Coping and a sense of control among the oldest old: An exploratory analysis. *Journal of Aging Studies* 7(1):67.

———. 1997. *Life beyond 85 years: The aura of survivorship.* New York: Springer Publishing Company.

Kaakinen, Joanna Rowe. 1992. Living with silence. *The Gerontologist* 32(2):258–64.

Kalymun, Mary. 1990. Toward a definition of assisted living. *Journal of Housing for the Elderly* 7:97–131.

Kane, Rosalie. 1995. Autonomy and regulation in long-term care: An odd couple, an ambiguous relationship. In *Enhancing autonomy in long-term care: Concepts or strategies*, Lucia Gamroth, Joyce Semradek, and Elizabeth Tornquist, eds. New York: Springer Publishing Company.

Kane, Rosalie, and Arthur Caplan. 1990. *Everyday ethics: Resolving dilemmas in nursing home life*. New York: Springer Publishing Company.

Kane, Rosalie, Iris Freeman, Arthur L. Caplan, Mila A. Aroskar, and E. Kristi Urv-Wong, 1990. Everyday autonomy in nursing homes. *Generations* 14(supplement):69–71.

Kane, Rosalie, Laurel Illston, Robert Kane, and John Nyman. 1990. *Meshing services with housing: Lessons from adult foster care and assisted living in Oregon*. Minneapolis: University of Minnesota Long Term Care Decisions Resource Center.

Kane, Rosalie, and Keren Brown Wilson. 1993. *Assisted living in the United States: A new paradigm for residential care for frail older persons?* Washington, DC: Public Policy Institute, the American Association of Retired Persons.

Kapp, Marshall B., and Keren Brown Wilson. 1995. Assisted living and negotiated risk: Reconciling protection and autonomy. *Journal of Ethics, Law, and Aging* 1:5–13.

Kayser-Jones, Jeanie. 1981. *Old, alone, and neglected: Care of the aged in the United States and Scotland*. Berkeley: University of California Press.

Keith, Jennie. 1979. The ethnography of old age: Introduction. *Anthropological Quarterly* 52(1):1–5.

———. 1980. Old age and community creation. In *Aging in culture and society: Comparative viewpoints and strategies*, Christine L. Fry, ed. New York: Praeger Publishers.

———. 1981. The "back to anthropology" movement in gerontology. In *Dimensions: Aging culture, and health*, Christine L. Fry, ed. New York: Praeger Publishers.

———. 1982. *Old people as people: Social and cultural influences and old age*. Boston: Little, Brown, and Company.

Keith, Jennie, Christine L. Fry, and Charlotte Ikels. 1990. Community as context for successful aging. In *The cultural context of aging: Worldwide perspectives*, Jay Sokolovsky, ed. New York: Bergin and Garvey.

Kertzer, David J., and Jennie Keith. 1984. *Age and anthropological theory*. Ithaca, NY: Cornell University Press.

Kidder, Tracy. 1993. *Old friends*. Boston: Houghton Mifflin Company.

Knoerl, Annmarie. 1993. Perceptions of self-care ability and morale in the elderly living in assisted living facilities. Master's thesis, Wayne State University.

Korosec-Serfaty, Perla. 1985. Experience and use of the dwelling. In *Home environments*, Irwin Altman and Carol M. Werner, eds. New York: Plenum Press.

Kron, Joan. 1990. It's not chic, it's not plain. It's homey. *New York Times*, 26 July, C1.

Laird, Carobeth. 1979. *Limbo: A memoir of life in a nursing home by a survivor.* Novato, CA: Chandler and Sharp.

Lasky, William. 1999. *Shopping for assisted living: What consumers need to make the best buy.* Testimony before the Special Committee on Aging, U.S. Senate, GAO/T-HEHS 99–111, 26 April.

Lawrence, Roderick J. 1985. A more humane history of homes: Research method and application. In *Home environments*, Irwin Altman and Carol M. Werner, eds. New York: Plenum Press.

———. 1987. What makes a house a home? *Environment and Behavior* 19:154–68.

———. 1989. Translating anthropological concepts into architectural practice. In *Housing, culture, and design: A comparative perspective*, Setha M. Low and Erve Chambers, eds. Philadelphia: University of Pennsylvania Press.

Lawton, M. Powell. 1988. Three functions of the residential environment. *Journal of Housing for the Elderly* 5:35–50.

———. 1990. Knowledge resources and gaps in housing for the aged. In *Aging in place: Supporting the frail elderly in residential environments*, David Tilson, ed. Glenview, IL: Professional Books on Aging, Scott, Foresman, and Company.

Lawton, M. Powell, Maurice Greenbaum, and Bernard Liebowitz. 1980. The lifespan of housing environments for the aging. *The Gerontologist* 20:56–63.

Lemke, Sonne, and Rudolph H. Moos. 1988a. *Multiphasic Environment Assessment Procedure: Handbook for users.* Palo Alto, CA: Social Ecology Laboratory, Veterans Administration and Stanford University Medical Center.

———. 1988b. *Multiphasic Environment Assessment Procedure: Manual.* Palo Alto, CA: Social Ecology Laboratory, Veterans Administration and Stanford University Medical Center.

Lemke, Sonne, Rudolph H. Moos, and Amy Marder. 1988. *Multiphasic Environment Assessment Procedure: Hand scoring booklet.* Palo Alto, CA: Social Ecology Laboratory, Veterans Administration and Stanford University Medical Center.

Lewin-VHI. 1996. *National study of assisted living for the frail elderly: Literature review and update.* Report prepared for the Assistant Secretary for Planning and Evaluation and U.S. Department of Health and Human Services. Research Triangle Park, NC: Research Triangle Institute. Contract number HHS-100-94-0024.

Lidz, Charles W., and Robert M. Arnold. 1990. Institutional constraints on autonomy. *Generations* (supplement):65–68.

———. 1995. The medical model and its effect on autonomy: A comparison of two long-term care settings. In *Enhancing autonomy in long-term care: Concepts or strategies*, Lucia Gamroth, Joyce Semradek, and Elizabeth Tornquist, eds. New York: Springer Publishing Company.

Litwak, Eugene, and Charles Longino. 1987. Migration patterns among the elderly: A developmental perspective. *The Gerontologist* 27:266–72.

Lucas, Nancy. 1999. Assisted living and nursing home: An exploration of these two paradigms of long-term care using subjective reports by residents of their quality of life. Masters thesis, Smith College School for Social Work, Northampton, MA.

Manard, Barbara. 1999. Assisted living for changing needs. *Health Progress* (March–April):24–34.

Manard, Barbara, William Altman, Nancy Bray, Lisa Kane, and Andrea Zeuschner. 1992. *Policy synthesis on assisted living for the frail elderly: Final report.* Submitted to the Office of the Assistant Secretary for Planning and Evaluation, U.S. Department of Health and Human Services. Contract number HHS-100-89-0032.

Mangum, Wiley P. 1994. Planned housing for the elderly since 1950: History, policies, and practices. In *Housing and the aging population: Options for the new century*, W.E. Flots and E.E. Yeatts, eds. New York: Garland Press.

Marans, Robert, Michael Hunt, and Kathleen Vakalo. 1984. Retirement communities. In *Elderly people and the environment*, I. Altman, M.P. Lawton, and J.F. Wohlwill, eds. New York: Plenum Press.

Marek, Karen Dorman, and Mailyn Rantz. 2000. Aging in place: A new model for long-term care. *Nursing Home Administration Quarterly* (Spring):1–11.

Marsden, John Patrick. 1993. The architecture of assisted living for the elderly: Achieving the meanings of home. Master's thesis, University of Arizona, Tucson.

———. 1997. Assisted living housing for the elderly: Symbolic and physical properties of homeyness. Ph.D. dissertation, University of Michigan.

Martz, Sandra, ed. 1987. *When I am an old woman I shall wear purple.* Watsonville, CA: Papier-Mache Press.

Melia, Mark. 2000. Regulation: The state of the states. *Nursing Homes: Long Term Care Management* (May):54–56.

Merrill, John, and Michael Hunt. 1990. Aging in place: A dilemma for retirement housing administrators. *Journal of Applied Gerontology* 9:60–76.

Meyerhoff, Barbara. 1978. *Number our days.* New York: Simon and Schuster.

———. 1984. Rites and signs of ripening: The intertwining of ritual, time, and growing older. In *Age and anthropological theory*, David Kertzer and Jennie Keith, eds. Ithaca, NY: Cornell University Press.

———. 1992. *Remembered lives: The work of ritual, storytelling, and growing older.* Ann Arbor: University of Michigan Press.

Millard, Peter H., and Chris S. Smith. 1981. Personal belongings: A positive effect. *The Gerontologist* 21(1):85–90.

Mitchell, Judith, and Bryan Kemp. 2000. Quality of life in assisted living homes: A multidimensional analysis. *Journal of Gerontology: Psychological Sciences* 2:117–27.

Moller, David Wendell. 1990. *On death without dignity: The Human impact of technical dying.* Amityville, NY: Baywood Publishing Company, Inc.

——. 1996. *Confronting death: Values, institutions, and human mortality.* Oxford: Oxford University Press.

Mollica, Robert. 1998a. Regulation of assisted living facilities: State policy trends. *Generations* (Winter):30–33.

——. 1998b. State regulation update: States are adopting new rules at a brisk pace. *Contemporary Long Term Care* (August):45–49.

——. 2000. *State assisted living policy, 2000.* Portland, ME: National Academy for State Health Policy.

——. 2001. State policy and regulations. In *Assisted living: Needs, practices, and policies in residential care for the elderly,* Sheryl Zimmerman, Philip D. Sloane, and J. Kevin Eckert, eds. Baltimore: Johns Hopkins University Press.

Mollica, Robert L., et al. 1992. *Building assisted living for the elderly into long term care policy: A guide for states.* A publication of the Center of Vulnerable Populations. Waltham, MA: National Academy for State Health Policy and the Bigel Institute for Health Policy, Brandeis University.

——. 1995. *Guide to assisted living and state health policy.* National Long Term Care Resource Center, Minneapolis, University of Minnesota.

Mollica, Robert L., and Kimberly Irvin Snow. 1996. *State assisted living policy: 1996.* Portland, ME: National Academy for State Health Policy.

Mollica, Robert L., Keren Brown Wilson, and Roberta Ryther. 1992. *Guide to assisted living and state health policy.* National Long Term Care Resource Center, Minneapolis, University of Minnesota.

Moon, Marilyn, George Gaberlavage, and Sandra Newman, eds. 1989. *Preserving independence, supporting needs.* Washington DC: AARP Public Policy Institute.

Moos, Rudolf H., Mary Gauvain, Sonne Lemke, Wendy Wax, and Barbara Mehren. 1979. Assessing the social environments of sheltered care settings. *The Gerontologist* 19(1):74–82.

Moos, Rudolf H., and Sonne Lemke. 1980. Assessing the physical and architectural features of sheltered care settings. *Journal of Gerontology.* 35(4):571–583.

——. 1984. Supportive residential settings for older people. In *Elderly people and the environment,* Irwin Altman, M. Powell Lawton, and Joachim Wohlwill, eds. New York: Plenum Press.

——. 1987. Priorities for design and management in residential settings for the elderly. In *Housing the aged: Design directives and policy considerations,* Victor Regnier and Jon Pynoos, eds. New York: Elsevier Science Publishing Company.

——. 1988. *Multiphasic Environment Assessment Procedure supplementary manual: Ideal and expectation forms.* Palo Alto, CA: Social Ecology Laboratory, Veterans Administration and Stanford University Medical Center.

——. 1996. *Evaluating residential facilities: The Multiphasic Environment Assessment Procedures.* Thousand Oaks, CA: Sage Publications.

Morgan, James. 1996. *If these walls had ears: The biography of a house.* New York: Warner Books, Inc.

Morris, John, et al. 1990. Aging in place: A longitudinal example. In *Aging in place: Supporting the frail elderly in residential environments*, David Tilson, ed. Glenview, IL: Professional Books on Aging, Scott, Foresman, and Company.

Morton, Alan. 1995. Camouflaging care for assisted living providers: The challenge is delivering care discreetly. *Contemporary Long Term Care* (July): 40–42, 44, 46–47.

Munroe, Donna J., et al. 1994. *Characteristics of assisted living in Illinois.* Hinsdale: Center for Eldercare Choices, Illinois Association of Homes for the Aging Foundation.

Murer, Matthew J. 1997. Assisted living, the regulatory outlook: An overview of those waiting for the federal regulatory "shoe to drop." *Nursing Homes* (July/August):24–27.

———. 1999. Assisted living regulations come of age. *Nursing Homes* 8:6–8.

Nader, Laura, and Thomas Maretzki. 1973. *Cultural illness and health: Essays in human adaptation.* Anthropological Studies Series, no. 9. Washington, DC: American Anthropological Association.

Namazi, Kevan H., and Paul K. Chafetz, eds. 2001a. *Assisted living: Current issues in management and resident care.* Westport, CT: Auburn House.

———. 2001b. The concept, the terminology, and the occupants. In *Assisted living: Current issues in management and resident care*, Kevan H. Namazi and Paul K. Chafetz, eds. Westport, CT: Auburn House.

Namazi, Kevan H., J. Kevin Eckert, Eva Kahana, and Stephanie Lyon. 1989. Psychological well-being of elderly board and care home residents. *The Gerontologist* 29:511–16.

Namazi, Kevan H., J. Kevin Eckert, Tena Tarler Rosner, and Stephanie Lyon. 1991. The meaning of home for the elderly in pseudo-familial environments. *Adult Residential Care Journal* 5(2):81–97.

Nasar, Jack L. 1989. Symbolic meanings of house styles. *Environment and Behavior* 21:235–257.

National Center for Assisted Living (NCAL). 1998. *Facts and trends: The assisted living sourcebook.* Washington, DC: National Center for Assisted Living.

———. 2000. Assisted living state regulatory review 2000. www.nacal.org.

———. 2001. Assisted living: Independence, choice and dignity. http://www.nacal.org.

National Investment Conference for the Senior Housing and Long Term Care Industries (NIC). 1998. *National survey of assisted living residents: Who is the customer?* Annapolis: National Investment Conference (NIC).

Nydegger, Corine. 1981. Gerontology and anthropology: Challenge and opportunity. In *Dimensions: Aging, culture, and health*, Christine L. Fry, ed. New York: Praeger Publishers.

O'Bryant, Shirley. 1982. The value of home to older persons: Relationship to housing satisfaction. *Research in Aging* 4:349–63.

———. 1983. The subjective value of "home" to older homeowners. *Journal of Housing for the Elderly* 1:29–43.

Oh, Chan Ohk. 1998. Toward a generic evaluation tool for assisted living facilities. Master of science thesis, University of Cincinnati.

Pallasmaa, Juhani. 1995. Identity, intimacy, and domicile, notes on the phenomenology of home. In *The home: Words, interpretations, meanings, and environments*, D. Benjamin, ed. Aldershot, UK: Avebury.

Pastalan, Leon A. 1990. Designing a humane environment for the frail elderly. In *Aging in place: Supporting the frail elderly in residential environments*, David Tilson, ed. Glenview, IL: Professional Books on Aging, Scott, Foresman, and Company.

Peace, Sheila, Leonie Kellaher, and Dianne Willcocks. 1997. *Re-evaluating residential care.* Buckingham, UK: Open University Press.

Peck, Richard L. 2000a. Accreditation comes to assisted living. *Nursing Homes* (March):26–28.

———. 2000b. What is assisted living? *Nursing Homes* (March):4.

Perin, Constance. 1970. *With man in mind: An interdisciplinary prospectus for environmental design.* Cambridge, MA: MIT Press.

Perlman, Robert, and Uhlmann, Richard. 1988. Quality of life in chronic diseases: Perceptions of elderly patients. *Journal of Gerontology: Medical Sciences* 43: M25–M30.

Pierson, Charon A. 2000. Issues in end-of-life decision making in the hospital and nursing home culture. In *Cultural issues in end-of-life decision making.* Kathryn L. Braun, James H. Pietsch, and Patricia L. Blanchette, eds. Thousand Oaks, CA: Sage Publications, Inc.

Powers, Thomas. 1982. Learning to die: The final lesson that few doctors know how to teach. In *Readings in aging and death: Contemporary perspectives.* Stephen H. Zarit, ed. 2d ed. New York: Harper & Row.

Pristic, Susan. 1991. Assisted living in the spotlight: New association eyes expanded Medicaid funding. *Contemporary Long-Term Care* 14(2).

Proshansky, H., W.H. Ittleson, and L.G. Rivlin. 1970. *Environmental psychology: Man and his physical setting.* New York: Holt, Rinehart, and Winston.

Pynoos, Jon. 1990. Public policy and aging in place: Identifying the problems and potential solutions. In *Aging in place: Supporting the frail elderly in residential environments*, David Tilson, ed. Glenview, IL: Professional Books on Aging, Scott, Foresman, and Company.

Rajecki, Ron. 1992. New regs promote aging in place. *Comtemporary Long-Term Care* (September):46–48.

Rapoport, Amos. 1969. *House form and culture.* Englewood Cliffs, NJ: Prentice-Hall.

———, ed. 1976. *The mutual interaction of people and their built environment: A cross-cultural perspective.* Chicago: Aldine.

———. 1977. *Human aspects of urban form.* Oxford: Pergamon Press.

————. 1981. Identity in cross-cultural perspective. In *Housing and identity*. James Duncan, ed. New York: Holmes & Meier.

————. 1982. Identity and environment: A cross-cultural perspective. In *Housing and identity: Cross-cultural perspectives*. James S. Duncan, ed. New York: Holmes & Meier.

————. 1995. A critical look at the concept "home." In *Home: Words, interpretations, meanings, and environments,* David N. Benjamin and David Stea, eds. Aldershot, UK: Avebury.

Redmond, Rosemary, and Paul K. Chafetz. 2001. Legal and ethical issues for assisted living facility operators: Managing risk by doing the right thing. *Assisted living: Current issues in management and resident care,* Kevan H. Namazi and Paul K. Chafetz, eds. Westport, CT: Auburn House.

Regnier, Victor. 1991. Assisted living: An evolving industry. *Seniors Housing News* (Spring).

————. 1992. Assisted living: Promoting independence, choice, and autonomy. *Supportive Housing Options* 1(1):1, 4, 5. Los Angeles: National Eldercare Institute on Housing and Supportive Services, Andrus Gerontology Center, University of Southern California.

————. 1995. Assisted living models from Northern Europe. *Assisted Living Today.*

————. 1996. *Critical issues in assisted living.* Los Angeles: National Resource and Policy Center on Housing and Long Term Care, Andrus Gerontology Center, University of Southern California.

————. 1999. The definition and evolution of assisted living within a changing system of long-term care. In *Aging, autonomy, and architecture: Advances in assisted living.* Benyamin Schwarz and Ruth Brent, eds. Baltimore: Johns Hopkins University Press.

————. 2001. Special care settings: Case studies/post occupancy reports on state-of-the-art facilities. New Directions in Alzheimer Care, the tenth National Alzheimer Disease Education Conference, Chicago, Illinois, 15–18 July.

Regnier, Victor, Jennifer Hamilton, and Suzie Yatabe. 1991. *Best practices in assisted living: Innovations in design, management, and financing.* Los Angeles: National Eldercare Institute on Housing and Supportive Services, Andrus Gerontology Center, University of Southern California.

Regnier, Victor, and Jon Pynoos. 1987. *Housing the aged: Design directives and policy considerations.* New York: Elsevier Publishing Company.

Retirement housing industry, 1998. 1999. Philadelphia: Laventhol and Horwath.

Retzlaff, Kay. 1996. Assisted living. *Continuing Care* (September):30–36.

Riesman, David. 1954. *Individualism reconsidered and other essays.* Glencoe, IL: Free Press.

Romano, Michael. 1994. Reinventing assisted living: An age-old alternative takes on a new look. *Contemporary Long Term Care* (July):30–35.

Rosenblatt, Robert A. 2001. Hearing focuses on spotty oversight of assisted living. *Aging Today: The Bimonthly Newspaper of the American Society on Aging* (May/June).

Rosenfelt, Rosalie H. 1965. The elderly mystique. *Journal of Social Issues* 21:37–43.

Rowles, Graham D. 1987. A place to call home. In *Handbook of clinical gerontology*, L. Carstensen and B. Edelstein, eds. New York: Pergamon.

———. 1993. Evolving images of place in aging and "Aging in Place." *Generations* 17:65–70.

Rubinstein, Robert L. 1989. The home environments of older people: A description of the psychological process linking person to place. *Journal of Gerontology: Social Sciences* 44(2).

Rybczynski, Witold. 1986. *Home: A short history of an idea*. Harrisburg, PA: R.R. Donnelley and Sons.

Sadalla, Edward K., Beth Vershure, and Jeffrey Burroughs. 1987. Identity symbolism in housing. *Environment and Behavior* 19:569–87.

Saegert, Susan. 1985. The role of housing in the experience of dwelling. In *Home environments*, Irwin Altman and Carol M. Werner, eds. New York: Plenum Press.

Saile, David G. 1985. Experience and use of the dwelling. In *Home environments*, Irwin Altman and Carol M. Werner, eds. New York: Plenum Press.

Savishinsky, Joel. 1991. *The ends of time: Life and work in a nursing home*. New York: Bergin and Garvey.

Schorr, Alvin L. 1970. Housing and its effects. In *Environmental psychology: Man and his physical setting*, Harold M. Proshansky, William Ittleson, and Leanne Rivlin, eds. Vol. 1. New York: Holdt, Rinehart, Winston.

Schwartz, Ronald M. 1998. Assisted living coalition urges regulation avoidance. *Nursing Homes* 47(10):10–12.

Schwarz, Benyamin, and Ruth Brent. 1999. *Aging, autonomy, and architecture: Advances in assisted living*. Baltimore: Johns Hopkins University Press.

Scott, Gregory J., Mary Kender, and Scott E. Townsley. 1999. Emerging trends in assisted living. *Nursing Homes Long Term Care Management* (August): 52–55.

Sebba, R., and A. Churchman. 1986. The uniqueness of home. *Architecture and Behavior* 3(1):7–24.

Seip, David E. 1987. Specializing in assisted living facilities: Bridging the gap between retirement housing and nursing homes. *Contemporary Long-Term Care* 10:32–34.

———. 1991. Facing the facts about assisted living: Design principles bind diverse industry. *Contemporary Long Term Care* (January):24–95.

Sheehan, Nancy H., and Steven K. Wisensale. 1991. Aging in place: Discharge policies and procedures concerning frailty among senior housing tenants. *Journal of Gerontological Studies* 16:109–23.

Sheidt, Rick, and Paul Windley, eds. 1998. *Environment and aging theory: A focus on housing*. Westport, CT: Greenwood Press.

Sherwood, Sylvia, Ruchlin Hirsch, and Clarence Sherwood. 1990. CCRCs: An option for aging in place. In *Aging in place: Supporting the frail elderly in resi-*

dential environments, David Tilson, ed. Glenview, IL: Professional Books on Aging, Scott, Foresman, and Company.

Shield, Renee Rose. 1988. *Uneasy endings: Daily life in an American nursing home*. Ithaca, NY: Cornell University Press.

———. 1990. Liminality in an American nursing home: The endless transition. In *The cultural context of aging: Worldwide perspectives*, Jay Sokolovsky, ed. New York: Bergin and Garvey.

Shulamit, Bernard L. 2001. Aging in place. In *Assisted living: Needs, practices, and policies in residential care for the elderly*, Sheryl Zimmerman, Philip D. Sloane, and J. Kevin Eckert, eds. Baltimore: Johns Hopkins University Press.

Siemon, Dorothy, Stephanie Edelstein, and Zita Dresner. 1996. Consumer advocacy in assisted living. *Clearinghouse Review* (October):579–588.

Simmons, Leo. 1945. *The role of the aged in primitive society*. New Haven, CT: Yale University Press.

Sixsmith, Andrew. 1986. Independence and home in later life. In *Dependence and interdependency in old age*, C. Phillipson, M. Bernard, and P. Strang, eds. London: Croom Helm.

Sixsmith, Andrew, and Judith Sixsmith. 1991. Transitions in home experience in later life. *The Journal of Architectural and Planning Research* 8:181–91.

Sixsmith, Judith. 1986. The meaning of home: An exploratory study of environmental experience. *Journal of Environmental Psychology* 6:281–98.

Smith, Sandy G. 1994. The essential qualities of a home. *Journal of Environmental Psychology* 14:31–46.

Smithers, Janice A. 1985. *Determined survivors: Community life among the urban elderly*. New Brunswick, NJ: Rutgers University Press.

Stacy-Konnert, C., and J. Pynoos. 1992. Friendship and social networks in a continuing care retirement community. *Journal of Applied Gerontology* 11:298–313.

Steinfeld, Edward. 1981. The place of old age: The meaning of housing older people. In *Housing and identity: Cross-cultural perspectives*, James Duncan, ed. London: Croom Helm.

Tarlach, Gemma M. 1998. What a difference a state makes! (Assisted living facilities). *Drug Topics* 142(4):72.

Tilson, David, ed. 1990. *Aging in place: Supporting frail elderly in a residential environment*. Glenview: Professional Books on Aging, Scott, Foresman, and Company.

Tilson, David, and Charles Fahey. 1990. Introduction. In *Aging in place: Supporting the frail elderly in residential environments*, David Tilson, ed. Glenview, IL: Professional Books on Aging, Scott, Foresman, and Company.

Tuan, Yi Fu. 1980. Rootedness versus sense of place. *Landscape* 24:3–8.

Tulloch, Janet. 1995. A resident's view of autonomy. In *Enhancing autonomy in long-term care: Concepts or strategies*, Lucia Gamroth, Joyce Semradek, and Elizabeth Tornquist, eds. New York: Springer Publishing Company.

Turner, Victor. 1977. Variations on a theme of liminality. In *Secular ritual*, Sally F. More and Barbara G. Meyerhoff, eds. Amsterdam: Van Gorcum.

————. 1982. *From ritual to theatre: The human seriousness of play*. New York: PAJ Publications.

Twersky, Ori. 1998. Close to home: Lack of uniform standards for assisted living fuels debate about federal intervention. *Consultant Pharmacist* (November).

U.S. Congress General Accounting Office. 1997. *Consumer protection and quality of care issues in assisted living*. Washington, DC: Government Printing Office.

U.S. General Accounting Office. 1997. *Long-term care: Consumer protection and quality-of-care issues in assisted living*. Report to the Honorable Ron Wyden, United States Senate. GAO/HEHS-97-93.

U.S. Senate, Special Committee on Aging. 1999. *Shopping for assisted living: What consumers need to make the best buy*. Hearing before the Special Committee on Aging, United States Senate, 106th Cong., 1st sess. 26 April.

————. 2001. *Assisted living in the 21st century: Examining its role in the continuum of care*. 107th Cong., 1st sess., 26 April.

Van Gennup, Arnold. 1960. *The rites of passage*. Chicago: University of Chicago Press.

Vesperi, Maria. 1985. *City of green benches: Growing old in a new downtown*. Ithaca, NY: Cornell University Press.

Vickery, Kathleen. 1998. States pick up speed on assisted living regulations: Many loosen admission and retention criteria. *Provider* (June):15.

————. 1999. Federal regulation unlikely for assisted living, committee says. *Provider* (June):10–11.

Wagner, Lynn. 1995. Aging in place fuels growth in assisted living. *Provider* (October):55, 67, 68.

Webster's new twentieth century unabridged dictionary. 1977. 2d ed. Cleveland, OH: William Collins and World Publishing Co., Inc.

Welch, Polly, Valerie Parker, and John Zeisel. 1984. *Independence through interdependence: Congregate living for older people*. Boston: Department of Elder Affairs, Commonwealth of Massachusetts.

Werner, Carol M. 1987. Home interiors: A time and place for interpersonal relationships. *Environment and Behavior* 19:169–79.

Werner, Carol M., Irwin Altman, and Diana Oxley. 1985. Temporal aspects of homes: A transactional perspective. In *Homes environments*, Irwin Altman and Carol M. Werner, eds. New York: Plenum Press.

Werner, Oswald, and G. Mark Schoepfle. 1987. *Systematic fieldwork: Foundation of ethnography and interviewing*. Vols. 1 and 2. Newbury Park, CA: Sage Publications, Inc.

White, Robert W. 1959. Motivation, reconsidered: The concept of competence. *Psychology Review* 66:297–333.

————. 1963. Ego and reality in psychoanalytic theory. *Psychology Issues* 3(11): 1–210.

————. 1971. The urge towards competence. *The American Journal of Occupational Therapy* 25(6):271–74.

Wilkin, David, and Beverley Hughes. 1987. Residential care of elderly people: The consumer's views. *Aging and Society* 7:175–201.

Willcocks, Diane, Sheila Peace, and Leonie Kellaher. 1987. *Private lives in public places*. London: Tavistock Publications.

Wilson, Keren Brown. 1990a. Assisted living: The merger of housing and long-term care services. *Long-Term Care Advances* 1(4):2–8. Chapel Hill, NC: Duke University Center for the Study of Aging and Human Development.

———. 1990b. Assisted living as a model of care delivery. In *Enhancing autonomy in long-term care: Concepts or strategies*, Lucia Gamroth, Joyce Semradek, and Elizabeth Tornquist, eds. New York: Springer Publishing Company.

———. 1993. Assisted living: A model of supportive housing. In *Advances in long-term care*, Paul Katz, Robert Kane, and Mathew Mezey, eds. vol. 2. New York: Springer Publishing Company.

———. 1996. *Assisted living: Reconceptualizing regulation to meet consumers' needs and preferences*. Washington, DC: The American Association of Retired Persons, Public Policy Issue.

Yee, Donna L., et al. 1999. Resident-centered care in assisted living. *Journal of Aging and Social Policy* 10: 7–27.

Young, Robert. 1986. *Personal autonomy: Beyond negative and positive liberty*. New York: St. Martin's Press.

Zaner, Laura O. 1997. Managing care. *Urban Land* (June):51–63.

Zarit, Stephen H., ed. 1982. *Readings in aging and death: Contemporary perspectives*. 2d ed. New York: Harper & Row.

Zedlewski, Sheila, et al. 1990. *The needs of the elderly in the 21st century*. Washington, DC: The Urban Institute Report.

Zeisel, John. 1987. Assisted living design trends: Residential or health care model. Unpublished paper prepared for the National Real Estate Development Center Conference, Boston, MA.

Zimmerman, Sheryl, Philip D. Sloane, and J. Kevin Eckert, eds. 2001. *Assisted living: Needs, practices, and policies in residential care for the elderly*. Baltimore: Johns Hopkins University Press.

Index

Activities, 119, 121, 126; residents' opinions of, 121–24, 126; similar to children's activities, 119–20

ADLs (activities of daily living), 24, 49, 52, 75, 108, 132–33, 138, 149, 184; assistance with, 69, 149–50; levels of assistance offered with different assisted living models, 132–33; as part of admission criteria, 67–69; reasons for moving into assisted living, 138; related to the continuum of care, 82–85; related to functioning, 149; in relation to control, 108–9

Admission criteria: admission agreements, 143–44; Chicago providers' experiences, 67–71, 142; national data on, 142–44; in relation to marketing literature, 142–44

Aging in place, 1, 2, 5, 12, 17, 21, 41, 131, 135, 165; accommodating approach, 63; confusion surrounding, 162–63; constant approach, 63; definitions, 1, 62–65; as dying in place, 178–81; "full" aging in place, 17, 135, 161, 177, 181, 183, 185; in-

terpretations of by assisted living industry, 161–62; in marketing literature, 163–64; as a marketing tool, 160–63; national data, 183; opposing interpretations, 183–84; policies and perspectives, 160–64; provider's comments, 76; related to marketing, 64; related to prolonged residence and aging in place, 182–87; versus the continuum of care (residents' views), 176–78

ALFA (Assisted Living Federation of America), 1, 49–51, 55–56, 132; defining assisted living, 49–50

Anthropologists, and aging research, 13–15, 21

Anthropology, 5, 9; approaches to aging, 12–14; fieldwork, 17–19

Assisted living, 1, 2, 4, 15, 17, 41, 83; benefits according to providers, 76–78; compared to one's home, 34–39; decision to move into, 136–37; definitions, 47, 49–53; design, 11, 25, 50, 59, 148–49, 167; different names for, 49; history of, 47–49; as "home," 35–38, 92, 183;

About the Author

JACQUELYN BETH FRANK is Assistant Professor and Coordinator of Gerontology Programs in the sociology-anthropology department at Illinois State University.